DATE DUE

DEMCO 38-296

TOPOPHILIA

topophilia

A STUDY OF ENVIRONMENTAL
PERCEPTION, ATTITUDES, AND VALUES

WITH A NEW PREFACE BY THE AUTHOR

YI-FU TUAN

COLUMBIA UNIVERSITY PRESS
NEW YORK

Columbia University Press Morningside Edition
Columbia University Press
New York   Oxford

© 1974 by Prentice-Hall Inc., Englewood Cliffs, New Jersey

Morningside Edition, with new preface
copyright © by Columbia University Press
All rights reserved

Library of Congress Cataloging-in-Publication Data

Tuan, Yi-fu, 1930–
    Topophilia : a study of environmental perception, attitudes, and
values / Yi-fu Tuan ; with a new preface by the author.
        p.   cm.
    Originally published: Englewood Cliffs, N.J. : Prentice-Hall,
1974.
    "A Morningside book."
    Includes index.
    ISBN 0-231-07394-1.—ISBN 0-231-07395-X (pbk.)
    1. Human ecology—Public opinion.   2. Geographical perception.
I. Title.
[GF41.T82   1990]
304.2—dc20
90-1965
    CIP

Morningside Edition 1990

Casebound editions of Columbia University Press books are Smyth-
sewn and printed on permanent and durable acid-free paper

Printed in the U.S.A.
c 10 9 8 7 6 5 4 3 2 1
p 10 9 8 7 6 5 4 3 2 1

All science should be scholarly, but not all scholarship can be rigorously scientific. . . . The *terrae incognitae* of the periphery contain fertile ground awaiting cultivation with the tools and in the spirit of the humanities.

John Kirtland Wright

The geography of the world is unified only by human logic and optics, by the light and color of artifice, by decorative arrangement, and by ideas of the good, the true, and the beautiful.

David Lowenthal

Humanist, quantifier, what you will—it is never wrong to plug your own line; it is almost always wrong to write off others.

O. H. K. Spate

One of my lasting memories of *The Gallic Wars,* read when I was in high school, is that Caesar was always in *medias res.* I have never reread him to discover whether in fact this was the case, but like him we are moving into the heart of the matter.

Clarence J. Glacken

contents

acknowledgments

Acknowledging one's intellectual debts would be unmitigated pleasure but for the realization that it is an impossible undertaking. Intellectual debts are endless and innumerable. This is, of course, especially true when one is rash enough to write a book that aspires toward the synthesis of a broad range of disparate topics. However, I do want to express my deep gratitude to four happy influences without which *Topophilia* would have remained a private fantasy: the Berkeley ambiance of free but intense intellectual inquiry when I was a graduate student there between 1951 and 1956; the example and encouragement of John Brinckerhoff Jackson; the beauty of New Mexico; the liberal structure of the Minnesota Department of Geography which encourages its faculty to "profess" their real interests, that is, to be professors rather than "resource persons" holding information in the generally approved slots of the discipline.

I wish to express my gratitude to the John Simon Guggenheim Foundation for a fellowship, which made it possible for me to reflect on environmental attitudes at leisure in the Australian desert.

Thanks are extended to the following authors and publishers for permission to quote briefly or paraphrase from copyrighted material: Robert Payne for *The White Pony* (The John Day Company, Inc., 1947); Colin

Turnbull and Simon & Schuster, Inc. for *The Forest People* (1961) ; T. G. H. Strehlow for *Aranda Tradition* (Melbourne University Press, 1947) ; the Association of American Geographers for *Man and Nature* (Resource paper No. 10, 1971) ; George Steiner and Random House, Inc. for *Tolstoy or Dostoevsky* (1959) ; Harcourt Brace Jovanovich, Inc. for *To the Lighthouse* (1927) by Virginia Woolf; The Viking Press, Inc., for *Stop-time* (1967) by Frank Conroy; Doubleday & Company, Inc., for *Seven Pillars of Wisdom* (1936) by T. E. Lawrence; Random House, Inc. for *The Levittowners* (1967) by Herbert J. Gans; University of Pennsylvania Press for *Culture and Experience* (1955) by A. Irving Hallowell; The Macmillan Company for *Manchild in the Promised Land* (1965) by Claude Brown; Yale University Press for *Life in Ancient Rome* (1940) by Jérôme Carcopino; William Stringfellow and Holt, Rinehart and Winston, Inc. for *My People is the Enemy* (1964) ; Harper & Row, Publishers for *Dark Ghetto* (1965) by Kenneth Clark; Prentice-Hall, Inc. for *Class in Suburbia* (1963) by William M. Dobriner; Kevin Lynch and the M.I.T. Press for *The Image of the City* (1960).

preface to the morningside edition

In 1952, a few friends and I, all Chinese graduate students at the University of California–Berkeley and all novices at camping, arrived at the Death Valley National Monument at about three in the morning, exhausted by the long drive and exhausted by an unsuccessful attempt to set up tent in the dark, buffeted by strong wind. In the end, we slept out in the open in our sleeping bags. When I woke up, the sun had risen high enough to throw its rays on the range of mountains across the valley and presented me with a scene, totally alien to my experience up to that time, of such unearthly beauty that I felt transported to a supernal realm and yet, paradoxically, also at home, as though I had returned after a long absence.

The desert, including the barren parts and (I would even say) especially those, appeals to me. I see in it purity, timelessness, a generosity of mind and spirit. The bleached skull in the desert, far from evoking the odor of death, suggests something clean and noble that may crumble into dust but is exempt from the humiliation of decay. I have also lived close to the tropical rainforests of the Philippines and Panama. In the tropical forest, where life is displayed in all its diversity and luxuriance, all I can see and smell is decay and death. The rainforest is clearly not my niche on earth.

These are strong prejudices, but they are not unique to me. Of course, peoples of the desert (nomads as well as sedentary farmers in oases) love their homeland: without exception humans grow attached to their native places, even if these should seem derelict of quality to outsiders. But the desert, despite its barrenness, has had its nonnative admirers. Englishmen, in particular, have loved the desert. In the eighteenth and nineteenth centuries, they roamed adventurously in North Africa and the Middle East, and wrote accounts with enthusiasm and literary flair which have given the desert a glamor that endures into our time, as the continuing interest in the exploits of T. E. Lawrence shows. Why this attraction for Englishmen? The answers are no doubt complex, but I wish to suggest a psychogeographical factor—the appeal of the opposite. The mist and overpowering greenness of England seem to have created a thirst in some individuals to seek their opposite in desert climate and landscape.

As a geographer, I have always been curious about how people live in different parts of the world. But unlike many of my peers, the key words for me are not only "survival" and "adaptation," which suggest a rather grim and puritanical attitude to life. People everywhere, I believe, also aspire toward contentment and joy. Environment, for them, is not just a resource base to be used or natural forces to adapt to, but also sources of assurance and pleasure, objects of profound attachment and love. In short, another key word for me, missing in many accounts of livelihood, is *Topophilia*.

When the book appeared in 1974, it met with unexpected success. It was widely and favorably reviewed, and it sold well. At a time when the Whole Earth Catalog was a bestseller, perhaps the modest success of *Topophilia* could be predicted. The sixties and early seventies were a time when Americans grew newly conscious of the environment. They saw in the American landscape—more often than not—prosperity rather than beauty, urban renewals and gleaming skyscrapers rather than any deep concern for the human attachment and love of place. Indeed, the words "attachment" and "love" have no place in social-science discourse and sound more like poetry than a basis for serious argument in political and planning councils where hard budgetary decisions are made. We who believe in the preservation of not only wilderness but also (say) an older neighborhood that is threatened by the bulldozer have no convincing language with which to present our case to people and their political representatives. *Topophilia* is not such a language, much as I would like it to be. However, it does— perhaps for the first time—present a general framework for discussing all the different ways that human beings can develop a love of place.

In the course of the eighties, not only Americans and Europeans but thoughtful people everywhere have acquired a serious concern for environmental protection. They see everywhere a threatened earth. Even Antarctica is beginning to be visibly polluted by human debris. The environmental movement is by now a political movement of international scope. It is also becoming an intimate part of our culture—a subject for neighborly gossip over the picket fence. But, sad to say, the mountains of research and speech focus almost exclusively on what has gone wrong. I say "sad" because the polluted state of the earth is tragic for us human beings largely because we are aware of what the earth could be like, and sad also because in our passion to preserve nature we tend to become misanthropes—to look upon technological progress and large-scale creations, especially the city, with a jaundiced eye.

Let me offer two examples which reveal both our misanthropic tendency and my own inclination to look more kindly upon the human species. A favorite landscape of many cultivated Europeans and Americans is the English countryside of the eighteenth century. Jacquetta Hawkes sees the mid-eighteenth century as a time when "man and earth" reached its greatest intimacy and most sensitive pitch—a precious moment of balance before the Industrial Revolution unfortunately tipped the scale in man's favor. Another English writer, John Wain, in his biography of Samuel Johnson, lauds the rural charms of the English scene in Johnson's time, compared with which the modern landscape is an abomination. Yet he has to admit that there was an incongruous element in that vanished world of great beauty, namely, its large number of diseased and disfigured human beings and animals. Beauty and suffering are perfectly compatible, and in our nostalgia for an older time we tend to forget the early deaths, the diseases, and the deformities that were also a part of that "Eden"—horrors removed or greatly mitigated by advances in modern hygiene and medical science.

The second example is more personal. I was on an airplane, flying at 30,000 feet across the continent, when a hot meal was placed on my laptable. I wrestled with the food and, between bites, looked out of the window to admire a scene of pristine beauty composed of bright sun, blue sky, and a carpet of fluffy clouds. Here, I thought, was vivid contrast between the grandeur of nature and such tokens of the human world as the rubbery chicken, the lukewarm coffee, the flight magazine with its glossy pictures and bland essays, and my neighbor's elbow. Suddenly, my perspective shifted. I realized, with distressing acuteness, that only a plate of glass separated me from instant death. The beauty of nature is something I can admire only from the safety of a humanly constructed world. The atmosphere at 30,000 feet is not my native element. What nourishes me is not that thin cold air, so alien to terrestrial life, but—well, yes, the rubbery chicken. Suddenly, that tinfoil plate with its micro-ovened food, the magazine, and my neighbor's elbow take on a more friendly air. I learn to appreciate more

my fellow human beings, and their brave—not always successful efforts—
to make a comfortable and pleasing home for themselves.

The rising tide of the environmental movement is a reason for hope.
We have shown that we are not entirely blind to our own folly and greed;
we have indicated occasionally a will to act. But the movement, in its in-
dignation and zeal, has blind spots, the most prominent of which is the
reluctance to recognize that intensely humanized worlds can have their own
ecological richness and beauty. The countrysides of many parts of the earth—
preeminently Western Europe, the Mediterranean borderlands, Eastern and
Southeastern Asia—are much richer now, ecologically speaking, than they
were in "pristine" prehistoric times. The human presence, contrary to the
message of the more hysterical environmental literature, has not always and
everywhere impoverished the earth. As for beauty, it seems a little mean-
spirited not to be able to say with Ada Louise Huxtable, when she saw a
Baroque church and plaza in Rome by moonlight, "I had no idea at that
time that cities could be so devastatingly beautiful, that stone could be so
sensuous, that architects dealt in such sublime stagesets for human drama,
that space could move one to such strong emotions, that architecture could
make men so much larger than life."

Topophilia was conceived and written in an earlier stage of the environmental movement, when the perception of a great need to preserve the
natural wealth of the earth was better balanced by, on the one hand, the
desire to understand the nature of environmental attitudes and values, how
they developed, how they differ from culture to culture, and, on the other
hand, the desire to build a better place—richer countrysides, more humane
neighborhoods, and cities that can lift the spirit. It may be that in the 1990s
we shall again wish to search both sides of the question. If so, *Topophilia*
may still have a part to play in the education of the young, until a more
comprehensive and better book comes along, which I hope will be soon.

Yi-Fu Tuan
Madison, Wisconsin
February 19, 1990

TOPOPHILIA

CHAPTER ONE

introduction

What are our views on the physical environment, natural and man-made? How do we perceive, structure, and evaluate it? What have been, and what are, our environmental ideals? How do economy, life style, and the physical setting itself affect environmental attitudes and values? What are the links between environment and world view?

These are some of the questions that I wish to explore. They are broad but not all-inclusive. Environmental pollution and ecology, two topics of major importance and concern to the world, lie outside the scope of this book. The themes to be taken up here—perception, attitude, and value—prepare us, first of all, to understand ourselves. Without self-understanding we cannot hope for enduring solutions to environmental problems, which are fundamentally human problems. And human problems, whether they be economic, political, or social, hinge on the psychological pole of motivation, on the values and attitudes that direct energies to goals. Since the mid-1960s the thrust of the environmental-ecological movement has been in two directions. One is applied: what can be done about rat-infested tenements and polluted water? The other is theoretical and scientific, the attempt to understand the complex forces that maintain the natural world. Neither approach is directly concerned with the formation of attitudes and values. Threatened environments and environments that are bad enough to endanger health require immediate action; questions of attitude and value seem beside the point. The scientist and theorist, on his part, tends to overlook human diversity and subjectivity because the task of establishing linkages in the nonhuman world is already enormously complex. However, in the larger view we know that attitudes and beliefs cannot be excluded even from the practical approach, for it is practical to recognize human passions in any environmental calculus; they cannot be excluded from the theoretical approach because man is, in fact, the ecological dominant and his behavior needs to be understood in depth, not merely mapped.

A general survey of environmental attitudes and values does not at present exist. The studies known to me are mostly specialized and are of limited scope. Since research in the field was pursued for different ends the resulting works are highly heterogeneous in content and presentation. They fall into five main types: (1) How human beings in general perceive and structure their world. Universal human traits are sought. (2) Environmental perception and attitude as a dimension of culture or of the interaction between culture and environment. Nonliterate peoples and small communities are examined in some detail and in a holistic framework. (3) Attempts to extract environmental attitudes and values with the help of surveys, questionnaires, and psychological tests. (4) Changes in environmental evaluation as part of a study of the history of ideas or of culture history. (5) The meaning and history of environments such as the city, the suburb, the countryside, and wilderness.

. The disparateness in aim, method, philosophical assumption, and in scale—temporal and spatial—is bewildering. What can be the common ground between a detailed analysis of the shopping behavior of housewives in Ames, Iowa and a grand survey of the Christian doctrine of nature? Or between the study of color symbolism as a universal trait and the history of landscape painting? A possible reply is that somehow they all bear on the way human beings respond to their physical setting—their perception of it and the value they put on it. The reply sounds lame because it lacks detailed exemplification. If a general survey of the field is called for, we are tempted to cull from the different disciplines and make an anthology. Anthologies invade the market when new and pressing interests develop and we are unsure what they are about and where they lead. Anthologies have a smorgasbord appeal and threaten us with indigestion should we be rash enough to run through the course. Ideally a single person should sort out the heterogeneous material and present a unified viewpoint. Given the paucity of overarching concepts the effort is almost certain to fail. Yet it is worth making, for unless we do we shall not confront the structural weaknesses of the field. Disparate streams of knowledge lead, ideally, to fruitful marriage in a capacious mind; at the other extreme they share a common bed only through the bookbinder's art. On this spectrum of achievement the present essay stands, at best, short of the midpoint between collage and the integral vision. I hope it will stimulate, if only by its evident weakness, others to do better.

No single all-embracing concept guides my effort. The best that I can do is to structure the theme of topophilia with a limited set of concepts. I have tried to (1) examine environmental perception and values at different levels: the species, the group, and the individual; (2) hold culture and environment, topophilia and environment, as distinct in order to show how they mutually contribute to the formation of values; (3) introduce the concept of change with a sketch of the displacement of the European medieval world view by a scientific model and what this has meant to environmental attitudes; (4) examine the idea of the search for environment in the city, suburb, countryside, and wilderness from a dialectical perspective; (5) distinguish different types of environmental experience and describe their character.

Research methods are not presented. Technical discussions on procedure appear in most publications on environment and behavior. As social scientists we have many skills but the crucial (as distinct from the socially urgent) problems often escape us because we lack sophisticated concepts to frame them. In the physical sciences even simple laws can defy common sense. In the social sciences common sense is repeatedly confirmed with a great show of professional solemnity. The means needed to achieve the results are often more impressive than the results themselves. Nonetheless, systematized findings are invaluable for they give precision to the hunches of common sense, and they sometimes challenge and overthrow mere opinion.[1]

An active front of research, especially by geographers, is the human response to natural hazards.[2] Eventually this type of work should give us basic understanding of how people react to uncertainty in natural events. The work contributes to environmental psychology and has important implications for planning. I have omitted the findings of hazard research with regret, but they have no direct bearing on topophilia. For a similar reason I have touched only lightly on blighted environments in chapters 12 through

---

1 For a recent review of the problems in research on environmental perception see David Lowenthal, "Research in Environmental Perception and Behavior: Perspectives on Current Problems," *Environment and Behavior*, 4, No. 3 (September 1972), 333–42.

2 For example, Kenneth Hewitt and Ian Burton, *The Hazardness of a Place: A Regional Ecology of Damaging Events,* University of Toronto Department of Geography Research Publication No. 6 (1971); see bibliography for other studies dealing with environmental hazards.

14, since my main concern is with the formation and nature of positive attitudes and values.

Perception, attitude, value, and world view are among the key terms of the present work; their meanings overlap. The sense of each term should be clear in the proper context. Here are some preliminary definitions. *Perception* is both the response of the senses to external stimuli and purposeful activity in which certain phenomena are clearly registered while others recede in the shade or are blocked out. Much of what we perceive has value for us, for biological survival, and for providing certain satisfactions that are rooted in culture. *Attitude* is primarily a cultural stance, a position one takes vis-à-vis the world. It has greater stability than perception and is formed of a long succession of perceptions, that is, of experience. Infants perceive but have no well-formed attitude other than that given by biology. Attitudes imply experience and a certain firmness of interest and value.[3] Infants live in an environment; they have barely a world and no world view. *World view* is conceptualized experience. It is partly personal, largely social. It is an attitude or belief system; the word *system* implies that the attitudes and beliefs are structured, however arbitrary the links may seem, from an impersonal (objective) standpoint.[4]

Topophilia is the affective bond between people and place or setting. Diffuse as concept, vivid and concrete as personal experience, topophilia is the recurrent theme of the book.

[3] Myra R. Schiff, "Some Theoretical Aspects of Attitudes and Perception," *Natural Hazard Research,* University of Toronto, Working Paper No. 15 (1970).
[4] W. T. Jones, "World Views: Their Nature and Their Function," *Current Anthropology,* 13, No. 1 (February 1972), 79–109.

common traits
in
perception:
the senses

The earth's surface is highly varied. Even a casual acquaintance with its physical geography and teeming life forms tells us as much. But the ways in which people perceive and evaluate that surface are far more varied. No two persons see the same reality. No two social groups make precisely the same evaluation of the environment. The scientific view itself is culture-bound—one possible perspective among many. As we proceed in this study, the bewildering wealth of viewpoints on both individual and group levels becomes increasingly evident; and we risk losing sight of the fact that however diverse our perceptions of environment, as members of the same species we are constrained to see things a certain way. All human beings share common perceptions, a common world, by virtue of possessing similar organs. The uniqueness of the human perspective should be evident when we pause to ask how the human reality must differ from that of other animals. Contrary to appearances, a person cannot enter imaginatively into the life of his dog: canine sense organs diverge too far from our own for us to leap into the dog's world of smells, sounds, and sights. But with good will one person can enter into the world of another despite differences in age, temperament, and culture. In this chapter I shall note how human senses differ in range and acuity from those of some other animals, and thus delineate the uniqueness of the human world insofar as this derives from man's perceptual equipment.

vision

The human being has more ways to respond to the world than the five senses of seeing, hearing, smelling, tasting, and touching known to us since the time of Aristotle. For instance, some people are remarkably sensitive to subtle changes in humidity and atmospheric pressure; others appear to be endowed with an unusually acute sense of direction, although the innateness of this faculty has been questioned. Of the traditional five senses man is more consciously dependent on sight to make his way in the world than on the other senses. He is predominantly a visual animal. A larger world is open to him, and far more information that is detailed and specific spatially reaches him through the eyes than through the sensory systems of hearing, smell, taste, and touch. Most people probably regard sight as their most valued faculty, and would rather lose a limb or become deaf or dumb than to sacrifice vision.

Human vision, like that of other primates, has evolved in an arboreal environment. In the dense complex world of a tropical forest, it is more important to see well than to develop an acute sense of smell. In the long course of evolution members of the primate line have acquired large eyes while the snout has shrunk to give the eyes an unimpeded view. Of mammals, only man and some primates enjoy color vision. The red flag is black to the bull. Horses live in a monochrome world. Light visible to human eyes, however, occupies only a very narrow band in the whole electromagnetic spectrum. Ultraviolet rays are invisible to man, though ants and the honey bees are sensitive to them. Man has no direct perception of infrared rays, unlike the rattlesnake which has receptors tuned in to wavelengths longer than 0.7 microns. The world would look eerily different if human eyes were sensitive to infrared radiation. Then, instead of the darkness of night, we would be able to move easily in a shadowless world where objects glowed with varying degrees of intensity. Human eyes are in fact remarkably discerning in color gradations. The chromatic sensibility of normal human vision boasts a degree of accuracy that is rarely surpassed in spectrophotometry.[1]

Man possesses stereoscopic vision. Human eyes are located at the front, a position that limits the visual field. Unlike, for example, the rabbit a human cannot see what lies behind his head, but the gain in having frontal eyes is that they give a double assurance of information: binocular vision

---

1 Committee on Colorimetry, *The Science of Color* (Washington, D.C.: Optical Society of America, 1966), p. 219.

helps man to see things sharply as three-dimensional bodies. This is an innate ability to the extent that an infant soon learns to take cues such as linear perspective and parallax to perceive the round form of the human face. Eight-week-old infants are more capable of discriminating depth and orientation, taking into account size and shape constancy, and are better at performing completion than an empiricist would have predicted.[2] Time and experience, however, are required for the full development of three-dimensional vision. We are so used to seeing things in the round and the world in depth that it is surprising to know that many tricks have to be learnt. People who have been blind from birth as a result of congenital cataract and then have their sights conferred in later life by operation are barely able to recognize objects, far less to see them three-dimensionally. They have to learn the significance of the distribution of light and shadow in the recognition of solids, curves, and relief.

hands and the tactile sense

Primates are better able to pick out static details than other mammals. Their food in the forest is largely static so that it is more important for them to perceive objects like fruits, seeds, and shoots by their shape, color, and texture than by minute movements. Like humans, apes and monkeys probably see the environment as a collection of things rather than merely as a pattern. In acquiring this ability, the development of hands, strong and dexterous, is almost as important as the evolution of three-dimensional vision. Monkeys, apes, and man are probably the only animals that can fiddle with things, pick them up, and examine them from all sides. Paws are far less effective than hands, and among primate hands those of the human being combine strength with unmatched precision.[3]

Touch, the haptic sense, in fact provides human beings with a vast amount of information concerning the world. It takes no special skill for a person to feel the difference between a smooth pane of glass and one etched in grooves 1/2,500 of an inch deep. Blindfolded and with ears plugged to remove auditory cues, a man can nevertheless tell the difference between plastic, metal, paper, or wood by gently tapping the surface with a finger nail. Practice improves the sensitivity. The professional cloth feeler in textile houses can judge subtle differences in the quality of fabrics with amazing

2 T. G. R. Bower, "The Visual World of Infants," *Scientific American,* 215, No. 6 (1966), 90.
3 Bernard Campbell, *Human Evolution: An Introduction to Man's Adaptations* (Chicago: Aldine-Atherton, 1966), pp. 161–62.

accuracy. It is not even necessary for him to use his fingers; passing a stick over the cloth will do.[4]

The fundamental nature of the sense of touch is brought home to us when we reflect that, without sight a person can still operate with a high degree of efficiency in the world, but without the tactual sense it is doubtful that he can survive. We are always "in touch." For instance, at this moment we may be feeling the pressure of the chair against our posterior and the pressure of the pencil in our hand. Touch is the direct experience of resistance, the direct experience of the world as a system of resistances and pressures that persuade us of the existence of a reality independent of our imaginings. To see is not yet to believe: hence Christ offered himself to be *touched* by the doubting apostle. The importance of touch to knowledge is suggested by the English idiom "to keep in touch" or "to be out of touch," used not only with regard to persons but to fields of learning.

hearing

Auditory sensitivity in man is not especially acute. Hearing is less essential to primates, including humans, than to carnivores who track their prey. Compared with the ears of tracking killers those of primates are small and they lack twisting mobility. The average young human's hearing has a range extending roughly from 16 to 20,000 cycles per second. If a person is sensitive to pitch lower than 16 cycles, he may suffer the annoyance of being able to hear his own heartbeat. The upper limit of the human hearing range is modest compared with that of cats and bats: these mammals respond to sound of up to 50,000 and 120,000 cycles per second respectively. The human ear appears to be most sensitive to sound at a pitch corresponding to a child's or woman's cry. It is adapted specifically to the survival of the species and generally to engaging the world through auditory cues.

The eyes gain far more precise and detailed information about the environment than the ears but we are usually more touched by what we hear than by what we see. The sound of rain pelting against leaves, the roll of thunder, the whistling of wind in tall grass, and the anguished cry excite us to a degree that visual imagery can seldom match. Music is for most people a stronger emotional experience than looking at pictures or scenery. Why is this? Partly, perhaps, because we cannot close our ears as we can our eyes. We feel more vulnerable to sound.[5] "Hearing" has the connotation

---

[4] Lorus J. Milne and Margery Milne, *The Senses of Animals and Men* (New York: Atheneum, 1962), pp. 18–20; Owen Lowenstein, *The Senses* (Baltimore: Penguin, 1966).

[5] G. M. Wyburn, R. W. Pickford, and R. J. Hirst, *Human Senses and Perception* (Edinburgh: Oliver and Boyd, 1964), pp. 66.

of passivity (receptivity) that "seeing" does not have. Another reason may be that one of the most important sensations of the human infant, and perhaps even of the foetus, is the beat of the mother's heart. Desmond Morris, for example, thinks that this explains the fact that a mother (even when she is left-handed) normally holds the infant in such a way that his head rests against the left breast.[6] It also seems true that a human infant is sensitive to sound, making distinctions between the pleasant, the soothing, and the disturbing, long before it can discriminate with any subtlety visually.

The importance of hearing to the human grasp of reality is emphasized by the acute sense of loss for those who have suddenly become deaf. Contrary to expectations, the psychological effects of sudden deafness can be as debilitating as the sudden loss of sight. Deep depression, loneliness, and paranoid tendencies are some of the consequences. With deafness, life seems frozen and time lacks progression. Space itself contracts, for our experience of space is greatly extended by the auditory sense which provides information of the world beyond the visual field. At first, a world that seems to have lost its dynamism appears less demanding and nervous; it induces a feeling of detachment and peace, as happens in a pleasant way when the sounds of the city are muffled by light rain or a blanket of snow. But soon the silence, the severe loss of information, induces anxiety, dissociation, and withdrawal in the deaf.[7]

smell

A man cannot project himself into a dog's world if for no other reason than the chasm in the olfactory sensitivity of the two species. The dog's sense of smell is at least a hundred times more acute than that of man. Though carnivores and some ungulates have sharp vision, they place greater reliance on their olfactory receptors to survive in their world, in comparison with the primates. Of course the sense of smell is also important to primates. It plays a large part in the fundamental processes of feeding and mating. Modern man, however, tends to neglect the olfactory sense. His ideal environment would seem to require the exclusion of "smells" of any kind. The word "odor" itself nearly always connotes bad odor. This trend is regrettable, for the human nose is in fact an amazingly proficient organ for sniffing out information. With practice a person can classify the world into

6 Desmond Morris, *The Naked Ape* (London: Transworld Publishers, Corgi edition, 1968), pp. 95–96.
7 P. H. Knapp, "Emotional Aspects of Hearing Loss," *Psychomatic Medicine,* 10 (July/August 1948), 203–22.

such odoriferous categories as alliaceous, ambrosiac, pepperminty, aromatic, ethereal, foul, fragrant, goaty, or nauseous.

Odor has the power to evoke vivid, emotionally-charged memories of past events and scenes. A whiff of sage may call to mind an entire complex of sensations: the image of great rolling plains covered with grass and specked by clumps of sagebrush, the brightness of the sun, the heat, the bumpiness of the road. Whence this power? Several factors come into play. For one, the power of an odor to cast us into the past may be related to the fact that the cortex with its vast memory store evolved from the part of the brain originally concerned with smell. For another, as children, not only were our noses more sensitive but they were closer to the earth, to flower beds, tall grass, and the damp soil that give off odors. In adulthood, a chance encounter with the fragrance of a haystack may jolt our memory back nostalgically to the past. A further point is that seeing is selective and reflects experience. When we return to the scene of our childhood, not only the landscape has changed but the way we see it. We cannot recapture fully the essential feel of a visual world belonging to our past without the help of a sensory experience that has not changed, for instance, the strong odor of decaying seaweed.

perceiving with all the senses

Responding to the world through sight differs from responding to it through the other senses in several important respects. For instance, seeing is "objective;" seeing—as the expression goes—is believing, but we tend to distrust information obtained through the ears; it is "hearsay" or "rumor." Seeing does not involve our emotions deeply. We can see through the window of an air-conditioned bus that the slum is ugly and undesirable, but how undesirable reaches us with pungent force only when we open the window and catch a whiff from the malodorous sewers. The person who just "sees" is an onlooker, a sightseer, someone not otherwise involved with the scene. The world perceived through the eyes is more abstract than that known to us through the other senses. The eyes explore the visual field and abstract from it certain objects, points of focus, perspectives. But the taste of lemon, the texture of warm skin, and the sound of rustling leaves reach us as just these sensations. The visual field is far larger than the fields of the other senses. Distant objects can only be *seen;* hence, we have the tendency to regard *seen* objects as "distant"—as not calling forth any strong emotional response—even though they may in point of fact be close to us.

A human being perceives the world through all his senses simultaneously. The information potentially available to him is immense. In man's daily projects, however, only a small portion of his innate power to experience is called into use. What sense organ is given special exercise varies with the individual and his culture. In modern society man comes to rely more and more on sight. Space for him is bounded and static, a frame or matrix for objects. Without objects and boundaries space is empty. It is empty because there is nothing to see even though it might be filled with wind. Compare this attitude with that of the Aivilik Eskimo on Southampton Island. To the Eskimo, space is not pictorial or boxed in, but something always in flux, creating its own dimensions moment by moment. He learns to orient himself with all senses alert. He has to during certain times in winter when sky and earth merge and appear to be made of the same substance. There is then "no middle distance, no perspective, no outline, nothing that the eye can cling to except thousands of smokey plumes of snow running along the ground before the wind—a land without bottom or edge."[8] Under such conditions the Eskimo cannot rely on the points of reference given by permanent landmarks: he must depend on the shifting relationships of snow contours, on the types of snow, wind, salt air, and ice crack. The direction and smell of the wind is a guide, together with the feel of ice and snow under his feet. The invisible wind plays a large role in the life of the Aivilik Eskimo. His language includes at least twelve unrelated terms for various winds. He learns to orient himself by them. On horizonless days he lives in an acoustic-olfactory space.

The medieval cathedral fascinates the modern tourist for various reasons, but one that has received little comment is this: the cathedral offers him an environment that stimulates the simultaneous use of three or four sense receptors. It has sometimes been said that the steel-and-glass skyscraper is the modern equivalent of the medieval cathedral. Actually, apart from the vertical bias the two buildings have very little in common. They do not illustrate the same principles of construction, they are not put to the same use, and their symbolic meanings are entirely different. Again, apart from verticality, the sensual and aesthetic experiences provided by these two structures are antipodal. The modern skyscraper caters largely to sight, though the varying types of floor covering provide changes in tactile stimuli. If there is sound, it is probably "musak" which is meant to be audible but not heard. By contrast, the experience of the interior of a cathedral involves sight, sound, touch, and smell.[9] Each sense reinforces the other so that together they clarify the structure and substance of the entire building, revealing its essential character.

8 Edmund Carpenter, Frederick Varley, and Robert Flaherty, *Eskimo* (Toronto: University of Toronto Press, 1959), pages unnumbered.
9 Richard Neutra, *Survival Through Design* (New York: Oxford University Press, 1969), pp. 139–40.

perception and activity

Perception is an activity, a reaching out to the world. Sense organs are minimally operative when they are not actively used. Our tactile sense is very delicate but to tell differences in the texture or hardness of surfaces it is not sufficient to put a finger on them; the finger has to move over them. It is possible to have eyes and not see, ears and not hear.

The playfulness of the mammalian young and, in particular, the human child, has often been observed. For the very young the playing is not directed by sustained purposes. A ball is thrown, blocks are piled up and knocked down largely as manifestations of animal spirit. In this aimless playing the infant learns about the world. He develops body coordination. By moving about, touching, and manipulating he learns the reality of objects and the structuring of space. However, unlike other primates, at an early stage in the human child's growth (three or four years), his playing begins to be governed by themes. It occurs in the context of stories he tells himself. These are transfigured versions of his experiences in a world ruled by adults, of tales told by them, and bits of conversation overheard. His activities and explorations, then, are increasingly directed by cultural values. Although all human beings have similar sense organs, how their capacities are used and developed begin to diverge at an early age. As a result, not only do attitudes to environment differ but the actualized capacity of the senses differs, so that people in one culture may acquire sharp noses for scent while those in another acquire deep stereoscopic vision. Both worlds are predominantly visual: one will be enriched by fragrances, the other by the acute three-dimensionality of objects and spaces.

common

psychological

structures

and

responses

Human beings possess exceptionally large brains; they have minds. Philosophers have debated through the millennia on the relation between body and mind. Neurophysiologists and psychologists have tried to see how human brains operate differently from those of other primates. The tendency in modern research is to narrow the gap between human and animal mental processes. The gap remains because human beings boast a highly developed capacity for symbolic behavior. An abstract language of signs and symbols is unique to the species. With it human beings have constructed mental worlds to mediate between themselves and external reality. The artificial environment they have built is an outcome of mental processes—similarly, myths, legends, taxonomies, and science. All these achievements may be seen as cocoons that humans have woven in order to feel at home in nature. We are well aware that peoples in different times and places have structured their worlds very differently; the multiplicity of cultures is a persistent theme in the social sciences. Here our purpose is to focus, as in the previous chapter, on the underlying similarities.

rationalization

If by rational we mean the conscious application of logical rules, then only a small part of most people's lives is rational. It has been said that the human being is a rationalizing, rather than a rational, animal. This is a revealing half-truth; it underlines the fact that the complex brain through which we organize sense data, and which distinguishes us from other animals, is not all of a piece. Man's brain consists of three basic cerebral types, greatly dissimilar in structure and chemistry, and yet all three must interconnect and function together. The brain's oldest heritage is basically reptilian. It seems to play a primary role in instinctually determined functions such as establishing territory, finding shelter, hunting, homing, breeding, forming social hierarchies, and the like. A later development is the primitive (limbic) cortex of mammals. This structure of the brain plays an important role in emotional, endocrine, and viscero-somatic functions. Finally, late in evolution there appears a more highly differentiated cortex which is the hallmark of the brains of the higher mammals and which culminates in man to become the rational brain of calculation and symbolic thinking. Human needs, emotional drives, and aspirations are largely nonrational, but the neocortex has a seemingly infinite capacity to provide "reasons" for what we are propelled by our lower brains to do.[1] Wishful thinking and delusion permeate all our ideals, political and environmental; they are woven into all concepts and plans that are complex enough, and generate sufficient emotional force, to command action. The rational brain is the primary power at man's disposal to translate his yearnings into semblances of reality.

scale of human perception

The objects we perceive are commensurate with the size of our body, the acuity and range of our perceptual apparatus, and purpose. The south Californian desert, uninhabitable to Spaniards, was ample home to the Indians. Bushmen learn to read the fine script of spoors in the sand and recognize the location of individual plants on the barest plains of the Kalahari. Though the size of perceived objects varies greatly from culture to culture, nonetheless they fall into a certain range. Neither the very small nor the very large come into our purview in the course of day-to-day living. We notice bushes, trees, and grass but rarely the individual leaves and

---

1 Paul D. MacLean, "Contrasting Functions of Limbic and Neocortical Systems of the Brain and Their Relevance to Psychophysiological Aspects of Medicine," *American Journal of Medicine*, 25, No. 4 (1958), 611–26.

blades; we see sand but not its individual grains. The emotional bond between man and animal seldom holds below a certain size—the size of the goldfish in the bowl and of small turtles that children play with. Bacteria and insects are beyond our ordinary perceptual range, and well beyond the human capacity to empathize. At the other end of the scale we can see the stars, but only as specks of light in a ceiling of modest height. The mind can calculate astronomical dimensions as abstract entities; we cannot, however, imagine distances of a million miles, or even a thousand miles. No matter how often one has traversed the breadth of the United States, it is not possible to see it in one's mind's eye as other than a shape, a small-scaled map.

segmentation

Three-dimensional vision and dexterous hands enable human beings to perceive their environment as consisting of objects against an unfocused background, and not just as patterns. Nature consists partly of discrete objects like fruits, trees, bushes, individual animals, human beings, rocks, mountain peaks, and stars; partly it consists of enveloping and background continua like air, light, temperature, space. Human beings tend to segment the continua of nature. For instance, the light spectrum visible to the human eye is perceived as discrete bands of color: violet, blue, green, yellow, orange, red. In the middle latitudes temperature changes continuously in the course of a year but it is common for people to divide it into four or five seasons, often with festivities marking the passage from one to the other. An infinite number of directions radiate from one point but in many cultures, four, five, or six directions are especially privileged. The earth surface possesses certain sharp gradients: for instance, between land and water, mountain and plain, forest and savanna, but even where these don't exist man has the tendency to differentiate his space ethnocentrically, distinguishing between the sacred and the profane, center and periphery, the home estate and the common range. Again, people in different parts of the world have used cardinal directions to differentiate space. In China, provinces are named north or south of a lake or river, west or east of a mountain. In England one finds Norfolk and Suffolk, Wessex and Essex. Or regions may be distinguished into upper, middle, and lower as with the subdivisions of Franconia in south Germany. California is divided into upper and lower rather than into north and south regions. The scientific procedure for dividing up space is rather similar. The regions of a geographer may be numerous and complicated but they often develop from simple dichotomies such as between humid and arid, pedocals

and pedalfers. Köppen's climatic classification was derived from five basic units carved out of the continuum of temperature with its two poles, "Tropical" and "Frost."

binary oppositions

The human mind appears to be disposed to organize phenomena not only into segments but to arrange them in opposite pairs. We break the color spectrum into discrete bands and then see "red" as the opposite of "green." Red is the signal for danger, and green is the signal for safety. Traffic lights use these colors for the readiness with which we read their messages.[2] In other cultures the colors may have somewhat different emotional associations, but the general point remains valid, namely the tendency for the human mind to pick pairs among segments perceived in nature's continuum and assign opposite meanings to each pair. This tendency may reflect the structure of the human mind, but the emotional force of some bipolar antinomies suggests that the total human being, at all levels of experience, is involved. One may speculate on some of the fundamental oppositions in human experience: life and death, male and female, "we" (or "I") and "they" are among the most important. These antinomies of biological and social experience are then transposed to the enveloping physical reality.

Some Basic Polarities

Biological and Social	Geographical	Cosmological
life—death	land—water	heaven—earth
male—female	mountain—valley	high—low
we—they	north—south	light—darkness
	center—periphery	

resolution of contradictions

Opposites are often mediated by a third term. Thus to the polarized meanings of red and green in traffic signals we select the color yellow to signify "caution," neither "stop" nor "go;" and in this case yellow is the band of wave length intermediate between red and green in the color spectrum and not just an arbitrarily selected color. In the cosmological schema earth mediates between the forces of the upper- and underworlds. The idea of center reconciles the bipolar tendencies of the cardinal directions.

2 Edmund R. Leach, *Claude Lévi-Strauss* (New York: Viking, 1970), pp. 16–20.

Myths and geometric figures of symbolic power can also be viewed as man's efforts to resolve the contradictions that he encounters through life. Among the most fundamental and painful antinomic pairs in human experience is that of life and death. Myths arise as attempts to resolve the dilemma. For example, in myth it is possible to envisage a state in which a person is dead and yet alive, or is dead and will return to life.[3] Myths, legends, and folktales from widely different parts of the world have been identified as so many efforts to make death intelligible and acceptable. One type of myth views death in a quasi-Malthusian framework. Humankind has early recognized the importance of instituting order or equilibrium in a world in which resources are limited and the potential for human reproduction is great. Mythical thought has transfigured death, inescapable and horrible to man, into an agent (angel) of mercy who brings relief to an overburdened earth.[4]

The contradictions of life are usually resolved in narration. A geometric figure may serve the same purpose of harmonizing the opposites, and of such figures the most important is the circle or mandala.[5] The circle, a symbol of wholeness and harmony, is a recurrent motif in the arts of ancient Eastern civilizations, in the thinking of ancient Greece, in Christian art, in the alchemical practices of the Middle Ages and in the healing rites of some nonliterate peoples. Jungian psychoanalysts see the circle as an archetypal image of the reconciliation of opposites, common to all mankind. The specific form of the mandala varies greatly, as well as the context in which it appears. The mandala may take the form of the petals of a lotus, the rays of a sun wheel, the healing circle of the Navaho, the rose windows of churches, and the halos of Christian saints. As a symbol of perfection the circle has strongly influenced the Western world's conception of the cosmos. Planetary motions enact the harmony of the heavenly spheres and must therefore be circular. Their elliptic paths were conceded with the greatest reluctance; likewise the irregularities of the earth's surface were viewed as defects that had to be explained away. Architecturally, the mandala pattern appears in the layout of certain Indian and Chinese temples as well as in the design of traditional and idealized cities. At the world's primary centers of urbanism, cities arose not only in response to economic and commercial forces but also to the call for the establishment of sacred space, modeled after the cosmos. Such cities tended to have regular geometric outlines oriented to the cardinal directions, to their intermediate points, or to the position of

[3] Edmund R. Leach, "Genesis as Myth," in John Middleton (ed.), *Myth and Cosmos* (Garden City, N. Y.: Natural History Press, 1967), p. 3.

[4] H. Schwarzbaum, "The Overcrowded Earth," *Numen*, 4 (1957), 59–74.

[5] Aniele Jaffé, "Symbolism in the Visual Arts," in C. G. Jung (ed.), *Man and His Symbols* (New York: Dell, 1968), pp. 266–85; José and Miriam Argüelles, *Mandala* (Berkeley and London: Shambala, 1972).

the rising sun. A Jungian might say that every building, sacred or secular, that has a mandala (or isometric) ground plan is the projection of an archetypal image from within the human subconscious onto the outer world. The city, the temple, or even the dwelling may become a symbol of psychic wholeness, a microcosmos capable of exercising a beneficent influence on the human beings who enter the place or live there.

substances and cosmological schemata

The contents of nature are enormously varied. Each culturally-differentiated human group has its own nomenclature to cope with this variety. However, in different parts of the world people have recognized a few basic substances or elements that underlie the multiplicity of phenomena, for example, earth, water, wood, air, metal, and fire. Each substance or element is identified with a distinctive quality. One speaks of the earthiness of earth, the hardness and coldness of metal. Each element is also a process or the embodiment of a principle for action. Thus the idea of wetness and downward motion is associated with water, and the idea of change, heat, and upward motion with fire. Beneath the veneer of scientific sophistication, modern man still tends to think of nature in these elemental categories. Moreover, he relates to them personally: wood is warm and friendly, metal is cold.

The desire to bring nature and man's world into a coherent system is widespread. In different parts of the world we find the substances or elements, commonly four to six in number, identified with spatial directions, colors, animals, human institutions, and personality traits. Some cosmological schemata are elaborate, others are relatively simple. In cultures that we know, the associations appear natural or appropriate. With alien cultures they seem completely arbitrary. Needless to say, to the native, although he may not grasp the cosmological frame in its entirety, the parts he knows are, for him, meaningful and reasonable. The net of associations arises in the first place in response to the need for order, for establishing significant relationships among the overwhelming wealth of phenomena that confronts every individual. Here are four partial sets of cosmological correspondences:

1. CHINESE

wood	spring	east	lesser *yang*	green	anger
fire	summer	south	greater *yang*	red	joy
earth	————	center	balance	yellow	desire
metal	autumn	west	lesser *yin*	white	sorrow
water	winter	north	greater *yin*	black	fear

2. INDONESIAN

fire	north	black	unbending
earth	center	multicolored or grey	
alcohol (gold)	west	yellow	luxurious
mountain	south	red	avaricious
water, wind	east	white	comprehensive

3. KERESAN PUEBLO INDIAN (AMERICAN SOUTHWEST)

north	yellow	Shakak (God of winter and snow)	puma
east	white	Shruwisigyama (bird-like god)	wolf
south	red	Maiyochina (gopher-like god, helps crops to grow)	bobcat
west	blue	Shruwitira (man-like god)	bear
zenith	brown	—— (fox-like god) (middle)	badger
nadir	black	—— (mole-like god)	

4. OGLALA SIOUX (GREAT PLAINS)

north	white	great, white, cleansing wind
west	black	thunder brings rain
center of the world		
south	yellow	summer, growth
east	red	light, morning star, wisdom

What do these cosmological schemata have in common? First, the continua of nature, such as the color spectrum, the seasonal cycle, and the vectors from a point are subdivided arbitrarily into a small number of categories. Second, all four schemata relate directions to colors. Third, the principle of action or a behavioral trait is either implied or stated explicitly. The Chinese schema relates inanimate elements to anger, joy, etc.; the Indonesian schema to such qualities as eloquence, avariciousness, comprehensiveness; the Pueblo Indian schema to zoomorphic gods and animals; the Sioux Indian schema to actions in nature such as "cleansing wind," "thunder brings rain." Fourth, the concept of "center" exists in all four world views. If the elements are structured around the cardinal points and the center, we shall see what the tabular form masks: namely, the "closed" or circular nature of these world views. The multivarious elements of the cosmos are mediated by the center.[6]

harmonious whole, binary oppositions, and cosmological schemata

What are the relationships between the cosmological schemata of substances, directions, colors, etc., and the simpler categories of bipolar opposites, and the concept of a primordial "matter" or force? It is tempting to see an evolutionary process through which simple categories based on binary oppositions and the mediating third pass into schemata of increasing complexity, and that behind these efforts to structure segmented nature is the idea of a primal unity and harmony. Such a process of elaboration is possible and likely at certain stages in the structuring of the world; on the other hand it is also likely that the simpler categories are a later philosophical attempt to explain the inchoate richness of an earlier structure. In China the idea that *yin* and *yang* are complementary principles of an essential whole appears to have preceded the idea of five elements and the system of correspondences noted earlier. In ancient Egypt, Babylonia, and Greece, the world's substance was conceived as fundamentally one—water. Earth arose out of the primordial waters. The primordial substance dichotomized and life was generated through the union of the parts, often presented as the union of the Sky Father and the Earth Mother. The Greek idea of four elements—earth, fire, air, and water—appeared during the fifth century B.C., at roughly the time when the idea of five elements surfaced in China.

Both a dualistic and a five-fold ordering of society and nature can be found in Indonesia. Van der Kroef has attempted to show the relations between the two.[7] First, he notes that in virtually all areas of the Indonesian archipelago, despite its diversity of cultures, there is a persistent structural motif: the functional antithesis of social groups. The antithesis extends beyond the social system to art, religion, and nature. For example, the village in Amboina (south Moluccas) is divided into two parts: each part is not only a social unit but a category in cosmic classification comprising all objects and events around the villager. A list could be set up classifying all objects

---

6 Emile Durkheim and Marcel Mauss, *Primitive Classification*, trans. Rodney Needham (Chicago: University of Chicago Press, Phoenix Books, 1963), and Marcel Granet, *La Pensée Chinoise* (Paris: Albin Michel, 1934).
7 Justus M. van der Kroef, "Dualism and Symbolic Antithesis in Indonesian Society," *American Anthropologist*, 56 (1954), 847–62.

and characteristics associated with each of the two divisions:

Left	Right
Female	Male
Coast or seaside	Land or mountainside
Below	Above
Earth	Heaven or sky
Spiritual	Worldly
Downward	Upward
Peel	Pit
Exterior	Interior
Behind	In front
West	East
Younger brother	Old brother
New	Old

Three points are worth noting in connection with Indonesian dualism. One is that the native may not be aware of it. The native Amboinese, for example, is likely to see a tripartite rather than a dualistic division of his world. To him, implicit in each paired opposition is a mediating third term. Another point is that though the two parts of a duality are seen as complementary, they are clearly unequal; thus societies are often divided into *sacred* (leader) and *profane* (follower). The third point is the idea, implied by legends and rituals, that duality is the precursor of multiplicity. In Java and Sumatra, for instance, the marriage ceremony is believed to be the reenactment of the ancient and mysterious marriage of *heaven* (the groom as "king") and *earth* (the bride as "queen") from which all things have their beginning.

The relation between the concept of a harmonious whole, a bipolar, tripartite, and five-fold ordering of society and nature is suggested by the following diagrams of Javanese and Balinese world views.

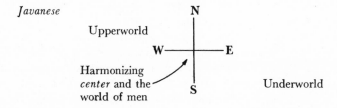

Balinese

Mountain: Upperworld—water, symbol of life

Madiapa:—Middleworld of man

Sea: Underworld—calamity, sickness, death

Confrontation of mountain-sea/is translated into confrontation of opposite directions:

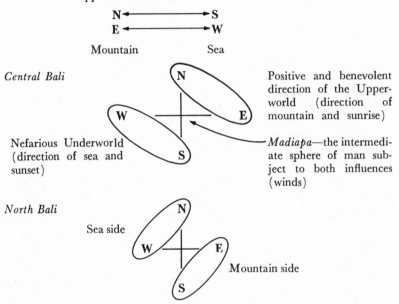

Javanese and Balinese world views are very much alike. Consider the Balinese schema, which is the simpler of the two. Dualism is evident in identifying the mountain as the upperworld and the sea as the underworld. These are polar opposites: from the mountain comes fresh water which symbolizes life, whereas the direction of the sea is that of calamity, sickness, and death. Mediating between the extremes, and receiving influences from both, is *madiapa*, the middle world of man. The antinomic pair of mountain and sea on the vertical axis is viewed on the horizontal plane of compass points as oppositions between north and south, east and west. In central Bali, north and east (the directions of mountain and sunrise) symbolize the positive and beneficent influences of the upperworld; west and south (the directions of sea and sunset) symbolize the nefarious effects of the underworld. The center is *madiapa,* the intermediate sphere of man which is buffeted by "winds" from both sources. Here, then, in Bali the duality of mountain and sea is mediated by the middle human sphere to constitute a tripartite division; and on the horizontal plane the tripartite division becomes the five-fold schema of four cardinal points and center. In Java and Bali both society and nature tend to be structured and ranked in a five-fold schema.

symbolism and cosmological schemata

A symbol is a part that has the power to suggest a whole: for instance, the cross for Christianity, the crown for kingship, and the circle for harmony and perfection. An object is also taken as a symbol when it casts a penumbra of meanings, when it calls to mind a succession of phenomena that are related analogically or metaphorically to each other. The practice of structuring the world into substances, colors, directions, animals, and human traits promotes a symbolical world view. In a cosmological schema, a substance immediately suggests a color, which suggests in turn a direction, the animal emblem of that direction, and perhaps a human personality trait or mood. In such a richly symbolical world, objects and events take on meanings that to an outsider may seem arbitrary. To the native, the associations and analogies are in the nature of things and require no rational justification: to the Chinese, "wood," "spring," "east," and "green" implicate each other. The meanings of most symbols are culture-bound. We may say that human beings have a tendency to structure their worlds in a limited number of categories which often include substances, colors, directions, etc., but the detailed ordering of the components varies greatly from culture to culture.

Yet certain substances have meanings of wide currency—for instance, fire and water. In the Chinese schema, fire is *yang,* male, directed upward, joyful, and phallic; water is *yin,* female, and passive. These interpretations are far from unique. They have become part of the modern lore through the works of Freud and Jung, works that derive their insight in part from the analysis of primitive folktales and ancient literature. In psychoanalysis, fire signifies striving consciousness.[8] Water is an image of the unconscious; it is formless but fertilizing, a source of potential power. Water symbolizes the feminine side of human personality. Immersion in water means the extinction of fire and of consciousness. It means death. Perhaps this explains

[8] Gaston Bachelard, The Psychoanalysis of Fire, trans. A. C. M. Ross (Boston: Beacon Press, 1968), and *L'eau et les Rêves* (Paris: José Corti, 1942).

why the emotion associated with water in the Chinese system is fear. As the feminine principle, water also signifies wisdom and regeneration; it is feared but the striving conscious self must accept the immersion and death if he is to be revitalized and achieve wholeness. This interpretation finds unexpected support in a ceremony of the Congo Pygmies, far from the high civilizations of Eurasia. The Pygmies of the rain forest recognize five elements: wood, fire, earth, water, and air. Wood, naturally, is the dominant element. Surprising is the fact that fire plays an important role in the Pygmies' economic and ceremonial life although they do not know how to start it. Fire is carried with them wherever they go. During the *molimo* death ceremony, the women try to stamp out the precious fire while the men try to fan it to life by a wild erotic dance.[9]

color psychology and symbolism

Human sensitivity to color is manifest at an early age. Even infants three months old appear capable of making discriminations. Colors, which play an important role in human emotions, may constitute man's earliest symbols. The relation between a chromatic band and emotion, however, is muddied by amateurish attempts at generalization: universal rules turn out to be culture-bound if not idiosyncratic. One generalization that does seem to have wide applicability is the distinction between "advancing" and "receding" colors. Red, orange, and yellow are described as advancing colors because they seem nearer to the observer than other hues. Red, or red-orange in particular, "reaches out." It stimulates the nervous system and suggests warmth. Red color also has the effect of making an object seem heavier than it is. Green, blue, and blue-green are known as receding colors; they suggest coolness.[10] Blue is antithetical to red; an object painted blue is often judged lighter than it is. Colors that affect our sense of weight also affect our sense of up and down. Where elevators have colored lights, the red arrow invariably points down, the blue arrow up.

Primary colors designate strong emotions. Young children appear to have little interest in mixed or impure colors apparently because they denote ambiguities that lie outside their experience. Among chromatic colors, red is the most dominant and its meaning is the most widely shared by peoples of different culture. Red signifies blood, life, and energy. Since Upper Paleolithic times red ocher has been used in burials. Greek, Etruscan, and

---

9 Colin Turnbull, "The Mbuti Pygmies of the Congo," in James L. Gibbs (ed.), *Peoples of Africa* (New York: Holt, Rinehart & Winston, 1965), p. 310.

10 S. M. Newhall, "Warmth and Coolness of Colors," *Psychological Record*, 4 (1941), 198–212.

Roman sarcophagi bear traces of red paint in their interior, and the red shroud has been in use for interment down to the present, although the practice is now limited to the burial of a pope. In China, red is the color used in weddings for it symbolizes life and joy. On the other hand, a red sky means calamity and warfare. Here is no contradiction: red is the color of blood and blood is life, but spilt blood leads to death. Red also symbolizes energy and action—action aimed at life though it may result in death. The red flag is the flag of revolutionary fervor.

All peoples distinguish between "black" and "white" or "darkness" and "light." Everywhere these colors carry powerful symbolic reverberations; only red among chromatic colors matches them in importance. Black and white have both positive and negative meanings, thus:

> *Black:* (positive) wisdom, potential, germinal, maternal, earth-mother.
> (negative) evil, curse, defilement, death.
> *White:* (positive) light, purity, spirituality, timelessness, divine.
> (negative) mourning, death.

Nonetheless the chief associations of white are positive, and those of black negative. The two colors symbolize opposed and yet complementary universal principles: analogous pairs are light and darkness, appearance and disappearance, life and death. These antinomies are different ways of saying the same thing. They are the necessary halves of a total reality: one merges into the other in space and evolves out of the other in time. In rituals, myths, and philosophical synthesis, the complementarity of black and white is emphasized. In isolation, however, these terms often appear to represent irreconcilable values. It is well known that in the Western tradition black stands for all the negative values of curse, evil, defilement, and death, whereas white signifies joy, purity, and goodness. But similar interpretations are given in a large number of non-Western cultures. For example, to the Bambara—a west African negro tribe—white is a regal color, representing wisdom and purity of spirit. The dark tones of indigo, on the other hand, are identified with sadness and impurity. To the Nupe tribe of Nigeria, black signifies sorcery, evil, and frightening prospects. Among the peoples of Malagasy (Madagascar) the word black is associated with inferiority, evil, suspicion, and disagreeableness; the word white with light, hope, joy, and purity. Examples can be multiplied easily. A reason for the negative response to black may lie in the child's horror of the night—a time of isolation, disturbing dreams, and nightmares, when invisibility of the familiar encourages fantasy to run wild. There is also the fear of blindness.[11]

[11] Kenneth J. Gergen, "The Significance of Skin Color in Human Relations," *Daedalus* (Spring 1967), pp. 397–99.

White, black, and red thus appear to be colors of universal significance. According to Victor Turner, they are among man's earliest symbols. Turner believes that these colors are important to man because they represent products of the human body whose emission, spilling, or production is associated with a heightening of emotion. The human individual is caught by sensations beyond the normal range; he is possessed by a power the source of which he posits outside of himself in nature and society. Thus the symbol, a superorganic cultural product, is intimately connected with organic bodily experiences in its early stages.[12] The physiological events associated with the three colors are also experiences of social relationships, which may be summarized as follows:

White = semen (man and woman tie).
      = milk (mother and child tie).

Red = bloodshed (war, feud, social discontinuities).
     = obtaining and preparing animal food (male productive role; sexual division of labor).
     = transmission of blood from generation to generation (index of membership in corporate group).

Black = excreta (bodily dissolution; change from one status to another— mystical death).
      = rainclouds, fertile earth (shared life-values).

Almost every language has special words for black and white. Among chromatic colors red occupies a special position. The term for red is usually one of the oldest color terms in a given language; as a rule it is a native word. "Yellow" in many respects follows the pattern of red. Like red, a special term develops for it which is old in the color vocabulary. Next come green and blue. Unlike red, for which comparison is readily made with blood, neither yellow, nor green, nor blue is the outstanding color of any ubiquitous phenomenon in nature. In China, yellow dominates because it is perceived to be the color of earth and of the center; but this attribution is not widespread. The evident object of comparison for green is given in plants, and in the great majority of languages the term for green is related to the words for plants and growth. In English, "green," "growth," and "grass" are derived from the Germanic root *grō* which probably meant "to grow." It would seem natural to associate the color blue with the sky; yet the influence of sky on the development of terms for blue has not been as

12 Victor Turner, "Color Classification in Ndembu Ritual," in Michael Banton (ed.), *Anthropological Approaches to the Study of Religion,* A.S.A. Monograph No. 3 (London: Tavistock Publications, 1966), pp. 47–84.

great as one might expect.[13] Almost everywhere, blue is the last of the color primaries to be indicated by a special term. In many languages there is no word for blue at all. Brent Berlin and Paul Kay believe that the basic color terms evolve through stages: first, black plus most dark hues and white plus most light hues; then red, orange, and yellow; then green and blue; then brown.[14]

spatial psychology and symbolism

The idea of "center" and "periphery" in spatial organization is perhaps universal. People everywhere tend to structure space—geographical and cosmological—with themselves at the center and with concentric zones (more or less well defined) of decreasing value beyond. This theme will be taken up in the next chapter. Spatial values that transcend individual cultures appear to be based on certain basic traits of the human body. For example, the human body has a back and front. What are the implications of this asymmetry? "Follow your nose" is the clearest direction we can give to the lost. Going forward is easy; going backward is not. Moreover, "turning back" is psychologically unpleasant, since it suggests error and defeat. "Front" and "back" are unequal in social value. In some cultures it is unseemly to turn one's back on another person, particularly if the other person is superior in dignity. Assemblies of people are often hierarchically organized. A common characteristic is the sitting of important personages in front while the nameless are shunted to the back. Somatic and psychological asymmetry is projected into space, which acquires the meaning and value of back and front. This asymmetrical designation of space occurs at different scales. Most rooms have a front entrance and the furniture is arranged with respect to it. Public buildings and private houses, especially those of the upper and middle classes, have clearly demarcated front and back regions. Many old cities had front entrances. Only one route was the royal route and a magnificent gate stood over it.[15]

"Open" and "enclosed" are spatial categories meaningful to many people. Agoraphobia and claustrophobia describe pathological states, but open and enclosed spaces can also stimulate topophilic feelings. Open space signifies freedom, the promise of adventure, light, the public realm, formal

---

13 B. J. Kouwer, *Colors and Their Character: A Psychological Study* (The Hague: Martinus Nijhoff), pp. 12–18.

14 Brent Berlin and Paul Kay, *Basic Color Terms: Their Universality and Evolution* (Berkeley and Los Angeles: University of California Press, 1969), pp. 7–45.

15 Yi-Fu Tuan, "Geography, Phenomenology, and the Study of Human Nature," *Canadian Geographer*, 15, No. 3 (1971), 181–92.

and unchanging beauty; enclosed space signifies the cozy security of the womb, privacy, darkness, biologic life. It is tempting to speculate on the relation of these feelings to certain profound human experiences considered phylogenetically and ontogenetically. As a species, man's primate ancestors migrated out of the womb-like shelter of the tropical forest to the more open and unpredictable environment of the park-like savanna. Individually, every birth is a move out of the dark protective womb to a bright world that seems at first far less accommodating. On the time scale of cultural evolution, the onset of urbanism, with the concomitant development of ideas of transcendence, broke the shell of place-bound, life-nurturing neolithic communities. The appeal of cities lies in large part on the juxtaposition of the cozy and the grand, of darkness and light, the intimate and the public. *Megara* and *atrium* both connote darkness: the private house shelters life's vulnerable physiological processes, whereas in the open *agora* and *forum* a person fulfills his potential as free man. Much of the attraction of old European cities resides in the juxtaposition of crowded residential quarters (the dark warrens of life) and spacious public squares. Certain natural landscapes appeal to us. Paul Shepard sees the appeal as related to the human anatomy. The scenic attractions often correspond to a narrow defile, a gorge, water gap, or valley that opens out to a bright sunlit plain. In the Grail legends and in the Tannhaeuser epic the landscape theme is that of a river issuing from a cloven stone or from a mountain in paradise. In Edgar Allan Poe's story, "Domain of Arnheim," the narrator describes the passage by water through a gorge of overhanging foliage to a large basin of great beauty. In real life, Shepard notes that among the earliest scenes to attract Americans are the water gaps and ravines of New England and the Appalachians. In the frontier West, again gorges and canyons hold great fascination for travelers, even in the nineteenth century when traveling was often a hardship. The Devil's Gate in south-central Wyoming, for example, is on the Oregon Trail; wagons did not have to pass through it for there was an easy detour. Nonetheless many travelers deliberately explored this gorge through the Granite Range and found it awe-inspiring.[16]

What other spatial characteristics can be said to excite emotions that are widely shared? The vertical versus the horizontal dimension? Here a common response is to see them symbolically as the antithesis between transcendence and immanence, between the ideal of disembodied consciousness (a skyward spirituality) and the ideal of earth-bound identification. Vertical elements in the landscape evoke a sense of striving, a defiance of gravity, while the horizontal elements call to mind acceptance and rest. Architectural spaces are capable of evoking certain types of emotion. Ac-

---

16 Paul Shepard, Jr., "The Cross Valley Syndrome," *Landscape*, 10, No. 3 (1961), 4–8.

cording to Morse Peckham, we tend to associate closed solids and shallow plasticity with the feeling of fixity and inhibition; open pavilions and deep plasticity with the feeling of flexibility and expansion; deep axis with energy release and shallow axis with energy conservation.[17] The existence of a kinesthetic relationship between certain physical forms and human feelings is implied in the verbs we use to describe them: for example, mountain peaks and man-made spires "soar," ocean waves as well as architectural domes "swell," arches "spring," landscapes "unfold," Greek temples are "calm," and Baroque façades are "restless."[18] Moreover, architectural forms appear to influence our impression of size—of the way space expands and contracts to a degree that natural landforms rarely give. As Susanne K. Langer puts it, "Open, outdoor space, without limiting contours of hills or shore lines, is many times larger than the hugest edifice, yet the sense of vastness is more likely to beset one upon entering a building; and there it is clearly an effect of pure forms."[19] Architectural space of perfectly resolved proportions, as in the interior of St. Peter's, Rome, seems to have the effect of reducing somewhat its great size; on the other hand Baroque interiors, lacking this kind of proportion, expand unequivocally.[20]

[17] Morse Peckham, *Man's Rage for Chaos* (New York: Schocken Books, 1967), pp. 168–84, 199.

[18] Geoffrey Scott, *The Architecture of Humanism: A Study in the History of Taste* (New York: Scribner's, 1969), p. 159 (originally published in 1914); Max Rieser, "The Language of Shapes and Sizes in Architecture or On Morphic Semantics," *The Philosophical Review*, 55 (1946), 152–73.

[19] Susanne K. Langer, *Mind: An Essay on Human Feeling* (Baltimore: Johns Hopkins, 1967), p. 160.

[20] J. S. Pierce, "Visual and Auditory Space in Baroque Rome," *Journal of Aesthetics and Art Criticism*, 18, No. 3 (1959), 66; Langer, *Human Feeling*.

ethnocentrism, symmetry, and space

Human beings, individually or in groups, tend to perceive the world with "self" as the center. Egocentrism and ethnocentrism appear to be universal human traits, though their strengths vary widely among individuals and social groups. Since consciousness lies in the individual, an egocentric structuring of the world is inescapable; and the fact that self-consciousness enables a person to view himself as an object among objects does not negate the ultimate seating of that view in an individual. Egocentrism is the habit of ordering the world so that its components diminish rapidly in value away from self. Although egocentrism is a strong bias of human nature, it can be fully achieved only on rare occasions. This is because a person is clearly dependent on others for biological survival and for psychological comfort; and also because the self is directionally biased: what lies "ahead" is not equivalent to what lies "behind." Egocentrism is a fantasy that manages to survive the challenges of daily experience.

By contrast, ethnocentrism (collective egocentrism) can be fully realized. Unlike the individual, a group can be self-sufficient; at least delusions of self-sufficiency are easier to sustain. Individuals are members of groups, and all have learned—though in varying degree—to differentiate between "we" and "they," between real people and people less real, between home ground and alien territory. "We" are at the center. Human beings lose human attributes in proportion as they are removed from the center.

ethnocentrism

Ethnocentrism is a common human trait. The ancient Egyptians, cut off from their peers in Mesopotamia by desert and sea, took it for granted that they were superior to the peoples they encountered beyond the rims of the Nile Valley. Conscious of their own sophistication they believed their neighbors to be rustic and uninitiated. They made the distinction between "men," on the one hand, and Libyans, Asiatics, or Africans, on the other. The Egyptians were "men," and somehow it was implied that foreigners lacked the full human stature. In times of national stress, when the old order had broken down, a common Egyptian plaint was that "foreigners have become people everywhere."

The Greek historian Herodotus commented on ethnocentrism among the Persians, thus: "Of nations, they honour most their nearest neighbours, whom they esteem next to themselves; those who live beyond these they honour in the second degree; and so with the remainder, the further they are removed, the less the esteem in which they hold them."[1]

In the northwestern sector of New Mexico, five cultures maintain their unique ways despite geographical proximity, frequent social contacts, and the blending influence of mass media. Their strong ethnocentrism is a bulwark against the forces for cultural homogenization. For instance, all five groups refer to themselves as people, as *dineh* (Navaho), the "cooked ones" (Zuni), the "chosen people" (Mormon), *la gente* (Spanish-Mexican), and "real Americans" or "white man" (Texan); each group thus implies that the others are not fully human. To the hypothetical question, "If after a prolonged drought the area is emptied of people and a new community has to be established with the return of rain, what kind of community would you put up?" the responses indicate unvaryingly that each group will want to reestablish itself, with no thought for a utopia that transcends local traditions.[2]

The illusion of superiority and centrality is probably necessary to the sustenance of culture. When rude encounters with reality shatter that illusion the culture itself is liable to decline. In the modern world of rapid communications, it is difficult for small communities to believe that they are in any literal sense at the center of things, and yet some such faith is necessary if

[1] Herodotus, *History*, trans. G. Rawlinson, *The History of Herodotus* (New York: Tudor, 1932), p. 52.

[2] Evon Z. Vogt and Ethel M. Albert, *The People of Rimrock* (Cambridge: Harvard University Press, 1966), p. 26.

they are to prosper. City fathers and town counselors appear to recognize this fact, and valiantly try to maintain a sense of centrality by proclaiming their town to be, for example, the "Bratwurst Capital of the World" (Sheboygan, Wisconsin) or even, rather desperately, "The Largest City for Its Size" (Taunton, Massachusetts). Modern nations, too, maintain an ethnocentric view of the world despite the clear knowledge that they are not alone in making the claim. De Gaulle tried to restore the centrality of France to the Frenchmen. Britain once took its position at the hub of the world for granted. In the nineteenth century there was ample evidence for the belief. Since the second world war, however, the dismemberment of empire, economic stress, and the emergence of America and Russia as superpowers have forced Britain to abandon the illusion of centrality, and compelled it to seek another image that is more consonant with the facts and yet of sufficient distinction to sustain the necessary sense of national pride.

It may not seem strange to us that China should for so long have considered itself the Middle Kingdom, nor that Britain in the nineteenth century, and now the United States, should see itself as the hub of the world. However, the fact is that this ethnocentric viewpoint prevails among most— if not all—peoples so long as they are isolated and do not have to face the existence of others more numerous or superior to themselves. From the vantage point of present-day knowledge we are right to call ethnocentrism an illusion, but in the past experience often lent it support.

ethnocentrism and cosmic diagrams among nonliterate peoples

The Ostiak of the lower Yenisei River are a small group of hunters and fishermen in western Siberia. Their cosmography is based on geographical reality, transformed to give it a vertical dimension. At the center of their universe is the Yenisei which is known as the Holy Water. Here lies the world of man. The Ostiak believe that away from the banks of the river, that is, away from the center, population diminishes, since this has been their experience. Above the earth, in the south, is Heaven, and below the earth, in the north, is Hades. Like many other peoples in northern Siberia the Ostiak see the earth as slanting, and equate "south" with "above" and "north" with "below." The Holy Water begins in Heaven and flows across the middle earth to Hades.

Geographically, the broad and flat Mongolian plateau is the waterdivide for the great river systems of Siberia and eastern Asia. It has some claim to centrality. The Mongols are aware of this but they take Mongolia to be a great mound and the center of the world rather than as a plateau rimmed by higher mountains. They, the Mongols, live on the central mound whereas other peoples live below them, on its slopes. To most peoples of Siberia and Central Asia the world is either circular or rectangular. Evidence suggests that with some groups belief in a circular cosmos was displaced by one of rectangular shape. The folk poetry of the Yakuts, for example, speaks of the four corners of both heaven and earth, but it also contains the idea of a round sky and a round earth. The sky of the Buriat is shaped like an overturned cauldron, rising and falling over the earth disc, of which the Buriat occupy the central place.[3]

To the Indians of Santa Ana pueblo in New Mexico, the earth is the center and principal object of the cosmos. Sun, moon, stars, Milky Way are accessories to the earth; their function is to make the earth habitable for mankind. The earth itself is square and stratified. Cardinal directions are recognized; in addition the pueblo Indians perceive the vertical axis of zenith and nadir in line with their stratified view of the cosmos (Figure 1).[4] The Zuni Indians to the west hold similar ideas. Their compact settlement is called the *itiwana* or the Middle Place. All the universe is oriented to *itiwana*. Much of their origin myth is concerned with the problem of reach-

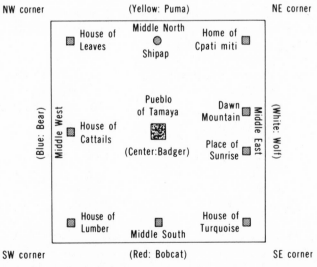

Figure 1 Cosmography of the Keresan Pueblo Indians, Santa Ana, New Mexico. (After White.)

3 U. Holmberg, "Siberian Mythology," in J. A. MacCulloch (ed.), *Mythology of All Races,* IV (Boston: Marshall Jones Co., 1927).
4 Leslie A. White, "The World of the Keresan Pueblo Indians," in Stanley Diamond (ed.), *Primitive Views of the World* (New York: Columbia University Press, 1964), pp. 83–94.

ing the Middle Place and ascertaining the correctness of its location. Their neighbor, the Navaho, have taken up sheepherding as well as agriculture. Unlike the pueblo Indians they live in dispersed hogans. The Navaho also believe that they have wandered in the past searching for the Middle Place. Each hogan is a middle place. Compared with the Zuni the Navaho hold less strongly to the idea of the center; more important to them is the idea of concentric zones of life-space that become successively more alien away from the center.

Eskimos live at the Arctic margin of the inhabited world. They did not, however, know this until they came into contact with large numbers of white men. Before the encounter they saw their habitat not only as the world's geographical center but also its cultural and population center. Early in the century, for example, Greenland Eskimos thought that Europeans were being sent to Greenland to learn virtue and good manners from them. In the Hudson Bay the hunter Agoolak, an Aivilik Eskimo of Southampton Island, entertained similar misunderstanding. He was amazed when the United States Army sent men to build an air strip near Coral Harbour. For years he had seen the same white faces—the faces of explorers and traders. Those who left often returned and they seemed to know one another well. Agoolak and other Aivilik hunters reasonably concluded that though white men were different they were far less numerous. This reassuring view was shattered during the second world war when many strange people from the outside world appeared.[5]

Before the true shape of Southampton Island was known through aerial photography, some Aivilik men were asked to sketch the shape of their island home. The outlines they drew turned out to be remarkably accurate down to the details of inlets (Figure 2). A notable distortion is in the size of Bell peninsula relative to the rest of the island; it is manifestly exaggerated. This is not surprising for most of the people live on the peninsula. The tendency to exaggerate the size of one's home ground at the expense of the territory of neighbors is well known. A Texan's view of the United States, for example, will probably show a huge Texas surrounded by smaller states becoming more and more midget-like the further away they are from the Lone Star. There may be some justification for this view, but a Bostonian's idea of the country is likely to show similar signs of self-inflation, exaggerating the size of Massachusetts out of all proportion to its true area. Aivilik Eskimos, then, like most people have acquired the ego-supporting habit of overestimating their own importance vis-à-vis the rest of the world. Their knowledge of the geography of Southampton Island is extraordinarily precise, and this detailed knowledge extends to the west coast of Hudson

5 E. S. Carpenter, "Space Concepts of the Aivilik Eskimos," *Explorations*, 5 (1955), 131–45.

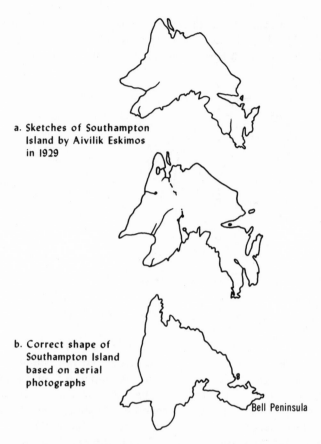

a. Sketches of Southampton
   Island by Aivilik Eskimos
   in 1929

b. Correct shape of
   Southampton Island
   based on aerial
   photographs

Bell Peninsula

Figure 2   Southampton Island, Hudson Bay. (After Carpenter.)

Bay where they do much of their hunting. Beyond the limits of personal experience, however, they have to depend on rumors and hearsay. The directions to some of the remoter spots, such as white man's trading posts and towns, are still fairly well represented on the sketch maps but their distances from Southampton Island are vastly compressed. Geography gives way to cosmography when the Aivilik attempt to understand the world beyond their home. They take Southampton Island itself to be the center of a flat, circular earth whose outer limit can be reached from the island in a journey of no more than several weeks.

The idea of the earth as a flat disc surrounded by water and floating on it appears in many parts of the world. The idea can take hold in people's minds despite the evidence of the environment, which may be a desert plateau, a mountainous country, or an island. The Yurok Indians of northern California, for example, appear to conceptualize their world two-dimensionally as a circular disc, despite the ruggedness of their home ground (Figure 3). The Yurok are fishermen of the Klamath River and gather

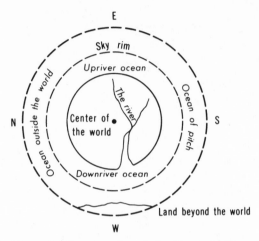

Figure 3 Cosmography of the Yurok Indians, Northern California.

acorns in its vicinity. They depend on the river for their principal food, the salmon, and for transportation. They tend to avoid the hill country; the large number of trails crossing it are not nearly so important for traveling and commerce as the river. The Yurok lack the idea of cardinal directions. They orient themselves by their principal geographical feature, the Klamath, and speak of directions as upstream or downstream. Since the river is crooked, upstream and downstream may designate almost all points of the compass. Yet the predominant trend of the river is clearly recognized: it bisects their world. The sense of cardinal directions is not necessary to the conception of a symmetrical world. The Yurok world, insofar as they know it intimately, is small, about one hundred and fifty miles in diameter. Beyond it the Yurok are vaguely aware that other human beings exist. The Yurok know that the Klamath River ends in the ocean but they also believe that by going upstream for ten or twelve days they shall reach salt water again. Water surrounds the circular earth; the Klamath crosses it in the middle. Somewhere on the bank of the Klamath, near the point where the Trinity comes in from the south, is *qe'nek* the center of the world. At this locality the sky was made. It is a solid dome. Above the dome is the sky country, which a ladder connects with the earth. Below the earth is the realm of the dead, which can be reached by going down a lake.[6]

[6] T. T. Waterman, "Yurok Geography," *University of California Publications in American Archaeology and Ethnography,* 16 (1920), 182–200.

chinese ethnocentrism

Ethnocentrism is strongly developed among the Chinese. If the Greenland Eskimos thought the Europeans had come to them to learn virtue and good manners, it is understandable that the Chinese should have assumed likewise when the Europeans attempted to open the empire to trade at the end of the eighteenth century. China had good reasons for thinking itself the center of the world. For some three thousand years of its recorded history it functioned as a civilization that was far superior to the tribal cultures with which it had contact. The Chinese for millennia lived in a secluded world. At the center are the fertile alluvial plains. Here population might already have reached twenty-five million by the fourth century B.C.; here a sophisticated literate culture had evolved which, in its essential features, owed little to ideas from the outside. Population declined sharply beyond the central plains. To the north is the steppe, to the west are deserts and the earth's highest mountain system; to the south lies the tropical forest, and to the east the sea.

China did not see itself as a nation among other nations of comparable stature. It stood at the center of the world; it was the Middle Kingdom. It was even more grandly known as *t'ien hsia* (under heaven) or *chung yuan* (center and source), or *sze hai chih nuai* (within the four seas). The last title is somewhat unexpected since the Chinese in antiquity knew the sea to exist only in the east. Here we have another illustration of the tendency to see a water-girdled earth. Under Buddhist influence, circular cosmic plans were drawn which show the Kunlun Mountains at the center. They are the world's axial peak. Next to them is the *chung yuan,* the fertile earth of China. In the later versions of this type of religious cosmography, which are the only ones that survive, realistic geographical details are shown such as the Great Wall, the Huang Ho, the Korean peninsula and the island of Japan, but away from the known world cosmographic fantasy holds sway. The land mass is surrounded by an island-dotted ocean stream; beyond it, however, lies another ring of land.

The circular pattern departs from the traditional Chinese conception of the earth as rectangular in shape. The idea of successive rectangular domains centered on imperial China is traditional. The earliest expression of this idea appears in the *Shu Ching* and possibly dates back to the fifth century B.C. The earth is conceived as a succession of zones of decreasing culture away from the imperial capital (Figure 4). The first zone is the zone of the royal domains. This is followed by the lands of tributary feudal lords; the zone of pacification or the frontier belt where Chinese culture is being adopted; the zone of allied barbarians, and the zone of cultureless savagery. This schema was popular with the Chinese but the Romans could

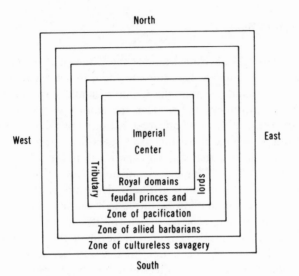

Figure 4 Traditional ethnocentric Chinese world view, dating back to fifth century B.C.

easily have adapted it for their own use. The two empires lay at opposite ends of the Eurasian continent. They were vaguely aware of each other's existence but neither felt the need to adjust their ethnocentric views to fit with the known facts.[7]

early greek maps

Ethnocentrism goes well with the idea of the circular cosmos. More than any other shape the circle implies a center. In the Occident numerous maps and diagrams exist to illustrate the pan-human habit of placing a symbol of self at the center of a symmetrically disposed world. The basic pattern shows land, roundish in shape, ringed by water. The earliest known example of this pattern is preserved on a Babylonian clay tablet: the sea is shown to encircle land with Babylon at the center. It expressed an Assyro-centric conception of the cosmos. In Greek antiquity Homer believed the earth to be round, flat, and girdled by a vast stream. Babylonian cosmology

---

[7] Yet the Roman world was known to the Chinese as Ta Ch'in, i.e., Greater China, a highly honorific term, while the Romans knew China merely as Seres, people of silk. Joseph Needham, "The Fundamental Ideas of Chinese Science," in *Science and Civiliation in China,* II (Cambridge: Cambridge University Press, 1956), 216–345; C. P. Fitzgerald, *The Chinese View of Their Place in the World* (London: Oxford University Press, 1964).

might have influenced this early Greek view. On the other hand we have seen that the conception is worldwide and held by peoples with no probable link with the ancient Near East. It may be a construct that is congenial to the human mind.

Ancient Greeks looked upon Homer as an authority on geography. His view of the earth was passed down to the time of Hecateus (fl. 520–500 B.C.). Hecateus divided the world into two great continents of equal extent: Europe in the north and Libya-Asia in the south (Figure 5). The two are

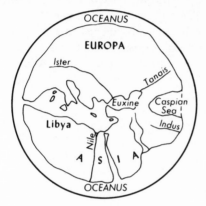

Figure 5   Hecateus of Miletus (fl. 520–500 B.C.).

connected at the Caucasus Mountains but are otherwise severed by a central belt of water consisting of the Mediterranean Sea, the Euxine (Black Sea) and the Caspian Sea. By the fifth century B.C., doubt concerning the perfect symmetry of land was expressed. Herodotus censured Hecateus for presenting the earth as "exactly round, as if drawn with a pair of compasses, and the Ocean flowing all around it." His own conception was far more detailed and the outline of his earth less regular; on the other hand the persistent hankering for symmetry is revealed by drawing the upper Nile River as a line that runs from west to east, thus paralleling the flow of the Ister (Danube) in Europe. Strabo (ca. 63 B.C.–21 A.D.) takes us to the beginning of modern geography. His earth is spherical, although unlike the Pythagoreans, Strabo placed it at the center of the universe. The habitable world is roughly an oblong island in the temperate latitudes. It is neatly bisected by the Mediterranean Sea and the Taurus Mountains. The elongation of the land mass follows from the increasing recognition of the great size of Asia. The area of Europe no longer dominates, although its size is still relatively exaggerated. With the diminishment and displacement of Europe, Greece could no longer pretend to a central location. Down to the fifth century B.C., however, Greece was assumed to be the center of the world, and Delphi the center of Greece.[8]

t-o (orbis terrarum) maps

In the Middle Ages a water-girdled circular earth again became a popular emblem of the world (Figure 6). The geometric elements of the wheel map are "O" and "T." One "O" marks the edge of the circumambient water, the other the edge of land. The "T" within the inner "O" of land consists of the two rivers, Don and Nile; they are aligned to form the horizontal bar of the "T," whereas the Mediterranean Sea forms the vertical stroke. The "T" thus divides the earth into three parts, with Asia east of

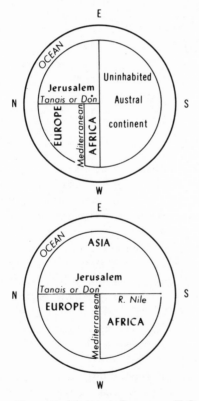

Figure 6 Medieval European T-O maps.

8 W. A. Heidel, *The Frame of Ancient Greek Maps* (New York: American Geographical Society, 1937); E. H. Bunbury, *A History of Ancient Geography Among the Greeks and Romans,* I (London: John Murray 1883).

the Don and Nile Rivers, Europe in the northwestern sector and Africa in the southwestern sector on two sides of the Mediterranean Sea. The top of the map is thus east, the place of the rising sun and of the risen Christ— the sun being one of the symbols for Christ. Europe seems to occupy a rather modest place in the T-O diagram; it is dwarfed by Asia, but this arrangement allows Jerusalem to be placed at the center of the world.

T-O maps date back to the sixth century. They continued to be drawn for more than a thousand years. Although we can appreciate why the ancient Greeks were content with the geometric simplicity of the circular maps, it is puzzling that they should be so popular in the Middle Ages and beyond. Before the fifth century B.C. few Greeks had any direct experience of geography outside of Egypt and the eastern Mediterranean basin. It is understandable that they should want to subsume their meager factual knowledge under a theoretical schema that they found congenial for other reasons. But scholars of the late medieval period had access to detailed information. Navigators made charts that showed the true shape of sea coasts, while travelers from the time of Marco Polo onward brought back geographical facts concerning the continental interior and eastern Asia. The T-O maps were clearly useless for navigation. They served no practical end and yet they were far from being idiosyncratic fantasies. The wheel maps of the Middle Ages expressed the beliefs and experiences of a theological culture that placed Christianity—and its topographic symbol, Jerusalem—at the center. They represented a way of thinking that colored action in nearly all spheres of medieval life, from the construction of cathedrals to the Crusades.[9]

europe at the world's center

Extended explorations overseas and the knowledge of densely peopled countries distant from Europe since 1500 made it more and more difficult to retain the religious world view of the T-O maps. The Holy Land lost its symbolic status as the world's center. Europe itself assumed that position. This Europocentric view is manifest in the idea of Europe. The history of this idea can be stated briefly. The division of the land masses into continents probably originated with Greek navigators. By the sixth century B.C. the Greeks were thoroughly familiar with the features of the Aegean Sea. They knew that great expanses of land blocked their courses to the west and east: these landmarks they called respectively Europe and Asia. Soon, however, the two terms that served navigators acquired political and cultural mean-

[9] C. Raymond Beazley, *The Dawn of Modern Geography*, II (New York: Peter Smith, 1949), pp. 549–642 (originally published in 1897).

ings. Herodotus discoursed on the feud between the continents. Aristotle noted the temperamental differences between Europeans and Asiatics, and called upon climate to explain the differences. No attempt was made to define the geographical limits of the continents. The idea itself lost currency in the post-Alexandrine period, and was revived only with the revival of classical learning during the Renaissance. Later, in the age of great oceanic navigation the terms Europe and Asia were found useful. Europe meant the hinterlands of ports from Cadiz to Trondheim, and Asia the hinterlands behind a scattering of ports from Arabia to Japan. The two continents are separated by the broad peninsula of Africa which seafarers have to circumnavigate. But "Europe" was to acquire once more political and cultural meaning. Toward the end of the seventeenth century the peoples of the Western world felt the need for a collective name designating their civilization. The traditional term "Western Christendom" seemed inappropriate after the Wars of Religion. "Europe" served that purpose.[10] It applied to an area that was unified by common roots in history, race, religion, and language. Europe has substance; Asia is simply that which is not Europe. It is defined negatively and from the European's viewpoint: so we have the Near East, the Middle East, and the Far East. Asia has never been an entity. Its peoples differ greatly in racial type, language, religion, and culture. The Arabs, the Indians, the Chinese, and the Balinese did not know they were all Asians until the Europeans told them. Asia was the shadow beyond the consciousness of Europe.[11] But Europe had the power to give a semblance of reality to the shadow. In time the word Asia acquired content and even a measure of effectiveness as a political weapon that could be used against the Europeans. For example, during the second world war the Japanese attempted to exploit the idea of Asia. They coined the slogan "Asia for the Asians" as a way of diverting the anger of the people they conquered from themselves to the allied powers.

the center of the land hemisphere

The Europocentric viewpoint is not often expressed cartographically. In school atlases, European countries are given great prominence. This is merely good sense for we naturally wish more detailed information of our own country and close neighbors than of remote lands. There is, however,

---

[10] Arnold Toybee, " 'Asia' and 'Europe'; Facts and Fantasies," in *A Study in History*, VIII (London: Oxford University Press, 1954), 708–29.

[11] John Steadman, "The Myth of Asia," *The American Scholar*, 25, No. 2 (Spring 1956), 163–75; W. Gordon East and O. H. K. Spate, "Epilogue: The Unity of Asia?" in *The Changing Map of Asia: A Political Geography* (London: Methuen, 1961), pp. 408–24.

one modern cartographic device that is egregiously ethnocentric—enough
to remind us of Greek circular maps centered on Greece and medieval maps
drawn with Jerusalem in the middle. The device shows the whole world on
a projection that is centered on southern Britain or northwestern France.
A circle is drawn on the map to enclose the area of half the globe (Figure
7). This is the land hemisphere.[12] It includes nearly the entire continental

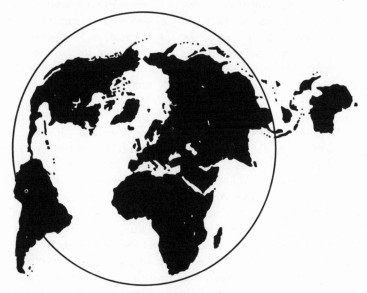

Figure 7 "The Land Hemisphere, showing the Mediterranean Ocean and
the central position of Britain." (After H. J. Mackinder, 1902.)

mass of Eurasia, the whole of Africa and North America and the northern
third of South America. Outside the circle is the water hemisphere. Exclud-
ing the uninhabitable ice plateaus of Antarctica and Greenland, nearly nine-
tenths of the land area of the globe is situated in the land hemisphere, where
95 percent of the world's population is located. The map enjoys a certain
popularity in Britain, which is understandable. Two influential textbooks,
Sir Halford Mackinder's classic study *Britain and the British Seas* (1902)
and the late Professor J. F. Unstead's *A World Survey,* volume 3 (1948)
use it to emphasize the island's centrality. Overlooked is the fact that the
same projection places the British Isles at the edge of the Arctic basin, far
from the core of the ecumene.

---

12 H. J. Mackinder, *Britain and the British Seas* (New York: D. Appleton & Co.,
1902), p. 4. Philippe Buache identified a land hemisphere as early as 1746.
See Preston E. James, *All Possible Worlds* (Indianapolis: Bobbs-Merrill, 1972),
p. 141.

exceptions

In some parts of the world people believed that a superior race, semi-divine, lived beyond the confines of their known territory. The capitulation of the Aztecs to Cortez and his small band of soldiers might have been facilitated by the Aztec belief in a divine people of white color. The ease with which Europeans colonized Africa was not solely a matter of military and technological superiority: they also enjoyed a psychological advantage in some encounters with the natives as, for example, in Madagascar where the natives anticipated the arrival of a powerful race in their legends. In the South Pacific, Marquesan islanders gazed on the first white woman they met as though she were a goddess. Clearly not every human group entertained the same degree of self-importance.

Ethnocentrism, whether this is to put oneself, one's country, or one's planet at the center of the universe, can also be overcome with imaginative effort. At the dawn of Occidental science astronomers of the Pythagorean school conceived the earth as a mere planet like Jupiter and the sun. Fire occupied the center of the universe, for fire and not earth was taken to be the worthiest element. In the Middle Ages earth occupied the central location. As Christ's birthplace this seemed proper. However, the medieval attitude was ambivalent. To some thinkers the central location did not in itself confer dignity. Medieval writers have described the earth in such unflattering terms as a mere geometrical point or a sort of dustbin for the offscourings of creation. Earth may be the hub around which the greater heavenly bodies moved but it also is located at the bottom of the cosmic hierarchy. Perhaps the best known example of ego transcendence in the Western world is the Copernican revolution, the substitution of the heliocentric for the geocentric theory. Less earth-shaking but as remarkable from the cultural and psychological perspective is the ego displacement of European savants during part of the seventeenth and eighteenth centuries. European statesmen and patriots might consider themselves a very superior people but European writers and scholars were inclined to be disillusioned with the tyrannical governments and religious bigotry of their homelands. At the same time they grew enamoured with the glowing reports of the virtues of peoples beyond the seas, in the Americas, in the South Seas, and in China. So, contrary to the ingrained habit of self-glorification, philosophers of the Enlightenment tended to see Europe as the center of darkness surrounded by a broad rim of light.[13]

---

13 Basil Willey, *The Eighteenth Century Background* (London: Penguin Books, 1965), pp. 19–21.

personal worlds: individual differences and preferences

As a species human beings are highly polymorphic. Outward physical variations among individuals are striking but they are minor when compared with the internal differences. Far from being "brothers under the skin," we are— in certain organic measures—almost different species. I should say at once that the significant contrasts occur among individuals; differences due to race are relatively unimportant.

Attitudes to life and environment necessarily reflect individual variations in biochemistry and physiology. A color-blind person's world must be somewhat less polychromatic than that of someone with normal vision. We also recognize temperamental differences among people. The outlook on life of a melancholic or placid person diverges far from that of a sanguine and excitable fellow. A root cause of variation in personality and temperament lies in the endocrine glands: even so-called normal people show important differences. Endocrine glands release hormones into the blood, which have a marked effect on a person's emotions and sense of well-being. To appreciate fully how environmental attitudes can differ, we need to know something of human physiology and temperament in all their diversity. As a homely illustration of the way individuality can transcend cultural forces that make for consensus, review the case of a family on a weekend outing.

This is not always the smooth happy affair that advertisements for the camp stove would have us believe. At the planning stage the members of the family may haggle over where to go, and once the party reaches its destination further disagreement may surface as to where to camp, when to stop for supper, which scenic places to visit, and so on. Age, sex, innate physiological and temperamental differences within a family easily override the social demand for harmony and togetherness.

physiological individuality

Chapter 2 treats briefly the senses of man. The stress is on what human beings have in common as a biological species. Consider now a few of the differences. With vision we know well that some people are blind, some are color-blind, some have 20–20 vision, and many have to correct defects in eyesight with spectacles. A less publicized visual endowment is the ability to see out of the corners of the eye (peripheral vision), an ability that varies widely in normal persons. Individuals especially favored with peripheral vision live, potentially, in a more panoramic world than people not so favored. As to individuality in color vision, red-green color blindness is a well-known defect; extreme sufferers see the world only in yellows, blues, and grays. There are, however, other kinds and degrees of sensitivity to color. Everyone, in fact, has his weaknesses and strengths in discriminating among fine color shades. Marked differences in aural perception exist. Tone deaf people fail to recognize popular melodies; they cannot tune keyboard instruments properly nor play string or wind instruments.[1] Responsiveness to pitch can be measured, and is found to show pronounced differences among people with no recognized hearing defects. Sensitivity to noise (and, in particular, to the kind of noise) also diverges conspicuously from person to person. Tactile sensitivity varies enormously. Some rare individuals appear to lack pain receptors. Cuts, bruises, and even broken bones may cause little pain. Pain is undesirable but it too is a means of knowing the world. Gross insensitivity to it is dangerous, since pain warns us of the bodily damages that may need attention. "Hot" and "cold" are subjective responses that vary greatly among individuals. We can readily observe how, for instance, a person goes to open the window at a time when another is about to put on a coat; how one person, in a hurry to catch the plane, is obliged to sip his coffee while another gulps it down. But differences in the brain are perhaps the most surprising of all. The brain is variable from person to person in

1 H. Kalmus, "The Worlds of the Colour Blind and the Tune Deaf," in J. M. Thoday and A. S. Parkes (eds.), *Genetic and Environmental Influences on Behaviour* (New York: Plenum Press, 1968), pp. 206–8.

every trait that has been observed and measured. We are encouraged to assume that people possess highly distinctive minds.[2]

temperament, talent, and attitudes

The association of physique with temperament and character is a commonplace of literature. One cannot think of such immortal creatures of the imagination, Falstaff and Mr. Micawber, Sherlock Holmes and Mr. Murdstone, without calling to mind their physiques. Body and personality seem all of a piece; it is as difficult to imagine a lean Micawber as a rotund Holmes. In everyday life people frequently infer character and talent from physical appearance without being conscious of the act: it comes so naturally. Scientists, however, have hesitated to make the association or even to give it much thought despite its obvious importance to the understanding of behavior. In the 1930s and 1940s, William Sheldon made a bold attempt to relate body type (somatotype) to temperament. His work was much criticized for its taxonomic naiveté, but recent studies tend to support some of his conclusions.[3] Sheldon classified people on three scales that represent visceral (endomorphy), muscular-skeletal (mesomorphy), and skin-and-nervous development (ectomorphy), thus:

Ectomorphy (tall, lean, fragile)

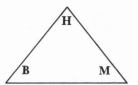

Mesomorphy (bony, muscular, athletic)

Endomorphy (soft, round, fat)

H: *Sherlock Holmes*
M: *Micawber*
B: *Tom Brown*

Each body type is associated with a cluster of temperamental traits which may exert an impact on environmental attitudes.

---

[2] Roger J. Williams, *You Are Extraordinary* (New York: Random House, 1967); H. J. Eysenck, "Genetics and Personality," in Thoday and Parkes, *Influences on Behavior*, pp. 163–79.

[3] William H. Sheldon, *The Varieties of Temperament* (New York: Harper & Row, 1942); Juan B. Cortés and Florence M. Gatti, "Physique and Propensity," *Psychology Today*, 4, No. 5 (October 1970), 42–44, 82–84.

Body Type	Temperamental Traits and Attitudes to Nature
Ectomorph	detached, thoughtful, shy, introspective, serious (contemplates nature-environment; interprets nature to reflect his own moods).
Mesomorph	dominant, cheerful, adventurous, optimistic, argumentative (enjoys dominating nature—for example, hunters, civil engineers).
Endomorph	relaxed, cooperative, affectionate, sociable (enjoys nature sensually; enjoys nature with others).

A weakness in Sheldon's characterization of body type is that the individual criteria of bone, fat, and muscle may vary independently. Physique and temperament are related, but as yet no entirely satisfactory way to score them has been found. Assuming that personality traits and temperament have an organic source (though it may be genetic and not correlatable with a Sheldonian body type), the question arises as to how they relate to certain specialized abilities important to the structuring of the world. Consider spatial visualization. It is a capacity that varies appreciably among people. The geneticist J. M. Thoday reports that a regular experience of his teaching career is to find a small proportion of students who seem totally incapable of visualizing the three-dimensional shape of a cell from observation of two-dimensional sections. Such people are severely handicapped in careers that require this knack.[4] The ability to visualize spatially and to orient oneself in space also seems to be associated with mathematical competence on the one hand and with inarticulateness of speech on the other. From the statistical analysis of a small population sample, Macfarlane Smith sees the following tentative correlations between personality traits and spatial/verbal skills:

1. Emotional instability is better associated with low scores in spatial as against verbal tests.
2. Personality characteristics such as self-confidence, perseverance, and vigor are related to high scores on spatial as against verbal tests.
3. People with high spatial and mechanical skills have masculine attitudes and interests; they tend to be introverted and asocial. By contrast, people with relatively high verbal ability are extroverted and likely to show feminine attitudes and interests.
4. A person of high spatial ability will grasp a figure mentally in relatively large units. He looks at it as a whole, instead of allowing his attention to stray away from one element to another. He tends to classify objects by shape rather than color.[5]

4 Thoday and Parkes, *Influences on Behavior*, p. 111.
5 I. Macfarlane Smith, *Spatial Ability and Its Educational and Social Significance* (San Diego: Robert R. Knapp, 1964), pp. 236–37, 243, 257.

The forceful and precise articulation of environmental attitudes requires high verbal skills. Literature rather than social science surveys provides us with the detailed and finely shaded information on how human individuals perceive their worlds. The realistic novel does not so much portray a culture accurately (which social science also attempts to do) as to highlight the particularity of persons within it. The unique voice escapes the matrix of sociological explanation. To interpret it the novelist hints at factors that are themselves little known: congenital endowment (temperament) on the one hand and the accidents of life (chance) on the other. Writers create fictional personalities; they are themselves personalities with voices that rise above the format discourse of their society. People have distinctive attitudes to life: the statement is pedestrian and we readily accept it. Writers, however, have succeeded in articulating subtly differentiated world views. From their writings we learn to recognize the singularity of persons. I shall illustrate this with the unique perspectives of several well-known writers, and then note a peculiar environmental attitude which seems to require, for its full explanation, the postulate of an ascetic temperament.

TOLSTOY AND DOSTOEVSKY

The Russian novelists, Tolstoy (1828–1910) and Dostoevsky (1821–1881), are titans of modern literature who viewed each other's works with a mixture of admiration and unease. Both were endowed with gigantic vitality and wrote massive works which excelled in depicting the labyrinthine ways of the human soul and of Russian society in the nineteenth century. Nonetheless the worlds they saw had little in common.

Tolstoy's world is Homeric. His perspective on life and nature overlapped more with the world view of the unknown bard of archaic Greece than with that of his contemporary Dostoevsky. According to George Steiner, the works of Tolstoy resemble the Homeric epics in the "archaic and pastoral setting...; the poetry of war and agriculture; the primacy of the senses and of physical gesture; the luminous, all-reconciling background of the cycle of the year...; the acceptance of a chain of being extending from brute matter to the stars...and deepest of all, an essential, a determination to follow 'the high road of life' (Coleridge) rather than the dark obliquities."[6] In the first epilogue of *War and Peace,* Tolstoy equates life in the country with the good life. In *Anna Karenina* the antithesis between the city and the land is the axis around which the moral and technical structure of the novel revolves. Dostoevsky, by contrast, is wholly immersed in the city. The city may be the inferno but salvation does not lie in the land; it can be found only in the Kingdom of God. Dostoevsky's fiction has few

6 George Steiner, *Tolstoy or Dostoevsky: An Essay in Old Criticism* (New York: Vintage Books, 1961), pp. 74–75.

landscapes. Even where he invokes natural beauty, the setting is urban: "I love the March sun in Petersburg. . . . The whole street suddenly glitters, bathed in brilliant light. All the houses seem suddenly, as it were, to sparkle. The grey, yellow and dirty-green hues for an instant lose all their gloominess."[7] The city may be cursed, but Dostoevsky is unable to conceive of any other setting in which meaningful human acts can take place. His home is the city though it be damp and comfortless. Tolstoy, on the other hand, appears to feel at ease in an urban environment only when it is being destroyed: his eloquence rises to a peak in the burning of Moscow.

MODERN POETS AND THE CITY

Three distinguished American poets, T. S. Eliot, Carl Sandburg, and E. E. Cummings, offer incompatible images of the city. Eliot's are consistently grim, sometimes sordid. In Eliot's city, yellow smoke slides along the street rubbing its back upon the window panes; lonely men in their shirt sleeves lean out of windows; gusty showers stir up withered leaves and grimy scraps of newspaper in vacant lots. When morning comes the poet invites us to think of all the hands that are raising dingy shades in a thousand furnished rooms, and of people who sit in despair on the bed's edge, clasping the yellow soles of their feet in soiled hands.[8] By contrast Sandburg's *Chicago* is full of gloating affirmations. Chicago is noisy, wicked, and brutal; it has hungry women and children. But the poet says, "Come and show me another city with lifted head singing, so proud to be alive and coarse and strong and cunning." Sandburg describes his metropolis in thundering epithets. Cummings, like Eliot, concentrates on the telling detail but his urban images are more kindly. One poem celebrates spring in the city. Spring does jolly things. It inveigles the unwary june-bug and the frivolous angleworm into crossing sidewalks, persuades the musical tom-cat to serenade his lady and stuffs the parks with overgrown pimperly cavaliers and gum-chewing giggly girls.[9]

THE EVANESCENT WORLD OF VIRGINIA WOOLF

A tremulous world that is about to dissolve with every shift of light is an important aspect of Virginia Woolf's sensibility. Consider this passage from her novel *To the Lighthouse:*

[7] Quoted in Steiner, *Tolstoy or Dostoevsky*, p. 199.
[8] Sordid urban images appear in several well known poems such as "The Love Song of J. Alfred Prufrock," "Prelude," "Rhapsody on a Windy Night," and "The Waste Land."
[9] Barclay Jones, "Prolegomena to a Study of the Aesthetic Effect of Cities," *The Journal of Aesthetics and Art Criticism*, 18 (1960), 419–29.

And now as if the cleaning and the scrubbing and the scything and the mowing had drowned it there rose that half-heard melody, that intermittent music which the ear half catches but lets fall, a bark, a bleat; irregular, intermittent, yet somehow related; the hum of an insect, the tremor of cut grass, dissevered yet somehow belonging; the dor-beetle, the squeak of a wheel, loud, low, but mysteriously related; which the ear strains to bring together and is always on the verge of harmonizing, but they are never quite heard, never fully harmonized, and at last, in the evening, one after another sound dies out, and the harmony falters, and silence falls. With the sunset sharpness was lost, and like mist rising, quiet rose, quiet spread, the wind settled; loosely the world shook itself down to sleep, darkly here without a light to it, save what came green suffused through leaves, or pale on the white flowers in the bed by the window.[10]

The effect of evanescence and fragility in this description of place is achieved by dwelling on the sounds. Compared with seeing, hearing is unfocused and passive. Noises are heard without context: "the ear strains to bring together and is always on the verge of harmonizing, but they are never quite heard, never fully harmonized." What we see is structured and harmonized in terms of background-foreground and perspective. Sound represents flux, visual image permanence. The world seems static to the deaf, contingent to the blind.

THE ASCETIC TEMPERAMENT

A preference for the stark environment, bare as the desert or the monk's cell, is contrary to the normal human desire for ease and abundance. Yet people are known to have sought, repeatedly, the wilderness, to escape from not only the corruption but the voluptuous luxury of city life. The yearning for simplicity, when it transcends social norms and requires the sacrifice of worldly goods, is a symptom of deep-seated bias; the behavior that it conduces cannot be explained solely by the cultural values of the time. What can be the positive appeal of asceticism? Asceticism is denial but denial is not only a means to an end but may in itself be a type of affirmation. Ascetic practice can be perceived as will, the lordship of spirit over matter, and the desert the austere stage for epiphany.

The Bible is a rich source of conflicting environmental attitudes. For example, the Israelites showed the normal human distaste for deserts. The home they sought was a land of milk and honey. But asceticism, identifying human merit and God's grace with the wilderness, persisted as a strong countervailing ideal. Encounters with God, both directly and indirectly through the prophets, took place in scenes of desolation away from the dis-

---

[10] Virginia Woolf, *To the Lighthouse* (New York: Harcourt Brace Jovanovich, 1927), pp. 212–13.

tracting sound of rivers and raucous men. The bare landscape mirrored the purity of faith. In the early Christian centuries, hermits sought strenuously for God in the silence and emptiness of the desert. Their attitudes toward nature and the environment could be highly eccentric. The Egyptian hermit, Anthony, declaimed against the rising of the sun for disturbing him in his prayers. Abba Abraham commended lands that lacked fruitfulness for not distracting men with thoughts of cultivation. St. Jerome wrote: "A town is a prison, the desert loneliness a paradise."[11]

In the modern age God has withdrawn from the world but the desert retains its ambivalent appeal to people of an ascetic temperament. It is difficult to think of Charles Doughty and T. E. Lawrence without seeing the desert as the stage natural to the enactment of their daunting personalities. There are people who shun the soft environment and long for the desert, or some other harsh setting, in which they may know reality's merciless hardness and naked splendor. A hint of the desert's intractable lure appears in the first paragraph of T. E. Lawrence's testament, *The Seven Pillars of Wisdom,* where he wrote: "For years we lived anyhow with one another in the naked desert, under the indifferent heaven. By day hot sun fermented us; and we were dizzied by the beating wind. At night we were stained by dew, and shamed into pettiness by the innumerable silences of the stars."[12]

Bleakness may be found in the country railroad station no less than in the desert. Heroic minds are drawn to it for reasons that common humanity finds difficult to understand. Simone Weil claimed that her proper niche in the world was the bare waiting room of a train station. George Orwell withdrew to spend his last years in the bleak Hebrides. Ludwig Wittgenstein could have enjoyed the comfortable and cultured life of a Cambridge don. But he disdained material comforts: his own rooms in Trinity College were bare except for the canvas cot. Albert Camus, at the height of his fame, reflected: "For me, the highest luxury has always coincided with a certain bareness. I love the bare interior of houses in Spain or North Africa. The place where I prefer to live and work (and, something more rare, where I would not mind dying) is a hotel bedroom."[13]

---

11 References in Yi-Fu Tuan, "Attitudes toward Environment: Themes and Approaches," in David Lowenthal (ed.), *Environmental Perception and Behavior* (University of Chicago Department of Geography Research Paper No. 109, 1967), pp. 4–17.

12 T. E. Lawrence, *Seven Pillars of Wisdom* (Garden City, N. Y.: Doubleday, 1936), p. 29.

13 Albert Camus, *Lyrical and Critical Essays,* trans. E. C. Kennedy (New York: Knopf, 1968), pp. 7–8.

sex

The relation between inborn capacity and the development of a special outlook on the world is very little understood. In our daily contacts with people we take for granted that eccentric attitudes exist and that they are not explained exhaustively by cultural factors such as family background, upbringing, and education. The examples given above are meant to suggest the existence of outlooks which, in their waywardness, invite us to postulate congenital influences—that is, to attribute certain inclinations to temperament, that uncertain mixture of humors. But there is little hard evidence. We are on surer ground when we relate the range of human attitudes to the biological categories of sex and age.

Male and female are not arbitrary distinctions. Physiological differences between man and woman are clearly specifiable, and these differences can be expected to affect their ways of responding to the world.[14] The average human male is heavier and more muscular than the average human female, a distinction between the sexes that is shared by almost all mammals. Man, having less fat in the tissue, is more sensitive to cold than woman. Woman's skin is more delicate, softer, and probably more sensitive than that of man; she is more responsive to tactile sensations. Smell sensibility is more acute in girls than in boys, especially after puberty. Other physiological differences that have an impact on the perception and behavior of man and woman can be readily specified. But we speak of the average or normal male and female. There are many exceptions to these general rules, and enough uncertainty as to the relationship between physiology and mental attitude to make one ask: Has the female a characteristic way of structuring the world that is different from the male? The overriding impact of culture on behavior and attitude confuses the problem further. In every known culture, male and female are assigned distinctive roles; they are taught in childhood to behave in differing ways, and yet the fact that there exist no exceptions argues for a cause rooted in biology.[15]

Behavioral psychologists tend to minimize the importance of sex whereas psychoanalysts influenced by Freud tend to stress it. Erik Erikson believes that sex plays a significant part in the way children structure space. In the book *Childhood and Society,* he has a section entitled "Genital Modes and Spatial Modalities." To the psychoanalytical way of thinking, and to

[14] Kenneth Walker, *The Physiology of Sex and Its Social Implications* (London: Penguin Books, 1964).

[15] On sexual differences and behavior see Walter Goldschmidt, *Comparative Functionalism* (Berkeley and Los Angeles: University of California Press, 1966), pp. 45–46.

Erikson in particular, "high" and "low" are masculine variables; "open" and "closed" are feminine modalities. Experiments with free play show that when a girl designs an environment, it is usually that of a house *interior*, represented either as a configuration of furniture without walls or by a simple *enclosure* built with blocks. In the girl's scene, people and animals are mostly *within* such an interior or enclosure, and they are primarily people or animals in a *static* position. Boy's scenes are either houses with elaborate walls, or façades with *protrusions* representing ornaments or cannons. There are *high towers*. In the boy's constructions more people and animals are *outside* enclosures or buildings, and there are more objects *moving* along streets and intersections. Along with tall structures boys play with the idea of *collapse;* ruins are exclusively male constructions.[16]

age

Shakespeare speaks of the seven ages of man and characterizes each with such eloquence and incisiveness that they seem seven different persons. If there remains doubt about the relationship between body type, sex, and other inborn traits to environmental behavior and perception, there can be no doubt concerning the role of the life cycle in extending the range of human responses to the world. In social science discourse, "man" is usually taken to be an active adult person; overlooked is the fact that adulthood is simply a stage people live through, like infanthood, childhood, and adolescence before it and senescence after. Each age has its own physiognomy and outlook: in the course of a long life we move inevitably from the infant "mewling and puking in the nurse's arms" to the second childishness "sans teeth, sans eyes, sans taste, sans everything."

INFANT

The infant is *worldless* to the extent that he cannot distinguish between self and environment. He perceives and responds to environmental stimuli; he is probably more discriminating in qualities of sound than in visual images. Above all, he is highly sensitive to touch. As every mother knows, the infant is uncannily aware of her mood from the way he is held. Or more precisely, he is aware of the subtle changes in pressure and temperature around him for the mother is not recognized as a separate individual. By about the fifth week a baby's eyes can fixate on objects. The first con-

16 Erik H. Erikson, "Genital Modes and Spatial Modalities," in *Childhood and Society* (Harmondsmith: Penguin, 1965), 91–102.

figuration he recognizes is the human face, even the abstraction of a face, such as two dots and a line drawn on a piece of paper. He cannot, however, discriminate among sharply-bounded geometrical objects like squares and triangles. Rectilinear shape is of no value to his survival but the human face is.[17] By around three to four months the infant can identify specifically the mother's face; yet the idea of a whole person continues to escape his grasp. When the baby looks at someone his eyes fixate-on parts of the body, the mouth, the hands, etc.; only at about six months does he give evidence of perceiving another person. The infant's experience of space is narrowly circumscribed. At the beginning of his life, space is primarily "buccal;" it is what he knows through exploration with his mouth. Respiration itself may provide the infant with a kind of spatial experience. The horizontal position of the cot and the vertical position against the mother's body as the infant is taken up to be burped instructs him in the reality of a spatial dimension. As to color, at age three months babies already appear to respond to it.

Young children appear to prefer warm colors to cool ones. As they grow older the preference for warm colors — particularly yellow — declines, and continues to decline with age.[18]

THE YOUNG CHILD

An infant smiles at the human face but also at a piece of paper with dots on it, which suggests that he does not distinguish visually between animate and inanimate objects. In a sensorimotor way, however, he can probably discriminate between living and lifeless matter. The young child is an animist: he responds to all moving bodies as though they are self-propelled and alive. Even a six-year-old may regard the clouds, sun, and moon as alive and able to follow him when he walks.[19] The young child's world is confined to his immediate surroundings; he is not by nature a star gazer. Distant objects and panoramic scenes are of no special appeal. Space is not highly structured to the five- and six-year-olds. A young child does not conceive space to be an ambiance analyzable into distinct dimensions. He is aware first of up and down, left and right, front and back, since these derive directly from the structure of the human body; other dimensions like

---

[17] R. A. Spitz and K. M. Wolf, "The Smiling Response: A Contribution to the Ontogenesis of Social Relations," *Genetic Psychology Monographs,* 34 (1946), 57–125.

[18] Ann Van Nice Gale, *Children's Preferences for Color: Color Combinations and Color Arrangements* (Chicago: University of Chicago Press, 1933), pp. 54–55.

[19] Jean Piaget, *The Child's Conception of Physical Causality* (New York: Humanities Press, 1951), p. 60.

open-delineated, compact-diffuse, acute-obtuse, are conceptualized later.[20] "Landscape" is not a meaningful word to the young child. To see the landscape requires, first of all, the ability to make the sharp distinction between self and others, an ability as yet weakly developed in a six- or seven-year-old. Then, to see the landscape and evaluate it aesthetically one needs to be able to identify an unbounded segment of nature and to be aware of the coherence of its spatial characteristics in such terms as: Are the vertical and horizontal components arranged in tense opposition? Are closed spaces harmoniously disposed on the open plain? Is the dense foliage on the right balanced by the line of willows on the left? Though the landscape escapes the young child, he is intensely aware of its separate components: a tree stump, a large boulder, bubbling water in a section of the stream. As the child grows older his awareness of spatial relations gains at the expense of the quiddity of the objects that define them. In color preferences the young child seems indifferent to mixed colors such as mauve, beige, lavender, but he is strongly drawn to bright hues, so much so that he tends to group geometrical objects according to similarity of color than of shape. All that glitters is gold. The young child's world, then, is animated and consists of vivid, sharply delineated objects in a weakly structured space.

THE CHILD AND OPENNESS TO THE WORLD

It is difficult for an adult to recapture the vividness of sense impressions that he has lost (except occasionally) as in the freshness of a view after the rain, the sharp fragrance of coffee before breakfast when the blood-sugar concentration is low, and the pungency of the world during convalescence after a long bout of sickness. A child, from about seven or eight years old to his early teens, lives in this vivid world much of the time. Unlike the toddler, the older child is not tied to proximate objects and surroundings; he is capable of conceptualizing space in its different dimensions; he appreciates subtleties in color and recognizes harmonies of line and volume. He has much of the adult's conceptual ability. He can see the landscape as a segment of artfully arranged reality "out there," but he also knows it as an enveloping, penetrating presence, a force. Unburdened by worldly cares, unfettered by learning, free of ingrained habit, negligent of time, the child is open to the world. Frank Conroy, in his autobiographical

---

20 Robert Beck, "Spatial Meaning, and the Properties of the Environment," in David Lowenthal (ed.), *Environmental Perception and Behavior* (University of Chicago Department of Geography Research Paper No. 109, 1967), pp. 20–26; Monique Laurendeau and Adrien Pinard, *The Development of the Concept of Space in the Child* (New York: International Universities Press, 1970); Yvonne Brackbill and George G. Thompson (eds.), *Behavior in Infancy and Early Childhood* (New York: Free Press, 1967), pp. 163–220.

novel *Stop-time,* describes what this childlike openness means to the experiencing of even the most commonplace type of environment. The author was then a boy of thirteen, riding a bicycle, and going nowhere in particular.

> At the first gas station I stopped for a Coke and checked the tire pressure. I liked gas stations. You could hang around as long as you wanted and no one took any notice. Sitting on the ground in a shady corner with my back against the wall, I took small sips at the Coke and made it last.
> Is it the mindlessness of childhood that opens up the world? Today nothing happens in a gas station. I'm eager to leave, to get where I'm going, and the station, like some huge paper cutout, or a Hollywood set, is simply a facade. But at thirteen, sitting with my back against the wall, it was a marvelous place to be. The delicious smell of gasoline, the cars coming and going, the fresh air hose, the half-heard voices buzzing in the background— these things hung musically in the air, filling me with a sense of well-being. In ten minutes my psyche would be topped up like the tanks of the automobile.[21]

OLD AGE

People are vaguely aware that their senses grow dull with age. The decline and its physiological cause can be measured. The child's taste buds are widely distributed about the hard and soft palate, the walls of the throat and the central upper surface of the tongue as well; these buds gradually disappear as a person matures with the result that taste sensitivity fades. Young adults can identify a sugar solution as sweet at a third the concentration required to give taste to an elderly person. Eyesight weakens. The elderly pay more attention to information channeled through the peripheral receptors of the eye which magnify movement. With age the world is a little greyer: discernment of color at the violet end of the spectrum suffers. The eye lenses become more yellow, filtering out the ultraviolet and some of the violet wavelengths. Hearing declines sharply at the high frequency range. While a young person of normal hearing is sensitive to sound at 20,000 cycles per second, in late middle age some people can no longer hear notes above 10,000 cycles. With increasing deafness the world seems static, lacking the pulsations of life. The perceived world shrinks as both eyesight and hearing weaken. Declining mobility further restricts the world of the old, not only in the obvious geographical sense but also from the fact that haptic-somatic encounters with the environment (in climbing, running, walking) become less frequent. Youngsters people the future with fantasies, whereas with the old it is the lengthening past that provides the material for fantasy and distortion. The world contracts for elderly people not only because their senses lose acuity but because their future is curtailed: as the future shrinks,

---

[21] Frank Conroy, *Stop-time* (New York: Viking, 1967), p. 110.

so does the spatial horizon and the old can become emotionally involved with immediate events and objects in a way that is reminiscent of the child.

The range of human response to the world is increased beyond what social scientists normally study when we remember to consider the stages of the life cycle. In addition, large differences in capacity occur within each age group. Rates of growth and senescence vary from person to person. At ninety Pablo Casals continued to play the cello and conduct the orchestra with distinction. Among artists and scholars of modern times, Tolstoy, Whitehead, Picasso, and Bertrand Russell led vigorous and creative lives in old age. De Gaulle remained an undiminished political figure as a septuagenarian.

CHAPTER SIX

culture,
experience,
and
environmental
attitudes

To understand a person's environmental preference, we may need to examine his biological heritage, upbringing, education, job, and physical surroundings. At the level of group attitudes and preferences it is necessary to know a group's cultural history and experience in the context of its physical setting. In neither case is it possible to distinguish sharply between cultural factors and the role of the physical environment. The concepts "culture" and "environment" overlap as do the concepts "man" and "nature." It is useful, however, to treat them as distinct initially. In this way we can focus first on culture and then on environment (chapter 7) : they provide complementary perspectives on the character of environmental perception and attitude. We shall start with culture and take note of the following themes: (1) culture and perception; (2) sex roles and perception; (3) differences in attitude between the visitor and the native; (4) differences in the evaluation of the same environment by explorers and colonists of disparate background and experience; (5) distinctive world views in a similar environment; and (6) changes in attitude toward environment.

culture and perception

Can culture influence perception to the degree that a person can see things that are nonexistent? Hallucination is known among individuals and groups of individuals. The phenomenon fascinates because the perception of a nonexistent object appears to follow the rules of normal perception. If a hallucinatory figure stands before a table, then part of the table is blocked out; and if the figure retreats it looks smaller. Hallucination is often a symptom of stress affecting the individual or the group. Excited pilgrims who expect a miracle may see the Virgin Mary. Many people claim to have seen flying saucers. The group affected is usually a small minority within a large society. An interesting question is: Can hallucination occur as a normal (i.e., commonly accepted) event in a culture? A. I. Hallowell believes that the Ojibwa Indians of the Lake Winnipeg area experience genuine perceptual illusion. It is a cultural trait of the people, and not merely a personal idiosyncracy. The Ojibwa see cannibal monsters known as *windigos*. One account told by an old man ends as follows:

> Between the shore and the islands there was a place where the water was not frozen. He [the *windigo*] was headed in this direction. I kept after him, I could hear him on the weak ice. Then he fell in and I heard a terrific yell. I turned back and I can't say whether he managed to get out or not. I killed some ducks and went back to my canoe. I was getting pretty weak by this time so I made for a camp I thought was close by. But the people had left. I found out later that they had heard him and were so scared that they moved away.[1]

It is not true that the Ojibwa are naive as to the sources of sights and sounds. On the contrary, they are expert woodsmen with detailed knowledge of their environment. Moreover, they typically give naturalistic explanations of sounds that startle them. In view of this fact, Hallowell says: "It is all the more significant then to discover cases in which the perceptions of individuals have been so thoroughly molded by traditional dogma that the most intense fears are aroused by objectively innocuous stimuli. It is the culturally derived *Einstellung*, rather than the stimuli themselves, that explains their behavior."[2]

When there is no time lapse between the sensation and its interpretation, as in the seeing of the *windigo*, it is proper to speak of the experience as perception in the narrow sense. With time lapse concepts may form; a person can stand back and interpret the perceptual cues in different ways as an exercise in rationality. One interpretation is preferred, and strongly

[1] A. Irving Hallowell, *Culture and Experience* (New York: Schocken Books, 1967), p. 258.
[2] Hallowell, *Culture and Experience*, p. 257.

adhered to, because it seems true. Truth is not given through any objective consideration of the evidence. Truth is subjectively embraced as part of one's total experience and outlook. The distinction may be illustrated by considering the Hopi Indian's understanding of space. It differs from the static, three-dimensional structure of Western man. The Hopi can see that too. Only to him, the white man's view is one possible view whereas his own is true in the sense that it conforms to his total experience.

The following dialogue between the anthropologist Dorothy Eggan and her Hopi informant makes this clear. The Hopi says: "Close your eyes and tell me what you see from Hopi House at the Grand Canyon." With enthusiasm Eggan describes the brilliantly colored walls of the canyon, the trail that winds over the edge of it reappearing and crossing a lower mesa, and so on. The Hopi smiles and says: "I see the colored walls too, and I know what you mean all right, but your words are wrong." The trail for him does not cross and does not disappear. The trail is only that part of the mesa which has been changed by feet. He continues: "The trail is still there even when you do not see it, because *I can see all of it*. My feet have walked on the trail all the way down. And another thing, did you go to the Grand Canyon when you described it?" Eggan says, "No, of course I didn't." The Hopi's answer to that is, "Part of you was there or part of it was here." Then with a broad smile: "It is easier for me to move you than to move any part of the Grand Canyon."[3]

sex roles and perception

In cultures of strongly differentiated sex roles, men and women will look at different aspects of the environment and acquire different attitudes toward them. For example, the mental maps of male and female Eskimos on Southampton Island diverge greatly. When an Aivilik hunter is asked to draw a map he shows in detail and accuracy the island's outline as well as the harbors and inlets of the neighboring coast of Hudson Bay. But a woman does not express her knowledge by outlines: her map is made of points each of which indicates the location of a settlement or trading post. These location maps are as admirably accurate with respect to direction and relative distance as the outline maps of the male hunters with respect to shape.[4]

Various methods are available to study differences in perception and environmental values. Joseph Sonnenfeld has applied a photo slide test to

---

[3] Dorothy Eggan, "Hopi Dreams in Cultural Perspective," in G. E. von Grunebaum and Roger Caillois (eds.), *The Dream and Human Societies* (Berkeley and Los Angeles: University of California Press, 1966), p. 253.

[4] C. S. Carpenter, F. Varley, and R. Flaherty, *Eskimo* (University of Toronto Press, 1959).

residents, native and nonnative, of Alaska. The slides depict landscapes that vary on one or more of four basic dimensions: topography, water, vegetation, and temperature. The result of the test shows that males tend to prefer landscapes with rougher topography and with indications of water, while females prefer vegetated landscapes in the warmer environments. The discrepancy is greater among the Eskimos than among the white residents and visitors.[5] The one unexpected element in the test is that men, rather than women, should show greater preference for water. In religious and psychoanalytic literature, water—especially still water—tends to be treated as a symbol for the feminine principle.

In Western society the mental map of a housewife with small children is likely to differ from that of her husband. Every workday the circulation routes of the married pair rarely parallel each other except in the home stretch. On a shopping expedition the man and woman will want to look into different stores. They may walk arm in arm but they do not thereby see and hear the same things. Occasionally they are jolted out of their own perceptual world to make a courtesy call on that of another, as, for example, when the husband asks his wife to admire some golf clubs in the shop window. Think of a frequented street and try to recall the shops along it: certain shops will stand out sharply while others dissolve in a dreamlike haze. Sex roles will account for much of the difference in pattern. This is especially true of lower-middle-class and lower-class adults in Western society. On the other hand, sex roles are less sharply drawn among members of the cosmopolitan upper class, and may be quite blurred among such specialized groups as the countercultural "street people" and scientists working in research centers. Their differences in perception are minimally based on sex.

Persistent differences in the perception and evaluation of environment between the sexes could lead to intolerable discord. However, in middle-class American society such conflict is rarely serious: husband and wife may agree to the same act but for different reasons. To illustrate, Herbert J. Gans, in his study of the Levittowners of New Jersey, asked the purchasers of houses in the new suburban development whether "they would prefer to live in the city if it were not for the children." Eighty-seven percent responded negatively. Jews were the most favorable to the city, and Protestants the least; the college educated were slightly more inclined to the urban environment than those who dropped out of high school. But sex

---

5 Joseph Sonnenfeld, "Environmental Perception and Adaptation Level in the Arctic," in David Lowenthal (ed.), *Environmental Perception and Behavior,* University of Chicago Department of Geography Research Paper No. 109 (1967), 42–53.

made no difference. On the other hand, sex accounted for the major source of diversity in the life values to which the Levittowners aspired. The man looked forward to the peace and quiet of the country after a day's work, as well as the opportunity to "putter around the house and yard." The women placed most stress on making new friends and "having nice neighbors."[6]

visitor and native

Visitor and native focus on very different aspects of the environment. In a stable and traditional society, visitors and transients form a small part of the total population; their views of the environment are perhaps of no great significance. In our mobile society the fleeting impressions of people passing through cannot be neglected. Generally speaking, we may say that only the visitor (and particularly the tourist) has a viewpoint; his perception is often a matter of using his eyes to compose pictures. The native, by contrast, has a complex attitude derived from his immersion in the totality of his environment. The visitor's viewpoint, being simple, is easily stated. Confrontation with novelty may also prompt him to express himself. The complex attitude of the native, on the other hand, can be expressed by him only with difficulty and indirectly through behavior, local tradition, lore, and myth.

Wilderness, to American settlers of the early colonial period, was viewed primarily as a threat, a place to be reclaimed and redeemed from the predations of Indians and demons. One's social and educational background made little difference to this outlook. By the middle of the eighteenth century, however, European nature-Romanticism had found followers among the growing leisured classes of America. A gap in environmental evaluation opened and continued to grow between the farmer who struggled against the wilderness and the cultured gentleman who appraised it as scenery. Wild nature received effusive laudations, and so too its lonely denizens—the woodsman, the hunter, and the trapper—but not the farmers who strove to make a living. Francis Parkman, as a young man, displayed this aristocratic disdain toward the farmer. During the summer of 1842 he traveled through northern New York and New England. After spending several days admiring the scenery along the shores of Lake George, he noted in his journal: "There would be no finer place of gentlemen's seats than this, but now,

6 Herbert J. Gans, *The Levittowners* (New York: Random House, Vintage Books edition, 1969), p. 38.

for the most part, it is occupied by a race of boors about as uncouth, mean, and stupid as the hogs they seem chiefly to delight in."[7]

Even William James, an open-minded philosopher, caught himself entertaining ill thoughts of the unkempt farms that belonged to the pioneers of North Carolina. Upon reflection he concluded that his view as someone merely passing through was superficial and frivolous: it mattered little compared with the attitude of the people who lived in the mountains. He explained:

> Because to me the clearings spoke of naught but denudation, I thought that to those whose sturdy arms and obedient axes had made them they could tell no other story. But when *they* looked on the hideous stumps, what they thought of was personal victory. The chips, the girdled trees, and the vile split rails spoke of honest sweat, persistent toil, and final reward. The cabin was a warrant of safety for self and wife and babes. In short, the clearing, which to me was a mere ugly picture on the retina, was to them a symbol redolent with moral memories and sang a very paean of duty, struggle, and success.[8]

The visitor's evaluation of environment is essentially aesthetic. It is an outsider's view. The outsider judges by appearance, by some formal canon of beauty. A special effort is required to empathize with the lives and values of the inhabitants. The unkempt farms of upstate New York and North Carolina offended the Eastern cultural establishment as represented, for example, by Francis Parkman and William James. In the second half of the twentieth century their successors may well judge harshly the raw, disorderly cityscapes of the American West—the endless rows of gas stations, motels, "dairy queens," and hamburger stands. The operator of an "eat" stand, however, can be proud of his business and his modest role in the community just as the backwoods farmer saw in his untidy patch of corn reassuring evidence of success in the struggle for an independent livelihood.

Differences of outlook between resident and passerby, between insider and outsider, are sensitively noted by Herbert Gans in his study of Boston's working-class district, the West End, before it was torn down in the interest

---

7 Mason Wade (ed.), *The Journal of Francis Parkman* (New York: 1947). Quoted in Henry Nash Smith, *Virgin Land* (New York: Random House, Vintage Books edition, first published in 1950), p. 54.

8 William James, "On a Certain Blindness in Human Beings," in *Talks to Teachers on Psychology: and to Students on Some of Life's Ideals* (New York: The Norton Library, 1958), pp. 150–52 (originally published in 1899). See David Lowenthal, "Not Every Prospect Pleases," *Landscape,* 12, No. 2 (Winter 1962–1963), 19–23. On the poets' low opinion of farmers, see R. H. Walker, "The Poets Interpret the Frontier," *Mississippi Valley Historical Review,* 48, No. 4 (1961), 622–23.

of urban renewal.[9] When the sociologist first saw West End, he was struck by its conflicting aesthetic qualities. On the one hand, West End's European character offered a certain appeal. The high buildings set on narrow curving streets, the Italian and Jewish stores and restaurants, and the crowds of people on the sidewalks in good weather all gave the district an exotic flavor. On the other hand, Gans noticed the many vacant shops, the abandoned tenements, and the alleys choked with garbage. After living in the West End for a few weeks his perception altered. He became selective, turning a blind eye to the empty and decaying quarters for those that were actually used by people; and these transpired to be far more liveable inside than their exteriors proclaimed. Gans also discovered that the outsider's view, even when it was sympathetic and generous, depicted a world alien to the native resident. For example, a settlement house memorandum for the training of new staff described the West End warmly as a multicultural residential area which, despite the poor housing, held "a charm and security for its residents"; and that what served to draw the people together were such pleasurable aspects of life as the stability of long-time residence, the nearness of the river, the neighborhood's parks and pools, and the richness of ethnic cultures. Actually, residents were not interested in ethnic variety; and though they used the riverbank and swimming pool they did not see them as part of the neighborhood. And no native resident would think of describing the neighborhood as having charm.[10]

The outsider's enthusiasm, no less than his critical stance, may be superficial. Thus a tourist to the medieval part of a European city expresses delight over its dark cobbled streets, intimate nooks and corners, picturesque compact housing, and quaint shops without pausing to wonder how the people had actually lived. A tourist in Chinatown is enchanted by the stimulation of his visual and olfactory senses; he departs in blissful ignorance of the overcrowding, the listless lives, the gambling behind the gaudy façades.

Obviously the visitor's judgment is often valid. His main contribution is the fresh perspective. The human being is exceptionally adaptable. Beauty or ugliness—each tends to sink into his subconscious mind as he learns to live in his world. The visitor is often able to perceive merits and defects in an environment that are no longer visible to the resident. Consider an example from the past. Smoke and grime badly polluted the industrial towns of northern England. This the visitor could easily see; but local residents tended to shunt unpleasant reality out of mind, turning a blind eye to what they

9 Herbert J. Gans, *The Urban Villagers: Group and Class in the Life of Italian-Americans* (New York: Free Press, 1962).
10 Gans, *Urban Villagers*, pp. 149–50.

could not effectively control. In northern England an adaptive response of the inhabitants to industrial pollution was to develop the institution of cozy chamber concerts and afternoon teas behind drawn blinds.

explorers and settlers at the pioneer fringe

At the pioneer fringe, explorers and settlers met with novel scenes and events which they had from time to time recorded in letters, diaries, reports, and books. Confrontation with novelty served to magnify a people's cultural bias: migrants saw the new environment through eyes that had adapted to other values. Consider New Mexico which received peoples of European origin from two directions, the south and the east.[11] From the south came the Spanish conquerors, missionaries, and colonists. From the east, at a much later time, came the Anglo-American explorers, military men, and settlers. A geography textbook might describe New Mexico as essentially a semiarid country with patches of real desert and islands of cool, moist, forest-clad mountains. The Spaniards and the early Anglo-American visitors perceived very differently.

Spanish conquerors were little concerned with the climate and soil of New Mexico. They did not move north in search of fertile soils and the peace of rural life. The familiar justifications for Spanish conquest were souls to save, private gain, and profits for the king. And the gain was to come primarily from mineral wealth. The Spaniards also failed to take much interest in climate and land because neither differed in any remarkable way from that of New Spain. In the march northward, the climatic change most evident to the conquerors and settlers was the drop in temperature. Coronado, in his report to Mendoza in 1540, wrote: "They [the people of Cibola] do not raise cotton, because the country is exceedingly cold;" "according to what the natives of the country say, the snow and cold are excessive," and "there are not many birds probably on account of the cold..." Since Coronado wrote the report in August, these remarks could have arisen only from hearsay, conjecture, and dark foreboding. Nearly sixty years later it was Don Juan de Oñate's turn to report to the Viceroy of New Spain. The report, written in March 1599, described rather optimistically the resources of the country, the minerals, salines, game, and Indian vassals, but there was no comment on the climate except "...by the end of August, I began to prepare the people of the Army for the rigorous winter of which the Indians and the nature of the land warn us."

11 This section is based on Yi-Fu Tuan and Cyril E. Everard, "New Mexico's Climate: The Appreciation of a Resource," *Natural Resources Journal*, 4, No. 2 (1964), 268–308.

In 1760 Bishop Tamarón visited New Mexico. His tract, *Kingdom of New Mexico,* surprises the modern reader with its frequent comments on floods and the abundance of water in the stream courses. Nowhere does he refer to aridity. He occasionally mentions the heat, but considering the fact that he traveled in New Mexico in the summer half of the year it is curious that he should also refer to the cold, to "freezing at dawn" on May 11, near Robledo, and to the fact that the stream at Taos is covered with ice every year. The strongest complaint against winter cold by a southern visitor occurs in the comments of Antonio Barreiro, a legal adviser to the government in Santa Fe. He wrote a booklet on the province's geography. In the section headed "climate" only winter is discussed because "the New Mexican winter so particularly impresses all who know that cold is to be experienced here." Barreiro had an eye for the picturesque detail. He noted, for instance, how "in the cow-houses, often times, the milk congeals almost on issuing from the cow's udder and one can carry it in a napkin to melt it in his house and to use it as desired."

Spaniards and Mexicans, when they moved north into New Mexico, did not find the country barren. On the contrary they remarked frequently on the presence of streams. Barreiro went so far as to say that "the greater part of the country consists of immense plains and delightful valleys, clothed with very abundant pasturage." In contrast to the Latins, Anglo-American explorers and surveyors moved into the Southwest from the humid East. The appearance of the Southwest made a strong impression on them, sometimes very unfavorably. Lieutenant J. H. Simpson, for instance, passed through the Navaho country of northwestern New Mexico in 1849. He concluded the journal of his reconnaissance with the comment: "But never did I have, nor do I believe anybody can have a full appreciation of the almost universal barrenness which pervades this country, until they come out, as I did, to 'search the land' and beheld with their own eyes its general nakedness." Elsewhere Simpson described the landscape as having a "sickening-colored'" aspect, one which "until familiarity reconciles you to the sight" you cannot even look upon "without a sensation of loathing." In May 1851, J. R. Bartlett, United States Commissioner of the United States and Mexico Boundary Commission, crossed the southwestern plains of New Mexico. He characterized them as "barren and uninteresting in the extreme." One became "sickened and disgusted with the ever-recurring sameness of plain and mountain, plant and living thing." "Is this the land," Bartlett asks, "which we have purchased, and are to survey and keep at such cost?" In a later report for the Boundary Commission, W. H. Emory claims that the Great Plains west of the one hundredth meridian are "wholly unsusceptible of sustaining an agricultural population, until you reach sufficiently far south to encounter the rains from the tropics...or westward until you reach the last slope of the Pacific."

indians and anglo-americans
in new mexico

Educated men exploring a country or intending to settle there often take notes. We have their impressions in writing. Such impressions are explicit. They tend also to be either specialized or somewhat superficial: specialized because explorers and surveyors are performing limited tasks, superficial because settlers perceive their new environment through the tinted glass of past experience. Once a people have settled down and adapted somewhat to the new setting, it is difficult to know their environmental attitudes for, having become native, they lose the urge to make comparisons and comment on their new home. Occasions to voice environmental values seldom arise; values are implicit in the people's economic activities, behavior and style of life. Having described the initial impressions of New Mexico, we may now turn to the environmental attitudes of the settled peoples.

In northwestern New Mexico, five groups of people—Navaho, Zuni, Spanish-Mexican, Mormon, and Texan—have been studied by Evon Vogt, Ethel Albert, and their colleagues.[12] Their work suggests that among the five peoples, the sharpest differences in environmental attitude occur between the Indians and the Anglo-Americans. The Indians have lived in the area for centuries. They have acquired detailed knowledge of the land and its resources. They do not regard nature as something to be subdued for purely economic gain, nor as occasions for testing one's manhood. They gather and hunt but these activities are linked not only to their economic life; they also have profound importance to their ceremonial life. The Navaho, for example, use plants in curing rituals and the Zuni require spruce boughs to decorate their *katchina* dancers. To Mormons and Texans alike, nature is to be subdued. God has given man lordship over the things of the earth; He has commissioned man to transform the desert into a garden. Such theological dogmas would inform the Mormon mind. God is a little more remote to the Texan farmer but his attitude to nature is as domineering. Both Mormons and Texans like to hunt. It is a male sport, a time to leave the women behind and assert one's manliness by shooting a deer and lugging it back to the hearth.

The Anglo-Americans have their differences, however. To the Texans, the Mormons are a peculiar people, and there is something unattractive in the chummy closeness of their dwellings. To the Mormons, the wide spacing

---

[12] Evon Vogt and Ethel M. Albert (eds.), *People of Rimrock: A Study of Values in Five Cultures* (Cambridge, Mass.: Harvard University Press, 1966).

of Texan houses is evidence that they lack communal life; they practice a type of dry farming that seems improvident; they do not irrigate their fields; they appear not quite civilized. Bragging and superstition are in them a curious mix. Consider the Texan pinto-bean farmer. He has to face a climate of unreliable rainfall. Success in any one year is never guaranteed. Drought is a force beyond his control and yet he needs to feel that he is the master of his fate. The result is evident in his personality: the desire to gamble and to brag even when there remains only the size of the crop failure to brag about. He also shows a readiness to believe in quack cures for defects in nature, such as water-witching and various unproven methods of rainmaking.[13]

Navaho and Zuni world views have this much in common. In both the sense of sacred power is widely diffused among humans, animals, places, and mythical beings, though some possess more of it than others. When all powers work together, harmony follows. Much of Navaho and Zuni ritual is oriented to keeping the harmony and to restoring it should it be disrupted. For both cultures harmony is the central value, and from it is derived a complex of attitudes toward man and nature. However, the Navaho and the Zuni differ in their social organization and economy, and these differences are reflected in some of their religious and environmental attitudes. Thus, as I have mentioned earlier, the Zuni have a strong sense of the center—the Middle Place—which corresponds to their compact settlement and is identified with their self-contained culture. The Navaho live in scattered hogans; their social organization is less structured, and their world view is correspondingly less organized. There is no one Middle Place; each hogan is a sort of center in which ceremonials may be performed. Space seems less well defined for the Navaho; yet they have a strong sense of the limits of their own grounds as sacred space—one that is bounded by the four sacred mountains. Both cultures admit the supremacy of the sun, share a common color symbolism, and embrace the sacred number four; but unlike the Zuni the Navaho people have no calendrical sequence that regulates ceremonial life and ensures the steady flow of blessings. The two peoples interpret the categories "pretty" and "ugly" differently. "Pretty" to the Zuni is a picture of abundance and well-being that is the fruits of labor. For the Navaho it is a vision of green, a summery landscape that supports life. "Ugly" to the Zuni means the difficulties inherent in livelihood and the maliciousness of human nature. The Navaho, on the other hand, tend to see "ugly" as the disruption of the natural order: it stirs memories of hardship, parched land, illness, accident, and aliens. Landscape symbols seem to

13 Evon Vogt, *Modern Homesteaders* (Cambridge, Mass.: Harvard University Press, 1955).

arise in the minds of the Navaho more often than they do in the minds of the Zuni who are more conscious of personal and social relationships.[14]

changes in environmental attitude: mountain

Changes in styles of architecture reflect changes in technology, economy, and in people's attitude toward what is desirable in the physical environment. Changes in agricultural land use, too, reflect technical innovations, new trends in marketing, and food preferences. However, certain aspects of nature defy easy human control: these are the mountains, deserts, and seas. They constitute, as it were, permanent fixtures in man's world whether he likes them or not. To these recalcitrant aspects of nature man has tended to respond emotionally, treating them at one time as sublime, the abode of the gods, and at another as ugly, distasteful, the abode of demons. In modern times the emotional charge of the response has greatly weakened but there remains a strong aesthetic element in our attitudes to nature that cannot be readily brought under the plow. The New Mexican landscape, we have noted, was once judged "disgusting," "sickening," and "monotonous." Now the state claims to be the "Land of Enchantment," and it boasts a substantial tourist industry.

To illustrate how attitude toward nature can change through time, consider the mountain. At an early stage in human history, the mountain was viewed with awe. It towered above the peopled plains; it was remote, difficult to approach, dangerous, and unassimilable to the workaday needs of man. People in widely different parts of the world regarded the mountain as the place where sky and earth met. It was the central point, the world's axis, the place impregnated with sacred power where the human spirit could pass from one cosmic level to another. Thus in Mesopotamian belief "the Mountain of the Lands" united earth and heaven. The stepped pyramid of Sumeria, the ziggurat, had the meaning of a hill visible from afar. Sumerians interpreted it as a cosmic mountain. In Indian mythology Mount Meru stood at the center of the world below the Polar Star. The Borobudur temple was an architectural translation of this symbol. In China and Korea, Mount Meru appeared on the circular cosmographic charts as the Kunlun. The Iranian Haraberazaiti was fastened to the sky at the world's center. The Uralo-Altaic peoples believed in a central mountain, and the Germanic peoples had their Himingbjorg (celestial mountain) where the rainbow touched the dome of heaven. We readily recall Mount Olympus of the

---

14 Vogt and Albert, *People of Rimrock,* pp. 282–83.

Greeks, Tabor of the Israelites, and Fuji of the Japanese. Other examples can easily be multiplied.[15]

Early aesthetic response to mountains varied from culture to culture. The Hebrews beheld them in confidence. They could feel the peace of the everlasting hills and had lifted up their eyes to the mountains, which were an index of the Divine. "Thy righteousness standeth like the strong mountains" (*Psalms* 36:6). They were creations for which one gave thanks (*Deuteronomy* 33:15). The early Greeks experienced awe as well as aversion before an aspect of nature they could not wholly grasp. Mountains were wild and terrifying, and yet the "sky-piercing rocks," "the star-neighbored peaks" (Aeschylus) also displayed sublimity in the modern sense. The Romans felt little sympathy for mountains which they described as aloof, hostile, and desolate.[16] In China mountains acquired numen in the earliest legends. T'ai Shan, the chief of the Five Sacred Peaks, was a divinity. The Emperor Wu (140–87 B.C.) sacrificed to Heaven and Earth there. Taoism enveloped mountains in an aura of mystery. Both Taoists and Buddhists built temples in their fastness. Mountains became familiar through ritual in ancient Greece as in China.[17] On the other hand, like the Greeks, the Chinese viewed them with fear and aversion. They were covered with dark forests. The habitation of monkeys and apes, mountains were wrapped in mist, and so high that the sun was hidden (viz. Chü Yuan 332–296 B.C.). A poem of the Former Han dynasty described mountains as broken and wild before which one's heart stood still, aghast.

Chinese attitudes toward mountains changed over time. The detailed shifts did not parallel those of the Occident, but in broad outline a common sequence can be discerned: in both civilizations the change was from a religious attitude in which awe was combined with aversion, to an aesthetic attitude that shifted from a sense of the sublime to a feeling for the picturesque; to the modern evaluation of mountains as a recreational resource. In China the aesthetic appreciation of mountains had its early beginnings in the fourth century A.D. when large numbers of people migrated to the rugged southern parts of the country.[18] Evidence from paintings, however, shows that as late as the T'ang dynasty (A.D. 618–907) human figures still dominated pictorial art. Man was the equal if not the measure of mountains.

15 Mircea Eliade, *Patterns in Comparative Religion* (Cleveland: World Publishing, Meridian, 1963), pp. 99–102.
16 W. W. Hyde, "The Ancient Appreciation of Mountain Scenery," *Classical Journal,* 11 (1915), 70–85.
17 Edouard Chavannes, *Le T'ai chan: essai de monographie d'un culte Chinois* (Paris: Ernest Leroux, 1910).
18 J. D. Frodsham, "The Origins of Chinese Nature Poetry," *Asia Major,* 8 (1960–1961), 68–103.

Toward the end of the period nature came to the fore, and during the Sung dynasty (A.D. 960–1279) paintings of the genre "mountain and water" achieved preeminence.

In the Occident the aesthetic appreciation of untamed nature came much later than it did in the Orient. During the Middle Ages writers tended to substitute abstraction and moralization (based on the symbolism of the Bible) for personal experience. But the epic *Beowulf* was composed in the early eighth century: it contains passages that describe direct experiences of nature, noting man's sense of awe touched with fear before "wolf-haunted valleys" and "wind-swept headlands."[19] In 1335 Petrarch climbed Mount Ventoux. A lover of wild nature well ahead of his time, Petrarch would sometimes get out of bed after midnight and go into the mountains for a moonlight stroll. This was a feat that even the bold Romantics of the early nineteenth century felt little inclined to emulate. Moreover, Petrarch's letters and poems give evidence of a sentimental attitude toward nature—a way of coloring the inanimate world to reflect the writer's mood—that is rare before the modern period.

Until well into the eighteenth century the prevailing view of mountains was unsympathetic. Literary evidence makes this distaste clear. Marjorie Nicolson refers to Joshua Poole's *English Parnassus,* published in 1657, in which the author suggested to aspiring poets the use of some three score epithets all descriptive of the mountain. A few adjectives were neutral (rocky, craggy); a few indicated a passing feeling for the grand (stately, star-brushing); and many expressed distaste: "insolent, surly, ambitious, barren, sky-threatening, supercilious, desert, uncouth, inhospitable, freezing, infruitful, crump-shouldered, unfrequented, forsaken, melancholy, pathless." In addition, mountains were described as "Earth's Dugs, Risings, Tumors, Blisters, Warts."[20]

Some one hundred odd years later, Romantic poets began to sing in praise of mountain splendor, of glorious heights that stirred their souls to ecstasy. No longer remote and ominous, mountains possessed a sublime beauty that was the closest thing on earth to the Infinite. Poets were not alone in their enthusiasm. Experience itself was unnecessary. Immanuel Kant, who never saw a mountain, nonetheless defined the idea of the sublime in terms of an Alpine scene. What brought about this remarkable change? Nicolson has traced some of the intellectual shifts in the seventeenth

[19] E. T. McLaughlin, "The Medieval Feeling for Nature," in *Studies in Medieval Life and Literature* (New York: Putnam's, 1894), pp. 1–33; Clarence J. Glacken, *Traces on the Rhodian Shore* (Berkeley: University of California Press, 1967), pp. 309–30.

[20] Marjorie Hope Nicolson, *Mountain Gloom and Mountain Glory* (New York: Norton, 1962).

and eighteenth centuries that contributed toward the reversal in mountain evaluation.

A major shift was the reluctant abandonment of the idea that the circle symbolized perfection. The belief has deep roots and was strongly held; it permeated many fields of thinking, from astronomy and theology to humane letters and art. If perfection existed any where it was in the heavens, and there indeed one found the planets in circular orbits. The earth, however, was not a perfect sphere. A viewpoint influential in the eighteenth century argued that the earth had only assumed its irregular shape, full of mountain protuberances and oceanic deeps, as a result of the Fall. The smooth innocence of the original earth's crust had collapsed into an inner layer of water. What we see as mountains and valleys are the deplorable ruins. For a time, noted scholars (including Newton) thought well of this thesis; but approval was steadily withdrawn as scientific evidence controverted it, and even more, as a new aesthetic denied the identification of simple geometrical shapes with beauty. In the course of the eighteenth century more and more writers and thinkers championed the irregular and the useless as possessing in themselves a beauty at once wonderful and terrible. The popularity of Chinoiserie, the novelty and acceptance of Chinese landscape design, further removed any lingering insistence on the formal and the regular as the only aesthetic canons. These, then, were some of the intellectual trends that opened the way toward the appreciation of mountains.

Attitudes toward the mountain changed also for other reasons. Traveling was easier as the century progressed. Mountains that became accessible lost much of their forbidding mien. Emotion waned with familiarity. Of course long before 1750 there were intrepid souls who tramped the mountains apparently without fear. Even in the sixteenth century some people crossed the Alps for enjoyment. More and more people traveled for pleasure and scientific purpose in the succeeding century so that by the 1700s numerous accounts of journeys through the Alps, mixing the fantastic with the scientific, were published. A great Alpine tourist, Johann Jacob Scheuchzer of Zurich, made nine extensive trips through the mountains between 1702 and 1711. He was a botanist and a geologist. He made barometric measurements of height and theorized on how ice moved but he also gave a reasoned catalogue of Swiss dragons, arranged according to cantons.[21]

Scheuchzer played another role in changing the evaluation of mountains. He developed a theory which explained why the light mountain air was good for health. In the exposition of his idea we catch the first intima-

21 G. Rylands de Beer, *Early Travellers in the Alps* (London: Sidgwick & Jackson, Ltd., 1930), pp. 89–90.

tion of the hotel prospectus. Mountains appeared in a different light when they were thought to generate recuperative power. Eventually this belief led to the construction of sanatoria, hotels, and tourist facilities, which became so successful that, in the eyes of the rich, Switzerland was a rest home and a playground. By the middle of the nineteenth century a complete reversal in the image of the mountain had occurred: far from being a place that induced shivers of horror agreeable only to hardy souls it was benign and well suited to the needs of those in poor health. America too recognized the attractiveness of its Western mountains at this time. A vigorous campaign was launched in the 1870s to draw attention to the limpid air, dry soils, and mineral springs of the Rockies. Colorado was proclaimed to be the Switzerland of America, or, in a more exuberant mood, Switzerland, the Colorado of Europe.[22]

---

[22] Earl Pomeroy, *In Search of the Golden West: The Tourist in Western America* (New York: Knopf, 1957).

environment, perception, and world views

In the last chapter I sketched the role of culture in conditioning people's environmental perception and values. Taking the physical setting as uniform and constant, we saw how people with different experience, socioeconomic background, and aim evaluated it; and also how, as society and culture evolve, attitude toward an environment can change—even reverse itself— over time. In this chapter I shall emphasize the effect of the physical setting on perception, attitudes, and world view, proceeding from the simple to the complex: from the impact of environment on the interpretation of visual cues to the structuring of the world based on the major physical characteristics of the habitat.

environment and perception

Human habitats vary greatly in character and are classifiable in various ways. A simple two-fold classification might distinguish the habitats into the categories "carpentered" and "noncarpentered." The carpentered world is replete with straight lines, angles, and rectangular objects. Cities are rectangular environment *par excellence*. Nature and the countryside, in contrast, lack rectangularity. In the landscape of primitive culture even the shelters may be round like bee-hives. Rural landscapes, however, are not devoid of orthogonals: the fields are often rectangular although their shape is seldom evident from the ground level. Farm houses are carpentered, and they are certain to contain many objects that are rectangular, such as tables, rugs, and beds. There is reason to believe that people who live in a carpentered environment acquire the tendency to perceive a nonorthogonal parallelogram drawn on a flat surface as the representation of a rectangular surface extending through space (Figure 8a). This tendency has great functional value in highly carpentered settings. A city dweller faces rectangular objects daily. On his retina these appear as nonrectangular images. To live in such a world a person must learn to interpret acute and obtuse angles in retinal images as deriving from orthogonal surfaces; the interpretation is automatic and constantly reinforced. We may therefore expect city and rural folk to interpret the length of straight lines and the size of angles rather differently. Residents of a cold climate live in a more carpentered world than residents of a hot climate because cold weather forces people to spend

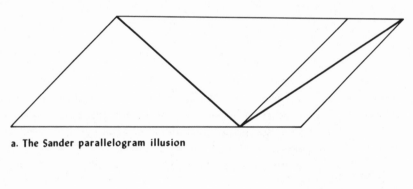

a. The Sander parallelogram illusion

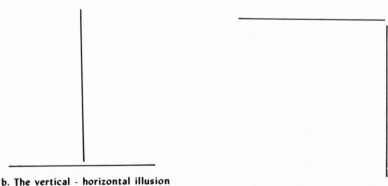

b. The vertical - horizontal illusion

Figure 8 Environment and illusion.

more time indoors. The perceptual judgments of these two groups might differ in a way similar to that between city and country folk.

Environment appears to affect a person's judgment of the length of a vertical line drawn on a piece of paper (Figure 8b). A short vertical line in a drawing may represent a relatively long horizontal line extending away from the observer. One can exaggerate the length of the vertical by supposing it to represent a foreshortened horizontal line. Take the case of a man who lives on a flat featureless plain over which he has plowed furrows. For him the only source of verticals on the retinal image are the furrows that extend away from him. These lines, which recede in the same direction as his line of vision, are much more foreshortened than the transverse horizontals. Such a person may acquire the adaptive habit of interpreting vertical retinal extensions as greatly foreshortened lines on the horizontal plane; he should be more subject to the horizontal-vertical illusion. Reasoning thus can lead one to suppose that rainforest dwellers and people who grow up in small courtyards surrounded by towering tenements are the least likely to suffer from illusions of this type.[1] Experimental evidence for all these postulates, however, is limited and difficult to evaluate with confidence.

*perceptual acuity
and the challenge of harsh environments*

People can develop exceptional perceptual acuity in the course of adapting successfully to the challenge of a harsh environment. In the Arctic, for example, there are times when no horizon separates the sky from the earth, when the scene is visually undifferentiated. The Eskimo is nonetheless able to travel a hundred or more miles across such wastes. His cues are less visual than acoustic, olfactory, and tactile. He is guided by the direction and smell of winds, and by the feel of ice and snow under his feet. Aivilik Eskimos have at least twelve different terms for the various winds, and their vocabulary for the different conditions of snow is equally rich. A city dweller, by way of extreme contrast, has a very limited vocabulary, not only in regard to snow and ice but also to aspects of nature that affect him daily such as weather and relief. Yet, if the city man should become an avid skier he soon learns to perceive different qualities in the snow surface and acquires a new vocabulary to designate them.

The Bushman of the Kalahari desert has successfully responded to the

---

[1] Marshall H. Segall, Donald T. Campbell, and Melville J. Herskovits, "Some Psychological Theory and Predictions of Cultural Differences," in *The Influence of Culture on Visual Perception* (Indianapolis: Bobbs-Merrill, 1966), pp. 69–97.

challenge of his sparse environment. Although an active Bushman's daily energy requirement is around 1,975 calories, the food that is available to him on an average day yields 2,140 calories. Thus contrary to popular belief the Bushman does not lead an existence on the edge of starvation.[2] To be successful, a hunter and gatherer in the desert has to develop his perceptual senses to a high degree of keenness, and particularly is this true of eyesight. Remarkable accounts are given of his visual acuity. According to Elizabeth Thomas, the Gikwe Bushmen can tell very quickly how long it is since a buck, lion, leopard, bird, reptile, or insect has passed. They can pick out one set of spoors from fifty, and deduce accurately the size, sex, build, and mood of the great antelope that has just made them. They know animals as much by their subtle script in the sand as by their physical presence. When they meet a new person their minds instinctively record not only the look on his face but also his footprint.[3]

As plant gatherers the Bushmen are equally keen in reading the ecological and botanical evidence for edible fruits and roots. Laurens van der Post notes: "A tiny leaf almost invisible in grass and thorn just above the surface of the red sand and to me indistinguishable from many others, would cause them to kneel down and grub deftly with their digging sticks to produce what I, in my ignorance of Kalahari botany, called wild carrots, potatoes, leeks, turnips, sweet potatoes, and artichokes."[4]

The part of the Kalahari desert in which the Gikwe Bushmen live is not only barren but devoid of landmarks, except for the baobab trees and even these grow far apart; some areas have none. To the Bushmen the desert is not featureless and empty. They have an extraordinarily detailed knowledge of their roaming area, which for each band of about twenty people may reach an extent of several hundred square miles. Within their own territory the Bushmen "know every bush and stone, every convolution of the ground, and have usually named every place in it where a certain kind of veld food may grow, even if that place is only a few yards in diameter, or where there is only a patch of tall arrow grass or a bee tree, and in this way each group of people knows many hundreds of places by name."[5]

The mainstay of Bushmen's diet during the hot season when the melons (*tsama*) are gone is a fibrous watery root known as the *bi*. The Gikwe can

2 Richard B. Lee, "What Hunters Do for a Living, or How to Make Out on Scarce Resources," in Richard B. Lee and Irven DeVore, *Man the Hunter* (Chicago: Aldine-Atherton, 1968), p. 39.
3 Elizabeth M. Thomas, *The Harmless People* (New York: Knopf, Vintage edition, 1965), p. 13.
4 Laurens van der Post, *The Lost World of the Kalahari* (Baltimore: Penguin, 1962), p. 217.
5 Thomas, *The Harmless People,* p. 10.

remember the location of individual *bi,* despite their inconspicuousness, after an absence from the area of several months.

Visual acuity is highly developed among the Gikwe Bushmen. In the northern part of the Kalahari, south of the Okovango River, live the Kung Bushmen. Their environment is still arid, but unlike the home of the Gikwe it has a rolling surface marked by clusters of small trees, by little hills and clay flats that become shallow lakes after rain. In a less harsh country the Kung live in somewhat grander style. They are less pressed for food and water; and although they know vast sections of their territory in detail, being sure of the whereabouts of game and veld food, they do not have to learn the cues for recognizing the location of individual roots as the Gikwe do.

environment and world view

Natural environment and world view are closely related: world view, unless it is derived from an alien culture, is necessarily constructed out of the salient elements of a people's social and physical setting. In nontechnological societies the physical setting is the canopy of nature and its myriad contents. Like means of livelihood, world view reflects the rhythms and constraints of the natural environment. To illustrate this relationship we may begin with the Congo rainforest and the semiarid plateau of the American Southwest: the one is a total ambiance in which a people can live immersed, whereas the other is noted for the architectural sharpness of its landmarks. We then move to consider how dualistic societies extend their polarities to the sharply dichotomized environments (mountain-sea, rainforest-grassland) they occupy; lastly, we note the extent that the cosmologies of the ancient Near Eastern peoples bear the imprints of their environments.

THE FOREST AMBIANCE

As a human habitat the chief distinction of the rainforest environment lies in its all-enveloping nature. It is not differentiated as to sky and earth; there is no horizon; it lacks landmarks; it has no outstanding hill that can be recognized, and no tree that exists in sharp isolation as the baobab on the Kalahari plain; there are no distant views. The BaMbuti Pygmies of the Congo rainforest live not so much on earth, with the heavens above and the underworld below, as within an all-encompassing element. The stars play no part in their cosmography. The sun itself is not a bright disc with a trajectory across the sky but rather patches of flickering light on the forest floor. Of the two hundred or so legends collected from the Pygmies only three are concerned with the creation of the world, with the stars and sky, and these would appear to be influenced by Negro legends.[6]

The sense of time is curtailed. Legends reveal a lack of interest in the past, and their memory with regard to genealogy is short. Seasonal variation in the rainforest is minimal; the immensely rich plant world goes through its complex life cycles without any salient visual evidence of change. Although the Pygmies have a detailed knowledge of the fauna and flora useful to them, this knowledge does not include cyclical activities. They are unaware, for example, that the aquatic larvae which they eat turn into mosquitoes, nor do they know that the caterpillar turns into a butterfly.[7]

An effect of the rainforest environment on perception is the curtailment of perspective. Anything that is seen is seen at close range. In hunting the game makes its presence known largely by the sound it makes until it appears suddenly within a few yards of the hunter. Outside the rainforest the Pygmy is bewildered by distance, the lack of trees and the sharpness of relief. He seems incapable of reading the cues for perspective. Colin Turnbull describes the bewilderment of the Pygmy, Kenge, when he was taken to the open grasslands near Lake Edward. A flock of buffaloes grazed several miles away, far below where they were standing. Kenge asked Turnbull, "What insects are these?"

> When I told Kenge that the insects were buffalo, he roared with laughter and told me not to tell such stupid lies. When Henri, who was thoroughly puzzled, told him the same thing, and explained that visitors to the park had to have a guide with them at all times because there were so many dangerous animals, Kenge still didn't believe but strained his eyes to see more clearly and asked what kind of buffalo they were that they were so small. I told him they were sometimes nearly twice the size of a forest buffalo, and he shrugged his shoulders and said he would not be standing out there in the open if they were. I tried telling him they were possibly as far away as from Epulu to the village of Kopu, beyond Eboyo. He began scraping the mud off his arms and legs, no longer interested in such fantasies.[8]

On another occasion Turnbull pointed to a boat in the middle of the lake. It was a large fishing boat with several people in it. Kenge thought it was a floating piece of wood.

The BaMbuti Pygmies lack the stars, the seasons, the sky, and the earth that figure prominently in the cosmic views of most other peoples.

6 Colin M. Turnbull, "Legends of the BaMbuti," *Journal of the Royal Anthropological Institute*, 89 (1959), 45.
7 Colin M. Turnbull, "The Mbuti Pygmies: An Ethnographic Survey," *Anthropological Papers*, The American Museum of Natural History, 50, Part 3 (1965), 164.
8 Colin M. Turnbull, *The Forest People* (London: Chatto & Windus, 1961), p. 228.

They have instead the all-sustaining forest, with which they maintain the closest identification. Closeness to the forest is expressed in many ways. Love making, for instance, takes place in a forest clearing rather than in a hut. A Pygmy may dance alone in the forest—*with* the forest. A newborn infant is bathed in water mixed with the juice of forest vine. Vine is tied around the waist, and circlets, decorated with small pieces of wood, are put around the wrists. At the time of puberty a girl renews her contact with the vines and leaves of the forest; she uses them for decoration, clothing, and bedding. During a crisis, such as failure in hunting, sickness, or death, the men would gather to sing songs that will waken the benevolent spirit of the forest. The *molimo* trumpet, a ritual instrument, is carried around to different parts of the forest; a young man echoes into it the songs the men sing. The sound of the trumpet, too, serves to draw the attention of the forest to the people in distress. In a pervasive environment undistinguished by landmarks, it is not surprising that the Pygmies should attribute special importance to the unfocused sound. In singing it is the sound rather than the words that matters. The clearest idea that the Pygmies have concerning the supernatural, as a state beyond death, beyond men and animals, and beyond men who could turn into animals, is the Beautiful Song of a Bird.[9]

THE STRUCTURED COSMOS OF THE PUEBLO INDIANS

The world view of the pueblo Indians of the American Southwest is, in many ways, the antithesis of that of the Congo Pygmies. It is also less distinctive in the sense that its major features are shared by other peoples. An Indian from Santa Ana pueblo should find it easier to accept the structured cosmography of the Egyptians and the Chinese than the undifferentiated ambiance of the Pygmies. We are perhaps inclined to assume that the greatest contrast in life style exists between a nonliterate tribe and the citizens of an urbanized society, when in fact the contrast may be as great among "primitives" who live in totally different natural environments.

The cosmos of the pueblo Indians is spatially well-defined, stratified, and rotatory. Their natural environment is the semiarid plateau, which presents to the eye sweeping vistas and prominent landmarks such as mesas, buttes, and cliffs of sculptured sharpness. The land is layered: cliffs expose multicolored strata of sandstone and shale, capped here and there by black basaltic lava. Color, when the sun is low in the sky, is brilliant. The blue of the sky, the buff and reddish soils, the dark green of scattered conifers, and the blue of springs and small lakes are juxtaposed but not merged on the bright palette of the Southwest. For livelihood the Indians raised crops.

---

9 Colin M. Turnbull, *Wayward Servants* (London: Eyre & Sottiswode, 1965), p. 255.

Before the conquest the main crops were corn, beans, and squash, and probably cotton. The Spaniards introduced wheat, oats, barley, peaches, apricots, apples, grapes, melons, chili, and other vegetables. The food repertoire has been greatly enriched but the agricultural rhythms, and the rituals that go with them, remain essentially the same.

Place, location, and direction figure prominently in the pueblo Indian's world view. The Santa Ana Indians conceive of the earth as a square and stratified. Each corner contains a house in which a spirit or god lives. Four other houses, corresponding perhaps to spirits, are distributed at the cardinal points. The idea of "house" seems important to pueblo Indians in general. All creatures, natural and supernatural, are assigned to houses: houses exist for the living and the dead, for clouds, the sun, butterflies, and dogs. Cardinal directions are known as "middle west," "middle east," "middle north," and "middle south." Zenith and nadir define the vertical axis. Each of the six directions has its own color and animal—an array of correspondences that resembles the cosmographic ideas of the Chinese. The geometric and oriented character of the cosmos is duplicated, though rather weakly, in the arrangement of the houses. In settlements such as Acoma, Santo Domingo, Santa Ana, and San Juan the houses stand in parallel rows; and in others the dwellings outline one or more courtyards. Streets rarely have names but parts of the town are occasionally given directional names. At Santa Ana pueblo there are three courtyards: the largest, where the principal dancing takes place, is called "middle plaza," and the other two are known as the "north corner" and "eastern" plazas.[10]

The vertical dimension of the pueblo cosmos is given emphasis by the directions zenith and nadir, by the stratification of the earth in colored layers (from white at the lowest level, through red and blue to the yellow layer at the surface), and in the creation myth. The latter usually tells of how the first people lived inside the earth, and how they climbed through the successive layers to emerge on the surface in the north, at Shipap. The place of emergence was too sacred to stay, so they moved south. In the Santa Ana legend, the move was to the White House; here they lived with the gods who taught them traditions, rituals, and songs that promoted fertility. The next move, again southward, took them to the middle place.[11] The Zuni myth is somewhat different. Their world is circular rather than square, and they call themselves the "ladder-descending children of the Corn Chiefs," thus suggesting an origin from above rather than from below.

Among objects the sun, the sky, the earth, and corn play prominent

10 Leslie A. White, *The Pueblo of Santa Ana, New Mexico,* American Anthropological Association, Memoir 60, 44, No. 4 (1942), 35–42, 80–84.
11 Leslie A. White, "The World of the Keresan Pueblo Indians," in Stanley Diamond (ed.), *Primitive Views of the World* (New York: Columbia University Press, paperback edition, 1964), pp. 83–94.

roles in pueblo Indian mythology. The sun is very powerful and is usually spoken of as "father" or "old man." It is prayed to for longevity, it is a hunt deity, and its warmth fertilizes the field. It makes its daily journey across the sky, reaching its house in the west at sundown. In ancient times the Indians sprinkled corn meal or pollen at sunrise and said a prayer. The sky is another important spiritual being. Earth is addressed as "mother" and "mother earth." And so is the corn—the body and spirit of pueblo life. Clouds house water spirits; they are also identified with the dead. Mountains and mesas have power; they house the supernaturals, and the four sacred mountains of the directions are themselves supernaturals. Springs are ritual centers.

The course of the sun marks the agricultural and ceremonial calendar. Among the Hopi, planting dates are established by the progress of the sun toward the summer solstice; the progress itself is calibrated by the successive positions of the rising sun relative to the landmarks on the horizon. There may be no further planting after solstice. The Zuni Indians have not organized a particular time for planting, but they observe the summer solstice which determines the beginning of the dance series for summer rainfall. Harvesting starts another round of activities with appropriate observations. Autumn and early winter is the time for hunting, housebuilding or repair; and winter is the time for story telling, playing games, and getting married.[12]

As the highly differentiated space of the pueblo Indians differs from the visually unorganized environment of the BaMbuti Pygmies, so does their full calendrical sequence of celebrations differ from the temporal monotony of the forest dwellers. The rainforest environment does not lack variety; far from it. Its monotony lies in the year that is unpunctuated by seasonal change. Even in a small and harmonious society, members who live in the closest association with each other need some form of release from the tensions that are bound to build up over time. Unlike the pueblo Indians, the Pygmies cannot find release in clearly marked seasonal changes of activity and in seasonal ceremonials; they have, however, one break—the honey season which lasts two months around June. This is a time when food is easy to obtain. The hunting band then breaks up into smaller units, drifting on their own through the forest, looking for honey, and regrouping at the end of the season into a band of different composition. The change allows old enmities to wane and the forging of new friendships.

DICHOTOMIZED ENVIRONMENT AND DUALISTIC ATTITUDES

We have noted earlier the tendency of the human mind to organize phenomena into polar opposites such as life and death, light and darkness,

12 Elsie Clews Parsons, *Pueblo Indian Religion* (Chicago: University of Chicago Press, 1939), Vol. 1.

heaven and earth, sacred and profane. In some societies this dualistic structure permeates several levels of thought: it affects a people's social organization as well as its cosmology, art, and religion. The natural environment may lend itself to this dualistic outlook: it can reinforce a tendency by serving as a clearly visible index of polarity. We have already seen in chapter 3 how the polarities permeate the thinking and social patterns of the Indonesian archipelago, and how the dichotomized natural environment of mountain and water symbolized (for the Balinese, in particular) the contrarieties of existence. Consider another example, the Lele of Kasai.[13] This African tribe has adapted successfully to a sharply differentiated environment. The dualistic organization of its economic, social, and religious life seems inextricably bound to the dichotomy in nature.

The Lele live in the southwestern part of the Congo rainforest, south and west of the Kasai River, in a zone where the dense equatorial rainforest gives way to the grassland. Their environment is split between thickly forested valleys and grass-topped hills. The Lele are hunters and agriculturalists. They live in villages built on the grassland. Each village is surrounded by a ring of raffia palm; beyond it lie the grass and scrub leading to the forest. Their staple food is corn, which is grown in the forest by the slash and burn method. Both men and women engage in this activity, but other economic activities are separated by sex. Hunting and the collection of medicinal plants are exclusively the work of men; women's job is to cultivate fishponds in the marshy streams and to grow groundnuts in the grassland. Ritual values and economic activity seem unrelated. The Lele religion is not centered on the raffia palm, despite the fact that it plays a major role in their economy. All the products of the palm are used: for hut building and basketry, for arrow shafts, for the fibers with which they weave their raffia cloth. In addition the palm yields an unfermented wine, which forms the second staple article of diet. The cultivation of corn has no ritual significance either. On the other hand, hunting is immensely important in the religious and social outlook of the Lele despite the fact that the Lele are mediocre hunters, and meat is not, from a nutritional viewpoint, indispensable to their diet.

The forest has a mystique that the grassland and the villages do not have. Mary Douglas reports:

> The Lele speak of [the forest] with almost poetic enthusiasm. God gave it to them as the source of all good things. They often contrast the forest with the village. In the heat of the day, when the dusty village is unpleasantly hot, they like to escape to the cool and dark of the forest.... Men boast that in

---

[13] Mary Douglas, "The Lele of Kasai," in Daryll Forde (ed.), *African Worlds: Studies in the Cosmological Ideas and Social Values of African Peoples* (London: Oxford University Press, 1954), pp. 1–26.

the forest they can work all day without feeling hunger, but in the village they are always thinking about food. For going into the forest they use the verb *nyingena,* to enter, as one might speak of entering a hut, or plunging into water, giving the impression that they regard the forest as a separate element.[14]

With the forest as the male domain, the grassland is left to women. The grassland, however, has no prestige; it is dry and barren and the only crop that thrives in the leached soil is the groundnut. And the groundnut is the only crop that the women tend from start to finish. Although women help men in cultivating corn in the forest and in making the many products of the raffia palm, men not only do not help the women in their work on the groundnut plots but they avoid even setting their eyes on the work in progress. Lele women have a far more detailed knowledge of the grassland than do the men. On days when the forest is taboo to women they often manage to find some substitutes in the grassland, such as grasshoppers in the dry season and caterpillars in the wet. The forest, a source of comfort to the men, is to the women dark and vaguely threatening.

riverine environments, cosmology,
and architecture

Two ancient civilizations, Egypt and Mesopotamia, developed on the riverine environments of the Near East. Their world views differed, reflecting the dissimilar experiences of a nature that ruled over nearly every facet of the people's lives—with order in Egypt, and somewhat capriciously in Mesopotamia.

EGYPT

The dominant geographical facts of Egypt are the desert and the Nile River. The desert cannot support agriculture without some form of irrigation: the Nile River introduces a meridional gash of great fertility across the brown sandy wastes. The flood waters of the Nile are remarkably dependable, giving not only water but rich silt yearly to the valley basins. The sun, brilliant in the cloudless sky, is another fact of overwhelming importance to the Egyptian. He hates darkness and the cold. An ancient prayer called for the triumph of the sun over cloud and storm.[15] Cloud may yield rain but Egypt does not depend on rain. Cloud hides the sun and, in winter, causes a sensible drop in temperature. When the sun is up the clear dry air permits

14 Douglas, "The Lele of Kasai, p. 4.
15 J. H. Breasted, *Development of Religion and Thought in Ancient Egypt,* introduction by John A. Wilson, (New York: Harper & Row, 1959), p. 11.

the temperature to rise sharply; when it is covered, and even more when it makes its daily plunge below the western horizon, cold sets in rapidly. The scantily clad Egyptian feels the cold which, together with darkness, is a premonition of death. Compared with the sun and the Nile, other aspects of nature are relatively unimportant.

The ancient Egyptian's environmental values were enshrined in the language. As one might expect, green was a favored color and identified with "blessed," whereas reddish brown was associated with the sandhills and foreign country; it also meant "despised." The hieroglyph for Egypt was ⬭ , a flat slice of fertile black soil; whereas a sign composed of three ridges ⌒⌒⌒ meant "desert," "highland," and "foreign country." Preserved letters indicate that the ancient Egyptian found foreign scenes outside his own fertile valley of little appeal: they were too rugged or had unpredictable floods; there were too many trees and the sky was "dark by day." The Egyptian also differentiated rainwater, known as "the Nile in the sky," from the real Nile which came from the lower world. Rain was appointed for the use of foreign peoples and the beasts of the highlands, whereas the Nile served the people of Egypt. The one was undependable, the other dependable.[16]

The course of the Nile exerted a powerful influence on the Egyptian's sense of direction. The word "to go north" meant also "to go downstream," and the word "to go south" meant "to go upstream" or against the current. When the Egyptian visited the Euphrates he would have had to describe its course in some such circumlocution as "that circling water which goes downstream in going upstream." At the time the Egyptian language was forming, the direction south dominated the Nile dweller's world. He faced south, the source of rising flood waters and of life. The word for south was also that for face, and the usual word for north was related to one which meant "back of the head." Facing southward, east came to be identified with left, and west with right.[17]

The main current in Egyptian religious history can be traced as one of rivalry between the two great phenomena of nature, the sun and the Nile.[18] In protohistoric time, following Lower Egypt's conquest of Upper Egypt, the sun challenged the supremacy of the Nile. In the delta region of Lower Egypt the anastomosing channels of the Nile spread out like the ribs of a fan; they no longer formed a single distinguishing landmark and could no longer serve as a guide to direction. Nothing caught the eye over the delta's broad and flat surface. The dominant feature in such a setting

16 Herodotus, *The History of Herodotus,* trans. George Rawlinson (Chicago: Encyclopaedia Britannica, Inc., 1952), Book II, chapters 13–14.
17 Henri Frankfort, H. A. Frankfort, John A. Wilson, and Thorkild Jacobsen, *Before Philosophy* (Baltimore: Penguin, 1951), pp. 45–46.
18 Breasted, *Ancient Egypt,* pp. 8–9.

was the sun making its daily trajectory across the sky. It is not surprising that the early inhabitants there should have looked to the sun for orientation and evolved a solar theology. Lower Egypt's theology of the sun was superposed on Upper Egypt's theology of the Nile; an east-west axis extended across the north-south axis. Adjustments in mythology became necessary. In a world view dominated by the Nile the region of the circumpolar stars was the goal of the dead, for it alone did not swing below the horizon. With the ascendancy of the sun mythology the place of entry to the underworld shifted westward, to the place where the sun itself underwent a daily death.

The Egyptian environment is symmetrically disposed about the Nile River. On either side of it stretch fertile fields; the west bank mirrors the east bank, the bounding cliffs of the valley on one side are balanced by those on the other; and beyond them the deserts are alike in their desolation. Could this symmetry in nature have influenced the development of the Egyptian view of the cosmos? The Nile civilization is outstanding in the simple grandeur with which the ideal of balance is expressed in cosmology, art, and architecture. The geographical symmetries of east and west are reiterated by symmetries along the vertical axis. At the center of the cosmos is the earth (*Geb*), which has the shape of the Nile Valley—a platter with high rims—and it floats on the primordial waters (*Nūn*) out of which life first issued. Above the earth is the inverted pan of the sky, the sky-goddess (*Nūt*), and below it is the counterheaven (*Naunet*), girding the underworld.[19]

Cosmic beliefs find expression in Egypt's monumental architecture. Consider the pyramid. It is made up of four equal isosceles triangles converging on a single point. The base is an exact square and it is oriented precisely to the cardinal directions. The Great Pyramid of Cheops departs no more than 3′ 6″ from the true north. The interplay between pyramid and cosmos is stressed by the precision of orientation. The square base and the isosceles triangles emphasize the urge toward symmetry that appears also in other expressive domains of Egyptian life. The upward pointing triangle is in itself associated with the uprising flame; it is probably a male fertility symbol, the polar opposite of the downward pointing triangle that appears frequently on Egyptian and Mesopotamian figurines of earth goddesses during the fourth millennium B.C.

The pyramid existed as part of a large architectural complex, the purpose of which was to provide the appropriate setting for the enactment of a major ritual, namely, the transformation of the dead king from an earthly, transient being into an eternal deity. As the sun moved from east to west, going through its daily cycle of birth, life, and death, so the steps in the final deification of the king entailed movement westward from the valley of

---

[19] Frankfort et al., *Before Philosophy*, pp. 52–57.

earthly life to the desert plateau. In the valley temple, on the borders of vegetation, the dead body was cleansed and mummified. A causeway led up for some one hundred feet from the valley temple to the mortuary temple on the east side of the pyramid. The atmosphere in the dimly-lit valley temple was mysterious, and the long vestibule of the causeway, dark. From it the mummy of the king was brought to the great open sun court, and then to the pyramid temple, where the king was ritually transformed into a god. The final step was the lowering of the sarcophagus into the heart of the pyramid through the northern entrance. The slope of the entrance, when projected skyward, met the polar star. The region of the polar star was the home of the dead, and likewise the western region of sunset; in the pyramid both ideas found expression. The pyramid was a tomb; yet it also symbolized —as the primeval hillock, the upsurging flame, and the sun—eternal life.[20]

The Egyptian king was a god, his government divine. Other powers did not dispute his authority. Egyptian religion promoted centralization to a high degree, culminating in the person of the king. Egypt was one and indivisible. It knew little of civil war and armed invasion by foreigners was rarer still. Hence, most towns did not have walls. Nor were they of great social and political importance. The only town that mattered was the capital, the home of the king, but even the capital was completely subservient to the king; it moved from place to place to suit the shifting taste of each new dynasty. The capital might have had wealth and magnificence but it could boast little civic function and spirit. Not much in fact is known about any Egyptian capital other than Akhetaton (Tell el Amarna), which was an unwalled town straggling for about five miles on the east bank of the Nile. Akhetaton lacked an inner city and had no sacred temenos. The temples, royal palaces and offices of state were sited almost at random. The haphazard appearance of the city is at odds with the urge toward symmetry and balance that found such precise expression in the pyramids and in other aspects of the Egyptian world view.[21] Egyptian settlements, unlike those in several other ancient centers of civilization, were not cosmicized: Egypt itself at one end of the scale and ritual structures on the other conformed to the cosmic paradigm.

MESOPOTAMIA

The natural environments of Egypt and Mesopotamia are similar in that both lack rainfall and that agriculture depends on water from the great perennial rivers that run through them. But there are important differences.

---

20 S. Giedion, *The Eternal Present: The Beginnings of Architecture* (New York: Pantheon, 1964), pp. 264–348.
21 Leonard Woolley, *The Beginnings of Civilization* (New York: Mentor, 1965), pp. 127–31.

The climate of Egypt is truly arid; that of Mesopotamia is less stringent from the viewpoint of the farmer. The lower portion of the Mesopotamian plain receives on the average four to eight inches a year, and in the upper portion, rain suffices for agriculture without irrigation. The special blessing of the Nile to Egypt is its dependability. The Tigris and the Euphrates, by contrast, have far less predictable regimes. Maximum flow of these rivers usually occurs in spring, with the melting of snow and the fall of rain. However, rain in the headstreams is highly variable. Over the upper Tigris basin, as much as ten inches of precipitation have been recorded in one week; when rainwater is augmented by snow-melt the result is disastrous flood. Deep flood waters that took months to drain off have repeatedly covered the lower plains of Mesopotamia. The Egyptian landscape is sharply defined and symmetrically disposed about the Nile River. In comparison the Mesopotamian landscape is undifferentiated: sand, alluvial plain, reed swamp, and lake merge into each other. The river courses themselves are not clearly marked off from the flooded lands around them: they are not the pointers to direction that the Nile is.

By the end of the third millennium B.C. the Mesopotamians had initiated an urban civilization and evolved a distinctive world view that reflected certain characteristics of their environment. In one myth on world origin, the beginning was depicted as a watery chaos made up of three elements, sweet waters (*Apsu*), the sea (*Ti'amat*), and mist (*Mummu*). The marriage of *Apsu* and *Ti'amat* gave birth to two gods which represented silt. The myth would thus seem to have transposed a readily observable phenomenon in nature, namely, when fresh water runs into the sea, mud is deposited and land appears. The completed cosmos consisted of the earth which was a flat disc. Over it lay a vast hollow space, enclosed by a solid surface in the shape of a vault. Between heaven and earth was *lil*—air, breath, and spirit—the expansion of which separated heaven from earth. Surrounding the heaven-earth (*an-ki*) on all sides, as well as top and bottom, was the boundless sea.[22]

A pantheon of gods, numbering in the hundreds, supervised the universe. They differed greatly in function and importance. The four most important deities were the heaven-god (*An*), the air-god (*Enlil*), the water-god (*Enki*), and the great mother-goddess (*Ninhursag*). They usually headed the god lists and were often portrayed as acting together in a group.[23] The Mesopotamian, unlike the Egyptian, did not take cosmic order as given;

---

[22] Thorkild Jacobsen, "Mesopotamia: The Cosmos as a State," in Frankfort et al., *Before Philosophy*, pp. 184–85; "Early Political Development in Mesopotamia," *Zeitschrift für Assyriologie*, 18 (1957), 91–140.

[23] S. N. Kramer, *The Sumerians* (Chicago: University of Chicago Press, 1964), p. 118.

it was something that had to be constantly maintained and administered like a state by a council of the gods. Mesopotamian nature, compared with Egyptian nature, was unruly.

> *Rising waters, grievous to eyes of man,*
> *All-powerful flood, which forces the embankments*
> *And mows down mighty* mesu-*trees,*
> *(Frenzied) storm, tearing all things in massed confusion*
> *With it (in hurtling speed).*[24]

At one time, *An* the heaven-god was supreme, but by 2500 B.C. *Enlil* seems to have taken his place as leader. *An* symbolized the majesty, authority, and power of the overarching sky, but it was power at rest. *Enlil,* as air—the turbulent element between heaven and earth—embodied active power. He was the executor of the will of the gods. He was conceived as a most beneficent deity with a hand in the planning and creation of most productive features of the cosmos. Unfortunately, his duty included the imposition of punishment, and although a paternal figure full of concern for the welfare of his people, he could be as violent and unpredictable as the storm.

Enki embodied wisdom. He was the creative, life-giving sweet waters— well water, springs, and rivers. While *Enlil* looked after the bigger projects and worked on the general plan, *Enki* lent his skills to the detailed workings of nature and culture. The goddess *Ninhursag* became a rather misty figure by the second millennium B.C. Her name might once have been *ki,* mother-earth, and she was probably the consort of heaven *An.* She was regarded as the mother of all living things.

While the cosmological ideas of Mesopotamia reflected certain aspects of its natural environment, they were also strongly colored by the socio-economic and political organizations of the period. It is tempting to think of the cosmic state as simply an ideational projection of the realities of the power systems on earth. According to this view, one pattern preceded the other and was, as it were, its cause. There is insufficient ground for this belief. It seems more probable that the Mesopotamian political system evolved *pari passu* with the ideas on the governing of the cosmos.

In contrast to Egypt the Mesopotamian civilization was essentially urban in character. By the third millennium B.C., lower Mesopotamia (Sumer) contained about a dozen city states, each of which was in the hands of free citizens and a chief, who exercised little more power than his peers. As there was no overarching power in nature, no domineering god among the deities, so there was—in the early period—no dictatorial ruler in the city state. However, as rivalry and fighting between the states grew,

[24] Jacobsen, *"Mesopotamia,"* p. 139.

and as they were increasingly threatened by barbarians from the east and west, leadership became a pressing need, and the "big man" or king, with large powers, was instituted.

Architecturally, the most prominent feature within the walled city was the temple, placed on a terrace inside the sacred compound (*temenos*). This dominance fitted well with the theological idea that the city belonged to its main god. At the start of the fourth millennium B.C., people still had free access to the temple. Later the chief temple was placed on a terrace, and the temple compound surrounded by a wall. Distance between god and people steadily increased. The terrace became higher and higher until, about 2000 B.C., it assumed the shape of a stepped pyramid or ziggurat, which was Mesopotamia's most distinctive contribution to architecture. The prominence of the temple and of the ziggurat, combined with the view that the city was the estate of the gods, would suggest that the state was organized as a theocracy. But, as we have noted, this type of rule did not necessarily hold. The temples in the city (there were usually several) owned only a fraction of the land in the city state; the remainder belonged to the nobles and commoners. Moreover, priests and temple retainers exercised little secular power.[25]

The architectural personality of the Mesopotamian city reflected its cosmic beliefs more closely than it did its political economy. Ziggurats could not compare with the great Egyptian pyramids in monumentality but they nonetheless loomed large on the flat landscape. The ziggurat of the moongod *Nanna* in Ur (2250–2100? B.C.) was a solid mass of brickwork that rose in three irregular stages to a height of about seventy feet. From its summit today one could see across the desolate plains to the ziggurats of Eridu and Al'Ubaid.

The stepped tower stood for many aspects of Mesopotamian thinking. Among its different names were "House of Mountain," "Mountain of the Storm," and "Bond between Heaven and Earth." As mountain it symbolized the center of the world; it was the earthly throne of the gods, a ladder to heaven, a monumental sacrificial altar. The immediate cause for building would appear to have been a natural disaster, such as drought, or in gratitude for a great blessing, such as the rich overflow of the Tigris. The people were said to respond enthusiastically to the labor of construction—just as, in another age of faith, peasants and nobles alike responded generously to the building of cathedrals. The ziggurat, then, played a part in Mesopotamian life that differed radically from that of the pyramid in Egyptian life. The one was located in the heart of the city, the other on the desert plateau in the land of the dead.

[25] Frank Hole, "Investigating the Origins of Mesopotamian Civilization," *Science,* 153 (August 5, 1966), 605–11.

topophilia
and
environment

Given the focal interest in environmental attitudes and values, I have tried to clarify their meaning through the simple device (in chapters 6 and 7) of dichotomizing culture-environment. This procedure enabled me to examine the dyad from two perspectives, first of culture, then of environment. In chapters 8 and 9 I shall adopt a similar strategy, but narrow the focus to specific manifestations of the human love of place or topophilia. The main topics of this chapter are: (1) the ways through which human beings respond to the environment, which may vary from visual and aesthetic appreciation to bodily contact; (2) the relations of health, familiarity, and awareness of the past to topophilia; (3) the impact of urbanization on the appreciation of the countryside and wilderness. This conglomeration of themes reflects the complexity of the idea of topophilia. The topics of chapter 8 do share, however, a common emphasis, which is the range, variety, and intensity of the topophilic sentiment. How the elements of environment permeate the content of topophilia is the theme of chapter 9. Again, we should remember that feeling and its object are often inseparable; the sundering of topophilia and environment serves a purpose if it facilitates exposition.

topophilia

The word "topophilia" is a neologism, useful in that it can be defined broadly to include all of the human being's affective ties with the material environment. These differ greatly in intensity, subtlety, and mode of expression. The response to environment may be primarily aesthetic: it may then vary from the fleeting pleasure one gets from a view to the equally fleeting but far more intense sense of beauty that is suddenly revealed. The response may be tactile, a delight in the feel of air, water, earth. More permanent and less easy to express are feelings that one has toward a place because it is home, the locus of memories, and the means of gaining a livelihood.

Topophilia is not the strongest of human emotions. When it is compelling we can be sure that the place or environment has become the carrier of emotionally charged events or perceived as a symbol. The order of priorities in human affection for the Greek tragedian, Euripides, is probably widely shared among all men: "Wife, dear in this light of the sun, and lovely to the eye is the placid ocean-flood, and the earth in the bloom of spring, and wide-spreading waters, and of many lovely sights might I speak the praises. But for the childless and those consumed with longings, nothing is so fair or lovely to behold as to see in their houses the light that newborn babies bring."[1]

aesthetic appreciation

Sir Kenneth Clark, the art historian, underlined the ephemerality of visual pleasure when he said, "I fancy that one cannot enjoy a pure esthetic sensation (so-called) for longer than one can enjoy the smell of an orange, which in my case is less than two minutes."[2] To attend to a great work of art for longer than that, knowledge of historical criticism has value for it keeps one's attention fixed on the work while the senses have time to get a second wind. Clark believes that as he remembers the facts of the painter's life and tries to fit the picture in front of him into its place in the development of the artist, his powers of receptivity are gradually renewing themselves; suddenly they make him see a beautiful passage of drawing or color which he would have overlooked had not an intellectual pretext kept his eye unconsciously engaged.

What Kenneth Clark says of art appreciation is equally true in the

---

1 Quoted in H. Rushton Fairclough, *The Attitude of the Greek Tragedians toward Nature* (Toronto: Roswell & Hutchison, 1897), p. 9.
2 Kenneth Clark, *Looking at Pictures* (New York: Holt, Rinehart & Winston, 1960), pp. 16–17.

appreciation of scenery. However intense, it is fleeting unless one's eyes are kept to it for some other reason, either the recall of historical events that hallowed the scene or the recall of its underlying reality in geology and structure. On the importance of historical association, F. L. Lucas wrote:

> The first time I saw the cloud-topped mountain ridges of Acroceraunia from the Adriatic, or the Leucadian Promontory white with sun and storm, or Hymettus, purpled with sunset, from the Saronic Sea, was something intenser even than poetry. But the same shapes and colours would not have seemed the same in New Zealand or the Rockies. Half their transfigured splendour came from the poetry of two thousand years before, or the memory of that other sunset on Hymettus when the hemlock was brought to Socrates.[3]

The most intense aesthetic experiences of nature are likely to catch one by surprise. Beauty is felt as the sudden contact with an aspect of reality that one has not known before; it is the antithesis of the acquired taste for certain landscapes or the warm feeling for places that one knows well. A few examples will make the nature of this experience clear.

One example is Wordsworth's dramatic perception of Mount Helvellyn in the Lake District. Wordsworth and De Quincey walked one night from the village of Grasmere to meet the postal carrier who usually brought them news of the war on the continent. They were anxious for news and waited in vain by the roadside for over an hour. No sound came up through the winding road. At intervals, Wordsworth would stretch himself on the road and press his ear to the ground in the hope of catching the sound of grinding wheels in the distance. Later he said to De Quincey,

> At the very instant when I raised my head from the ground, in final abandonment of hope for this night, at the very instant when the organs of attention were all at once relaxing from their tension, the bright star hanging in the air above those outlines of massy blackness of the Helvellyn, fell suddenly upon my eye, and penetrated my capacity of apprehension with a pathos and a sense of the Infinite, that would not have arrested me under other circumstances.[4]

The journals of explorers are rich in these sudden revelations of natural beauty: for example, Clarence King's description of the Yosemite Valley during a lull in the snow storm, and Sir Francis Younghusband's description of his encounter with Mt. Kinchinjunga—one of almost mystical intensity—when the mists that usually enshrouded the Himalayan peak unexpectedly parted to reveal its distant, ethereal splendor. This kind of experience occurs

---

[3] F. L. Lucas, *The Greatest Problem and Other Essays* (London: Cassell, 1960), p. 176.
[4] Thomas De Quincey, "William Wordsworth," *Literary Reminiscences* (Boston, 1874), pp. 312–17. Quoted in Newton P. Stallknecht, *Strange Seas of Thought* (Bloomington: Indiana University Press, 1958), p. 60.

even to people who do not pretend to any love of nature. The scholar William McGovern thought (and he is surely not alone in this) that too much landscape, whether in literature or in life, was apt to prove wearing and sleep-inducing. In the 1920s McGovern was a lecturer in London's School of Oriental Studies. He wanted to see Tibet and study the Buddhist scriptures at Lhasa. In India he found that permission to proceed to Lhasa was denied. Undaunted the scholar-explorer went in disguise—and nearly lost his life in the venture. For him the meeting of a physical challenge clearly counted for more than the enjoyment of scenery. Yet, one day on his perilous journey, when the sun at last appeared behind the cloud and shone on the peaks of the Himalayas, McGovern admitted that "it was far and away the finest view I had ever seen, and even so stolid and humdrum a person as myself had cause to drink in its grandeur."[5]

The visual enjoyment of nature varies in kind and intensity. It can be little more than the acceptance of a social convention. Much of modern sightseeing seems to be motivated by the desire to collect as many National Park stickers as possible. The camera is indispensable to the tourist, for with it he can prove to himself and to his neighbors that he has actually been to Crater Lake. A snapshot that failed to register is lamented as though the lake itself has been deprived of existence. Such brushes with nature clearly fall short of the authentic. Tourism has social uses and it benefits the economy, but it does not enjoin man and nature.[6] The appreciation of landscape is more personal and longer lasting when it is mixed with the memory of human incidents. It also endures beyond the fleeting when aesthetic pleasure is combined with scientific curiosity. Intense awareness of environmental beauty normally comes as a sudden revelation. Such awareness is least affected by received opinions and it also seems to be largely independent of the character of the environment. Homely and even drab scenes can reveal aspects of themselves that went unnoticed before, and this new insight into the real is sometimes experienced as beauty.[7]

physical contact

In modern life physical contact with one's natural environment is increasingly indirect and limited to special occasions. Apart from the dwin-

---

5 William McGovern, *To Lhasa in Disguise* (London: Grosset & Dunlap, 1924), p. 145.
6 Paul Shepard, "The Itinerant Eye," in *Man in the Landscape* (New York: Knopf, 1967), pp. 119–56; Daniel J. Boorstin, "From Traveler to Tourist," *The Image* (New York: Harper Colophon edition, 1964), pp. 77–117.
7 Vaughn Cornish, *Scenery and the Sense of Sight* (Cambridge: Cambridge University Press, 1935).

dling farm population, technological man's involvement with nature is recreational rather than vocational. Sightseeing behind the tinted windows of
a coach severs man from nature. On the other hand, in such sports as water
skiing and mountain climbing, man is pitted against nature in violent contact. What people in advanced societies lack (and countercultural groups
appear to seek) is the gentle, unselfconscious involvement with the physical
world that prevailed in the past when the tempo of life was slower, and
that young children still enjoy. In Chaucer, a simplicity of response is expressed in lines such as these:

> *And down on knees aright I me set,*
> *And as I could this freshe flow'r I grette,*
> *Kneeling always till it enclosed was*
> *Upon the small, and soft, sweete gras.*

(Prologue to the *Legend of Good Women*)

The childlike enjoyment of nature places little importance on picturesqueness. We know relatively little as to how a young child perceives the
playground, park, or seashore that he is taken to. The composed view is
sure to count for less than particular objects and physical sensations. A. A.
Milne, creator of the popular Pooh stories, has the gift of intimating the
kind of cozy, immediate world that a young child knows. Visual appreciation, discerning and reflective, creates aesthetic distance. For a young child
the aesthetic distance is minimal. When Christopher Robin goes down to
the "shouting sea," he feels the sand in his hair and the sand between the
toes. Happiness is to put on a new mackintosh and stand in the rain.

Nature yields delectable sensations to the child, with his openness of
mind, carelessness of person, and lack of concern for the accepted canons of
beauty. An adult must learn to be yielding and careless like a child if he
were to enjoy nature polymorphously. He needs to slip into old clothes so
that he could feel free to stretch out on the hay beside the brook and bathe
in a meld of physical sensations: the smell of hay and of horse dung; the
warmth of the ground, its hard and soft contours; the warmth of the sun
tempered by breeze; the tickling of an ant making its way up the calf of
his leg; the play of shifting leaf shadows on his face; the sound of water
over the pebbles and boulders, the sound of cicadas and distant traffic. Such
an environment might break all the formal rules of euphony and aesthetics,
substituting confusion for order, and yet be wholly satisfying.

The small farmer or peasant's attachment to land is deep. Nature is
known through the need to gain a living. French workers, when their bodies
ache with fatigue, say that "their trades have entered into them." For the

laboring farmer, nature has entered—and beauty insofar as the substance and processes of nature can be said to embody it.[8] The entry of nature is no mere metaphor. Muscles and scars bear witness to the physical intimacy of the contact. The farmer's topophilia is compounded of this physical intimacy, of material dependence and the fact that the land is a repository of memory and sustains hope. Aesthetic appreciation is present but seldom articulated.

A yeoman of America's deep South said to Robert Coles: "To me the land I have is always there, waiting for me, and it's part of me, way inside me; it's as much me as my own arms and legs." And "The land, it's friend and an enemy; it's both. The land, it runs my time and my moods; if the crops go well, I feel fine and if there's trouble with growing, there's trouble with me." The working farmer does not frame nature into pretty pictures, but he can be profoundly aware of its beauty. A young sharecropper, interviewed by Robert Coles, showed no desire to migrate north despite the hardness of his life at home. He would miss the farm, he explained. In a city one would miss watching the sun go down, "flicker out, like a candle that's lost its wax and is going away, disappearing."[9]

Topophilic sentiment among farmers differs widely in accordance with their socioeconomic status. The farm laborer works close to the soil; his relation with nature is a love-hate bond. Ronald Blythe reminds us that even in the 1900s the hired hand in England had few rewards other than a tie-cottage and a meager living. He had no greater source of pride than his own physical strength and the ability to plow a straight furrow—his ephemeral signature on the earth. The small farmer who owned his land was better off: he could nurse a pious attitude toward the land that supported him and that was his sole security. The successful proprietor-farmer took possessive pride in his estate, in the transformation of nature to a fruitful world of his own design. Attachment to place can also emerge, paradoxically, from the experience of nature's intransigence. In America, on the marginal farms of the Great Plains, farmers must constantly struggle against the threat of drought and dust storm. Those who cannot bear the hardship leave; those who hang on seem to develop a curious pride in their ability to endure. When Saarinen, in his study of drought on the Great Plains, showed some wheat growers a picture of a farm besieged by wind and dust, their characteristic response was that the dust-bowl farmer in the picture

8 Simone Weil, *Waiting for God*, trans. Emma Craufurd (New York: Capricorn Books, 1959), pp. 131–32.
9 Robert Coles, *Migrants, Sharecroppers, Mountaineers* (Boston: Little, Brown, 1971), pp. 411, 527.

knows he can do better elsewhere but remains because he loves the soil and the challenge of making a go of it.[10]

To live, man must see some value in his world. The farmer is no exception. His life is harnessed to the great cycles of nature; it is rooted in the birth, growth, and death of living things; however hard, it boasts a seriousness that few other occupations can match. In fact, little is known about the farmer's attitudes to nature. What we have is a vast, largely sentimental, literature on the farming life written by people with uncallused hands.

health and topophilia

From time to time we are infused by a sense of physical well-being so strong that it overflows and embraces, as it were, a part of the world: it makes us want to sing "O! What a beautiful morning, O! What a beautiful day," like the heroes in that popular musical of the late 1940s, *Oklahoma*. Young and healthy people experience the mood more frequently than older folks although they are less able to describe the sensation other than with the exuberance of their bodies. William James put it this way: "Apart from anything acutely religious, we all have moments when the universal life seems to wrap us round with friendliness. In youth and health, in summer, in the woods or on the mountains, there come days when the weather seems all whispering with peace, hours when the goodness and beauty of existence enfold us like a dry, warm climate, or chime through us as if our inner ears were subtly ringing with the world's security."[11] The seventeenth-century poet, Thomas Traherne, wrote: "You never enjoy the world aright, till the sea itself floweth in your veins, till you are clothed with the heavens, and crowned with stars." Poetic hyperbole—and yet in a sense the sea does flow in our veins: the chemical composition of our blood is a reminder of our remote ancestry in the primordial oceans.

It may seem far-fetched to detect any relation between the sense of well-being after, say, a good breakfast and the holy fervor of a Christian poet like Traherne. Yet the fact that the words "health," "wholeness," and "holiness" are etymologically related suggests a common meaning. An ordinary fellow embraces the world of golf in a temporary overflow of well-being, the holy (whole) person the world itself. Characteristically this feeling depends less on external circumstances than on the internal state of

10 Thomas F. Saarinen, *Perception of the Drought Hazard on the Great Plains*, University of Chicago Department of Geography Research Paper No. 106 (1966), pp. 110–11.

11 William James, *Varieties of Religious Experience* (New York: Modern Library, 1902), p. 269.

the subject, that is, whether he has put a good breakfast in his stomach, or, at a more exalted level, whether he enjoys the "peace that passeth all understanding." The authority on mysticism, Evelyn Underhill, reports, "I still remember walking down the Notting Hill main road and observing the (extremely sordid) landscape with joy and astonishment. Even the movement of the traffic had something universal and sublime in it."

familiarity and attachment

Familiarity breeds affection when it does not breed contempt. We are well aware of how a person can become deeply attached to old slippers that look rather mouldy to an outsider. There are various reasons for this attachment. A man's belongings are an extension of his personality; to be deprived of them is to diminish, in his own estimation, his worth as a human being. Clothing is the most personal of one's belongings. It is a rare adult whose sense of self does not suffer in nakedness, or who does not feel a threat to his identity when he has to wear someone else's clothes. Beyond clothing, a person in the process of time invests bits of his emotional life in his home, and beyond the home in his neighborhood. To be forcibly evicted from one's home and neighborhood is to be stripped of a sheathing, which in its familiarity protects the human being from the bewilderments of the outside world. As some people are reluctant to part with their shapeless old coat for a new one, so some people—especially older people—are reluctant to abandon their old neighborhood for the new housing development.

Awareness of the past is an important element in the love of place. Patriotic rhetoric has always stressed the roots of a people. To enhance loyalty, history is made visible by monuments in the landscape and past battles are recounted in the belief that the blood of heroes sanctified the soil. Nonliterate peoples can be strongly attached to their home grounds. They may lack the chronological sense of irreversible events characteristic of the modern Western man, but when they try to explain their loyalty to place they either point at the bonds of nurture (the mother-earth theme), or they reach into history. Strehlow, an ethnologist who knows the Australian aborigines intimately, says of the Aranda that he "clings to his native soil with every fiber of his being. . . . Today, tears will come into his eyes when he mentions an ancestral home site which has been, sometimes unwittingly, desecrated by white usurpers of his group territory. Love of home, longing for home, these are dominating motives which constantly re-appear also in the myths of the totemic ancestors." The love of the home ground is accounted for historically. Mountains and creeks and springs and water holes are to the Aranda not merely interesting or beautiful scenic features; they are the handiwork of ancestors from whom he himself has descended. "He sees recorded in the surrounding landscape the ancient story of the lives and the deeds of the immortal beings whom he reveres; beings, who for a brief space may take on human shape once more; beings, many of whom he has known in his own experience as his fathers and grandfathers and brothers, and as his mothers and sisters. The whole countryside is his living, age-old family tree."[12]

patriotism

Since the birth of the modern state in Europe, patriotism as an emotion is rarely tied to any specific locality: it is evoked by abstract categories of pride and power, on the one hand, and by certain symbols, such as the flag, on the other. The modern state is too large, its boundaries too arbitrary, its area too heterogeneous to command the kind of affection that arises out of experience and intimate knowledge. Modern man has conquered distance but not time. In a life span, a man now—as in the past—can establish profound roots only in a small corner of the world.

Patriotism means the love of one's *terra patria* or natal land. In ancient times it was strictly a local sentiment. The Greeks did not apply patriotism indiscriminately to all Greek-speaking lands, but to small fragments such as Athens, Sparta, Corinth, and Smyrna. The Phoenicians were patriotic to Tyre, Sidon, or Carthage; not to Phoenicia generally. The city aroused profound emotions, especially when it came under attack. When the Romans sought to punish the Carthaginians for disobedience by razing their city to the ground, citizens of Carthage begged their masters to spare the physical city, its stones and temples, to which no possible guilt could be attached, and instead, if necessary, exterminate the entire population. In the Middle Ages, allegiance was owed to the lord, or the city, or both, and by extension to a territory. But the sentiment covered variable extensions of the territory, not to a land of precise limit beyond which it must turn into indifference or hate. The modern nation as a large bounded space is difficult to experience in any direct way; its reality for the individual depends on the ingestion of certain kinds of knowledge. Decades or even centuries after the *literati* have accepted the idea of "nation" there may remain a substantial portion of the populace who have never heard of it. For example, the vast majority of peasants in nineteenth-century Tsarist Russia was entirely ignorant of the pretended fact that they belonged to a Russian society united by a common culture.

---

12 T. G. H. Strehlow, *Aranda Traditions* (Carlton: Melbourne University Press, 1947), pp. 30–31.

There are two kinds of patriotism, local and imperial. Local patriotism rests on the intimate experience of place, and on a sense of the fragility of goodness: that which we love has no guarantee to endure. Imperial patriotism feeds on collective egotism and pride. Such sentiment is extolled most vigorously at times of surging imperial ambition: for example, Rome in the first century B.C., Britain in the ninetenth century, and Germany in the twentieth. The sentiment does not attach itself to anything concretely geographical. Kipling's line, "I do not love my empire's foes," rings false, for no one can feel affection for a vast system of impersonal power like empire: no clear mind can conceive the empire as victim—an image of fragile goodness that may be destroyed and needs our compassion.[13]

England is an example of a modern nation small enough to be vulnerable and to arouse in its citizens visceral concern when it is threatened. Shakespeare has superbly voiced this kind of local patriotism. In the following lines from *Richard II* (act 2, scene 1), note the homely words "breed of men," "little world," "blessed plot."

> *This happy breed of men, this little world,*
> *This precious stone set in the silver sea,*
> *Which serves it in the office of a wall*
> *Or a moat defensive to a house*
> *Against the envy of less happier lands,*
> *This blessed plot, this earth, this realm, this England . . .*

Just as the pretense to "love for humanity" arouses our suspicion, so topophilia rings false when it is claimed for a large territory. A compact size scaled down to man's biologic needs and sense-bound capacities seems necessary. In addition, a people can more readily identify with an area if it appears to be a natural unit. Affection cannot be stretched over an empire, for it often is a conglomeration of heterogeneous parts held together by force. By contrast, the home region (*pays*) has historical continuity, and it may be a physiographic unit (a valley, coast, or limestone outcrop) small enough to be known personally. In between is the modern state. It has a degree of historical continuity; power is more diffused than in the empire and is not its most conspicuous bond. On the other hand the modern state is too large to be known personally, its shape too evidently artificial to be perceived as a natural unit. Not only for reasons of defense but also to buttress the illusion of organic unity, political leaders have sought to extend their country's frontiers to the river, mountain, or sea. If both empire and state are too large for the exercise of genuine topophilia, it is paradoxical

---

13 C. J. H. Hayes, *Essays on Nationalism* (New York: Macmillan, 1928); Simone Weil, *The Need for Roots*, trans. Arthur Wills (Boston: Beacon Press, 1955), pp. 103–84; Leonard Doob, *Patriotism and Nationalism: Their Psychological Foundations* (New Haven: Yale University Press, 1964).

to reflect that the earth itself may eventually command such attachment: this possibility exists because the earth is clearly a natural unit and it has a common history. Shakespeare's words "this blessed plot," "this precious stone set in a silver sea" are not inappropriately applied to the planet itself. Possibly, in some ideal future, our loyalty will be given only to the home region of intimate memories and, at the other end of the scale, to the whole earth.

urbanization and attitude to the countryside

Loyalty to home, city, and nation is a powerful sentiment. Blood is shed in their defense. The countryside, by contrast, evokes a more diffuse sentimental feeling. To understand this particular form of topophilia, it is well to be aware that an environmental value requires its antithesis for definition. "Water, is taught by thirst, Land—by oceans crossed" (Emily Dickinson). "Home" is a meaningless word apart from "journey" and "foreign country"; claustrophobia implies agoraphilia; the virtues of the countryside require their anti-image, the city, for the sharpening of focus, and vice versa. Here is a sample of rural sentiment taken from the works of three poets:

(1) This was one of my prayers: a little space of land, with a garden, near the house a spring of living water, and a small wood besides. Heaven has filled it, better and richer than my hopes. It is good. I ask no more now...but this: make it for ever my own.

(2) *In early summer the woods and herbs are thriving.*
Around my cottage thick sway the branches and shades.
The numerous birds delight in their sanctuaries,
And I too love my cottage.
After I have plowed and sown,
Then I return to read my books.

(3) And, in the summer, you would probably find me sitting under a tree with a book in my hand, or walking thoughtfully in some pleasant solitude.

The first excerpt expressed the sentiment of Horace (65–8 B.C.); the second that of Tao Yuan-ming, a Chinese poet of the fourth century A.D.; and the third that of the Englishman Henry Needler, who wrote at the beginning of the eighteenth century. The congruence of feelings among three poets who belonged to different worlds and times is instructive. They had one experience in common: they all knew the temptations and distractions of city life, and sought for ease in the country.

Once society had reached a certain level of artifice and complexity, people would begin to take note, and appreciate, the relative simplicities of nature. The earliest sundering of city values from the values of nature first appeared in the Epic of Gilgamesh, which was composed in Sumeria in the later part of the third millennium B.C. Gilgamesh was the lord of the wealthy and powerful city of Uruk. He enjoyed the civilized amenities though they failed to bring him ultimate contentment. Rather than seek consolation among the nobles he befriended the wild man Enkidu, who ate grass in the hills with the gazelle, jostled with wild beasts at the water-holes and knew nothing of the cultivated land. There was no real description of landscape in the Gilgamesh epic. The virtues of wild nature were embodied in a person, Enkidu. The type of sentiment for the countryside suggested by the excerpts given above could appear only when large cities were built, when the stresses of politics and bureaucratic life made rural peace seem attractive. The sentiment is romantic in the sense that it is far removed from any real understanding of nature. It is also suffused with melancholy: the literati retire for a time to the country and live in indolent ease with much thought for the vanity of office but no thought of how they are to be fed.

At the back of the romantic appreciation of nature is the privilege and wealth of the city. In archaic times man's enjoyment of nature was more direct and robust. The evidence of the *Shih Ching* suggests that in ancient China there was awareness of the beauty of earth but not of a countryside as a scene set apart and antithetical to the city. What we mostly find in this anthology of songs and poems are accounts of rural activities, such as clearing the grasses and trees, plowing up the land, and building dikes. These are probably good sketches of agricultural practice in the middle of the Chou period (ca. 800–500 B.C.) Later, in the fourth and third centuries B.C., cities of impressive size were built. The walls of one settlement enclosed an area of some ten square miles, while another, Lin-tzu, probably housed some 70,000 families. This was also a time of recurrent wars. It might seem that conditions were such that the court officials should not mind withdrawal from strife and retirement to the country. Banishment from the capital ought not be a great hardship. Yet it was so perceived perhaps because China, even in the Yangtze basin, still had vast expanses of wild nature that provided little security and gave no delight. Chu Yuan, who was banished in 303 B.C. for objecting to the war tactics of King Huai, wandered over the region of Tung-t'ing lake in northern Ho-nan. He found there "dark and interminable forests, the habitation of apes and monkeys. And mountains, wet with rain mists, so high that the sun was hidden."[14]

Toward the end of the Later Han dynasty (A.D. 25–220), a type of

[14] Robert Payne (ed.), *The White Pony: An Anthology of Chinese Poetry* (New York: Mentor Books, 1960), p. 89.

1. Edenic ideal

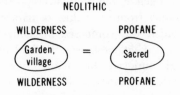

NEOLITHIC   HISTORICAL EXAMPLES

WILDERNESS   PROFANE   a. Eden and wilderness

b. Monastery and wilderness

c. The New England town and wilderness

WILDERNESS   PROFANE   d. The American seminary or college and wilderness

e. American utopian communities
(First half of 19th century)

2. Urban revolution and cosmic ideal

WILDERNESS (profane)

UTOPIA

a. Plato's Republic

b. New Jerusalem

WILDERNESS (profane)

3. The two juxtaposed ideals

PASTORAL ⎰ a. Alexandrian Greece
(bucolic) ⎱ b. Augustan Rome
GARDEN ⎰ c. T'ang-Sung China
⎱ d. Renaissance Europe
COUNTRYSIDE ⎰
⎱ e. 18th - 19th century England

4. The ideal of the "Middle Landscape" (Jeffersonian ideal: late 18th to mid-19th century)

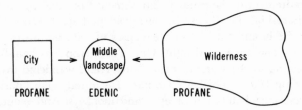

Figure 9   Wilderness, garden, city.

The "Middle landscape" of yeoman farmers is seen as threatened by the city on the one side and by wilderness on the other. In fact this was a time when both the city and the middle landscape were expanding at the expense of wilderness, thus:

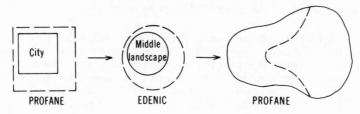

5. Late nineteenth-century values

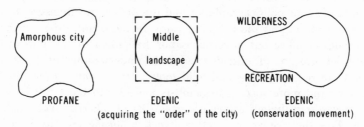

6. Middle and late twentieth-century values

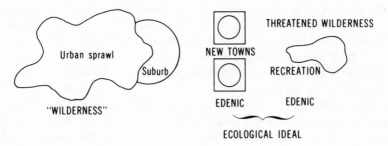

Figure 9 Continued.

appreciation for the countryside appeared that eventually became a cliché of nature sentiment among the gentry. T'ung Chung-chang (A.D. 180–220) lived in a time of great political upheavals and rebellions which were to end in the downfall of the dynasty. He wrote wistfully:

> All I ask is good lands and a spacious house, with hills behind and a flowing stream in front, ringed with ponds or pools, set about with bamboos and trees, a vegetable garden to the south, an orchard to the north. . . . Then with two or three companions of philosophic bent discuss the Way or study some book. . . and so ramble through life at ease, with a cursory glance of Heaven and Earth and all that lies between, free from the censure of my fellow-men.[15]

The scholar-officials who administered the Chinese empire for some two millennia wavered between city and rural lures. In the city the scholar could satisfy his political ambition but the price was submission to the Confucian rigidities and the risk of censure. In the country the scholar lost the trappings of office but in compensation he gained the delights of learning, the quiet pleasures of a life devoted to the understanding of the Way (Tao). The Chinese gentry class had solid roots in the country. From the land the cleverer and more successful members moved into the city where they led the rewarding, though rather uncertain life of officials. Wolfram Eberhard notes how they sometimes preferred to live outside the city in a luxurious cottage which they poetically called a "grasshut." There they became Taoists in psychological reaction against a life within the Confucian straitjacket. More often, they retired temporarily "when the political situation in the city had become unfavorable or dangerous. When things changed, our 'Taoists' often returned to the city and became 'Confucianists' again."[16]

In Europe preference for the countryside as against the city found eloquent literary expression in three periods: the Hellenistic or Alexandrian age of Greece, the Roman Augustan age, and the period of modern Romanticism which began in the eighteenth century. Before Alexander's time a wistful sentiment for the countryside already existed. Athenians, for instance, felt nostalgia for the simple rural life when they were cut off from their farms during the protracted Peloponnesian War (431–404 B.C.). However, rural idylls were unobtrusive in Hellenic literature. It took the rise of great cities in the Alexandrian Age to produce a strong reaction against urban sophistication and a longing for rusticity. The pastoral poems of Theocritus are redolent of the peace of the countryside. A poem that records

15 Arthur Waley, "Life Under the Han Dynasty: Notes on Chinese Civilization in the First and Second Centuries A.D.," *History Today*, 3 (1953), 94.
16 Wolfram Eberhard, *Conquerors and Rulers: Social Forces in Medieval China*, 2nd ed. (Leiden: E. J. Brill, 1965), p. 45.

a personal experience of a harvest festival describes a scene on the island of Cos in high summer. Note how much is made of rural sounds:

> Many a poplar and elm murmured above our heads, and near at hand the sacred water from the cave of the Nymphs fell plashing. On the shady boughs the dusky cicadas were busy with their chatter, and the tree-frog far off cried in the dense thornbrake. Larks and finches sang, the dove made moan, and bees flitted humming above the springs. All things were fragrant of rich harvest and of fruit time. Pears at our feet and apples at our side were rolling plentifully, and the branches hung down to the ground with their burden of sloes.[17]

Contrasting the splendors of Augustan Rome were the rural idylls, eloquently described in the poetry of Virgil and Horace. Virgil's country was the rich Po plain near Mantua. His poems evoked images of ancient beeches and dark oaks standing among the pastures, and of little herds of sheep and goat moving among them. His bucolics depicted ideally happy life in a beautiful land but every one of them had sadness mingled with its charm. The Virgilian Arcadia was threatened by the shadow of imperial Rome on the one side and by the inhospitable marshes and bare rocks on the other. Horace found solace and inspiration from his farm which lay outside of Rome, not far from Tivoli. He retired to it partly because of some failure in health, and partly because his taste for seclusion and a simpler life grew with the advancing years. He praised the country as against the city; he contrasted the peaceful life in his secluded valley not only with Rome's polluted air but with its ostentatious wealth, aggressive business, and violent pleasures.[18]

In the course of the eighteenth century the European cognoscenti deified nature. To philosophers and poets in particular, nature came to stand for wisdom, spiritual comfort, and holiness; from it people were supposed to derive religious enthusiasm, moral goodness, and a mystical understanding of man and God. Early in the century, praise for the countryside was more a neo-Augustan pose than any real flowering of interest in nature. As Samuel Johnson said in 1751, "There is, indeed, scarce any writer who has not celebrated the happiness of rural privacy." The literati of the age were citified because it was in the city (London, in particular) that all the opportunities, political and pecuniary, lay. But they would seem to have reacted against their condition. Neoclassicist poems written in the first half of the eighteenth century were full of the retirement theme. They told of

---

[17] Theocritus, "The Harvest Song," trans. A. S. F. Gow, *The Greek Bucolic Poets* (Cambridge: Cambridge University Press, 1953).
[18] Gilbert Highet, *Poets in a Landscape* (New York: Knopf, 1957).

the desire to leave the "gay town where guilty pleasure reigns" for the "humble plains." Gentlemen withdrew into the country for its solitude which encouraged study and contemplation. William Shenstone sought to "haunt this peaceful shade" where he could be free of the prick of ambition.[19] Henry Needler, as we have already noted, went into the country to read books rather than nature. To the extent that rural sentiments were genuine they were often steeped in melancholy. Poets described how one drifted "from solitude to brooding; to finding mournful pleasure in the subdued colors of evening, the darkness and mystery of night, the unlit churchward, the desolate ruin...the insignificance of man and the inevitability of death."[20] By the middle of the eighteenth century, however, there were clear signs of a more robust appreciation of nature that reached beyond the countryside to mountains, the desert, and the ocean.

In North America the theme of city corruption and rural virtue is popular enough to be classified as folklore. It is told repeatedly: first, decadent Europe and prelapsarian America provided the pleasing antithesis; later, as America took up manufacturing and was itself rapidly acquiring large cities, the opposition was perceived to lie between an industrialized and Mammon-seeking Eastern seaboard and the virtuous, agrarian interior. Thomas Jefferson had great influence in propagating what Leo Marx calls the "pastoral ideal." He was undoubtedly familiar with the literary pastoral. He could quote Theocritus in Greek; his fondness for the Latin poets is well known; and as a young man he had read diligently the poetry of James Thomson, who was one of the first to show in poetry the finger of God in all operations of nature, placid and sublime. To Jefferson, "Those who labour in the earth are the chosen people of God, if ever he had a chosen people, whose breasts he has made his peculiar deposit for substantial and genuine virtue." By contrast, "The mobs of great cities add just as much to the support of pure government as sores do to the strength of the human body."[21]

In Europe the sentiment for the countryside remained largely a literary convention—translated from time to time into substance through the propagation and design of country estates. In America the dream of human virtues flourishing in Arcadia reached the stage of a political program. The third president of the Republic was willing to subordinate national wealth and

---

19 George G. Williams, "The Beginnings of Nature Poetry in the Eighteenth Century," *Studies in Philology,* 27 (1930), 583–608.
20 Cornelis Engelbertus de Haas, *Nature and the Country in English Poetry* (Amsterdam: H. J. Paris, 1928), p. 150.
21 Thomas Jefferson, *Notes on Virginia*...Query 19. For a source book on rural behavior embracing the history of rural-urban thinking, see Pitirim A. Sorokin, Carle C. Zimmerman, and Charles J. Gilpin, *Systematic Source Book in Rural Sociology,* 3 vols. (Minneapolis: University of Minnesota Press, 1932).

power to an agrarian ideal; and there was no denying that the American public responded favorably to it. During the nineteenth century the image of a contented and virtuous rural people became a dominant emblem of national aspirations. The ideal did not stop, or even much hinder, the amassing of wealth and devotion to technological progress that combined to make America into a great manufacturing nation. Yet it was far from being an empty rhetoric. The sentiment permeates American culture. One finds it in the neglect of the cities and in the flight to the suburbs, in the weekend exodus to the country, and in preservation movements. Politically it is evident "in the 'localism' invoked to oppose an adequate national system of education, in the power of the farm block in Congress, in the special economic favor shown to 'farming' through government subsidies, and in state electoral systems that allow the rural population to retain a share of political power grossly out of proportion to its size."[22]

wilderness

The countryside is widely accepted as the antithesis of the city irrespective of the actual living conditions of these two environments. Writers, moralists, politicians, and even social scientists still tend to view the rural-urban spectrum as a fundamental dichotomy. Yet, from another perspective it is clear that raw nature or wilderness, and not the countryside, stands at the opposite pole of the totally man-made city. The countryside is the "middle landscape" (Leo Marx's term). In the agrarian myth it is the ideal middle world of man poised between the polarities of city and wilderness. The structuring of environment in binary opposition is analogous to the structuring of the world we have seen in other traditions: the American middle landscape is the Indonesian *madiapa*. But in the Indonesian world, mountain and sea are timeless polarities, while city and wilderness are shifting antinomies in the dynamic history of the Occident: in time the meaning of these two terms may be reversed and in the course of reversal both the city and the expanding farms (the middle landscape) are perceived as enemies of pristine nature. Let us review the meaning of wilderness in this framework.

In the Bible the term "wilderness" brings to mind two contradictory images. On the one hand, it is a place of desolation, the unsown land frequented by demons; it is condemned by God. "Their lands become a wilderness...because of [Yahweh's] wrath (*Jeremiah* 25:38)." Adam and Eve

---

[22] Leo Marx, *The Machine in the Garden* (New York: Oxford University Press, 1964), p. 5.

were driven from the Garden to the "cursed ground," overgrown with thorns and thistles. Christ was tempted by the devil in the wilderness. All these emphasize the negative—and dominant—meaning of wilderness in the Bible. On the other hand, wilderness may serve either as (a) a place of refuge and contemplation, or more commonly (b) any place where the Chosen are scattered for a season of discipline or purgation. Hosea (2:14 ff) recalls the nuptial period in the wilderness of Sinai. "Therefore, behold, I will allure her, and bring her into the wilderness, and speak tenderly to her...And there she shall answer as in the days of her youth, as at the time when she came out of the land of Egypt." In *Revelations* (1:9; 17:3), the Seer suggests that the wilderness enables the contemplative Christian to see the Divine more clearly, unencumbered by the world.

The ascetic tradition in Christianity maintained the dual and opposed meaning of wilderness. John Cassian (d. 435) claimed, on the one hand, that hermits went into the waste lands to engage in open combat with the devils; on the other, that in "the freedom of the vast wilderness" they sought to enjoy "that life which can only be compared to the bliss of angels." For the ascetics, the desert was in effect at once the haunt of demons and the realm of bliss in harmony with the creaturely world. Attitude toward wild animals was also ambivalent. They were seen both as the minions of Satan and as the denizens of paradise precariously restored in the environs of hermit or monk. Early in the history of Christianity the monk's cell in the wilderness and the church in the world were held to be small models of paradise. Their presence lent an aura of sanctity to the environs so that something of the paradisial innocence could be seen about them.[23]

In America the ambiguity of wilderness was retained. The New England Puritans believed that they were inaugurating a new age of the Church in the New World and that this reformed Church was to blossom like a garden in the protective wilderness. On the other hand, as John Eliot (d. 1690) put it, the wilderness was the place "where nothing appeareth but hard labour, wants, and wilderness-temptation." The writings of Cotton Mather (1663–1728) showed the same ambivalence toward the waste lands that we can find in the Old and New Testaments. Mather thought of the wilderness as the empire of Antichrist, filled with frightful hazards, demons, dragons, and fiery flying serpents. In another mood he held that the North American wilderness was ordained by Providence to be the protective refuge of the reformed Church.

Mather, who could speak seriously of demons and dragons in the forests, died in 1728. In that year the Virginian squire, William Byrd, caught sight of the Appalachian Mountains for the first time. He described

[23] George H. Williams, *Paradise and Wilderness in Christian Thought* (New York: Harper & Row, 1962).

the mountains with romantic fervor. When the fog blocked a view, Byrd lamented "the loss of this wild Prospect." And when he had to leave he expressed unwillingness to part with a scene that "was very wild and very Agreeable." While Mathér viewed wilderness through somber theological spectacles, Byrd saw it through the tinted glass of Romanticism, which was beginning to be popular at this time. Pioneers did not appreciate wilderness; it was an obstacle to overcome in the winning of a livelihood and it was a constant threat to that livelihood. The preachers of the early Colonial period saw wilderness as the habitation of demons and only rarely as the protective environment of the church. In the course of the eighteenth century, however, the gap widened between the pioneers, who continued to see wild nature as obstacle, and literary gentlemen who saw it through the eyes of the tourist familiar with the writings of European deistic philosophers and nature-poets.

As population increased and fields and settlements pushed rapidly westward into the wilderness, Easterners of literary and artistic bent grew more and more alarmed at the rapid disappearance of wild nature. John James Audubon, on his travels in pursuit of bird specimens in the Ohio Valley in the 1820s, had many opportunities to observe the destruction of the forest. Thomas Cole, the landscapist, lamented the doom of nature as "each hill and every valley is become an altar unto Mammon." He thought that the wilderness would vanish in a few years. And William Cullen Bryant was equally pessimistic. After touring the Great Lakes region in 1846 he sadly anticipated a future when wild and lonely woods would be filled with cottages and boarding houses. Sensitive and eloquent individuals, notably Henry David Thoreau, called for preservation. This call was to have effect. Yellowstone National Park (1872) and the Adirondack Forest Preserve (1885) were the first instances in the world in which large areas of wilderness were preserved in the public interest.[24]

By the end of the nineteenth century, a confusion of virtues were attributed to wilderness in America. It stood for the sublime and called man to contemplation; in its solitude one drifted into higher thoughts away from the temptations of Mammon; it has come to be associated with the frontier and pioneer past, and so with qualities that were thought to be characteristically American; and it was an environment that promoted toughness and virility. The growing appreciation of wilderness, like that of the countryside, was a response to the real and imagined failings of city life.

[24] Roderick Nash, *Wilderness and the American Mind* (New Haven: Yale University Press, 1967); David Lowenthal, "The American Scene," *Geographical Review*, 58 (1968), 61–88; Robert C. Lucas, "Wilderness Perception and Use: The Example of the Boundary Waters Canoe Area," *Natural Resources Journal*, 3, No. 3 (1964), 394–411.

But the move toward wilderness was not an extension of the agrarian ideal. The two ideals are in some respects antithetical, for it is the expansion of the countryside, rather than of cities, that poses the immediate threat to wilderness. The values of the middle region may be captured in three distinct images: shepherds in a bucolic landscape; the squire in his country estate reading a book under the elm; and the yeoman in his farm. None of these overlaps with the values associated with wilderness. The settled yeoman has little in common with the footloose pioneer, and the air of indolence which is the characteristic pose of the retiring scholar is the antithesis of the Rooseveltian cult of virility in the wilderness.

People rarely perceive the irony inherent in the idea of *preserving* the wilderness. "Wilderness" cannot be defined objectively: it is as much a state of the mind as a description of nature. By the time we can speak of preserving and protecting wilderness, it has already lost much of its meaning: for example, the Biblical meaning of awe and threat and the sense of a sublimity far greater than the world of man and unencompassable by him. "Wilderness" is now a symbol of the orderly processes of nature. As a state of the mind, true wilderness exists only in the great sprawling cities (see Figure 10d, p. 144).

environment
and
topophilia

The term *topophilia* couples sentiment with place. Having examined the nature of the sentiment, we may turn to the role of place or environment in providing images for topophilia so that it is more than a diffuse, unattached feeling. The fact that the images are taken from the environment does not, of course, mean that the environment has "determined" them; nor (from the evidence given in chapter 8) need we believe that certain environments have the irresistible power to excite topophilic feelings. Environment may not be the direct cause of topophilia but environment provides the sensory stimuli, which as perceived images lend shape to our joys and ideals. Sensory stimuli are potentially infinite: that which we choose to attend (value or love) is an accident of individual temperament, purpose, and of the cultural forces at work at a particular time.

environment and elysium

What is the environmental ideal of a people? We cannot know this fully by looking at the place they actually live in. One way to get closer to the ideal is to examine a people's idea of the world beyond death. Not all human groups, it is true, have notions of afterlife or conceive of a place—an Elysium—where the favored spirits go. The Nirvana of Buddhism is an explicit denial of such a place. Topophilia has no part in Buddhist doctrine although in practice Buddhist temples are often built on locations of exceptional beauty. Other than Buddhism and ascetic religions dominated by mysticism, many people in different parts of the world do have some form of belief in an afterlife that will be spent in a place above the sky, beyond the horizon, or underground. The furnishings of such a place, not surprisingly, are roughly the same as those on earth. They vary with the local geography but in all cases the unpleasing and distressing aspects of the terrestrial environment are removed. Paradises thus tend to be more alike than their earthly counterparts. For the Australian aborigine the "gum-tree country"—the land beyond the great water or in the sky—is like the Australian earth but more fertile, well watered, and abundantly supplied with game. For the Comanche the land where the sun sets is a "valley ten thousand fold longer and wider" than their own valley of the Arkansas. In that blissful world there is no darkness, no wind or rain, and game such as buffalo and elk exist in great abundance. For the Greenland Eskimo the life beyond for the favored is an underground region, a kindly place of sunshine and perpetual summer, with water, fish, and fowl in plenty, where seals and reindeer are easily caught or are found boiling alive in a great kettle.

environments of persistent appeal

People dream of ideal places. The earth, because of its varying defects, is not everywhere viewed as mankind's final home. On the other hand, no environment is devoid of the power to command the allegiance of at least some people. Wherever we can point to human beings, there we point to somebody's *home*—with all the kindly meaning of that word. The Sudan is monotonous and niggardly to the outsider, but Evans-Pritchard says that he can hardly persuade the Nuer who live there that better places exist outside its confines.[1] In a complex modern society, individual tastes in natural setting can vary enormously. Some people prefer to live in, and not just visit, the desert and windswept plains. Alaskans may develop a liking for their frozen landscapes. Most people, however, prefer a more accommodating environment as their home, although they may wish to stimulate their aesthetic palate with an occasional visit to the desert. The expansive steppe, desert, and ice field discourage settlement not only because of their meager biologic base, but because their taunt geometry and hardness seem to deny the idea of shelter. On a fertile plain the sense of shelter can be created

[1] E. Evans-Pritchard, *The Nuer* (Oxford: Clarendon Press, 1940), p. 51.

artificially with tree groves and houses grouped around an open space. The natural environment itself may produce a sense of shelter by being penetrable like the tropical forest, isolated and luxuriant like the tropical island, concave in geometry and diversified in resource as in a valley or along a protected seashore. In chapter 7 we have noted how, to the BaMbuti Pygmies and the Lele of Kasai, the tropical forest is an enveloping world that caters to their material and deepest spiritual needs. The sylvan environment was also the warm nurturing womb out of which the hominids were to emerge. Today the cabin in the forest clearing remains a powerful lure to the modern man who dreams of withdrawal. Three other natural settings have, at different times and places, appealed strongly to the human imagination. These are the seashore, the valley, and the island.

THE SEASHORE

The attractiveness to human beings of the sheltered cove by the sea is not difficult to understand. To begin with, its geometry has a two-fold appeal: on the one hand, the recessions of beach and valley denote security, on the other, the open horizon to the water incites adventure. Furthermore, water and sand receive the human body that normally enjoys contact only with the air and the ground. The forest envelops man in its cool shadowed recesses; the desert is total exposure in which man is repulsed by the hard earth and excoriated by the brilliant sun. The beach too is washed in the brilliance of direct or refracted sunlight but the sand yields to pressure, wedging in between the toes, and water receives and supports the body.

The sheltered sea- or lakeshore may be one of mankind's earliest homes, dating back in Africa to Lower and Middle Paleolithic times. If the forest environment is necessary to the evolution of the perceptual and locomotive organs of man's primate ancestors, the seashore habitat may have contributed to man's hairlessness, a trait that distinguishes him from apes and monkeys. Theories concerning the causes of evolutionary traits in the remote past are at best uncertain. Human agility in water is, however, a fact. The talent is not widely shared among the primates. Other than human beings, only certain Asian macaques forage for food along the seashores, and can swim. Could it be that our earliest home was a sort of Eden located near a lake or sea? Consider Carl Sauer's sketch of the advantages of the seashore: "No other setting is as attractive for the beginning of humanity. The sea, in particular the tidal shore, presented the best opportunity to eat, settle, increase, and learn. It afforded diversity and abundance of provisions, continuous and inexhaustible. It invited the development of manual skills. It gave the congenial ecologic niche in which animal ethology could become human culture."[2]

2 Carl O. Sauer, "Seashore—Primitive Home of Man?" in John Leighly (ed.), *Land and Life* (Berkeley: University of California Press, 1963), p. 309.

Primitive people who live near tropical and temperate shores are generally excellent swimmers and divers. Note further that in water the sexes differ little in ability, which means that they could participate as equals in work and in enjoying water sports. Carl Sauer suggested that the merging of recreation and economic activity might have attracted the primordial males to join in provision from the sea long before they amounted to anything as hunters on the land; and also that such participation helped to establish the bilateral family. In the prehistoric past the evidence of shell mounds suggests that the sea- and lakeshores were often capable of supporting population densities far in excess of those inland where the people had to depend on hunting and collecting. Perhaps only as agriculture became more sophisticated, late in the Neolithic period, did people begin to concentrate inland in large numbers, although even then fishing in the streams contributed importantly to their diet.

Fishing communities in the modern world are poor, generally speaking, when compared with farming communities in the interior; and if they endure it is less for the economic rewards than for the satisfactions to be got out of an ancient and lore-drenched way of life. In the course of the last century the seashore has become immensely popular, but health and pleasure, not the produce of the sea, have been the major attractions. Every summer hordes of people in Europe and North America migrate to the beaches. Take the example of Britain. In 1937, about 15 million people enjoyed a holiday away from home for a week or longer. By 1962, 31 million or sixty percent of Britain's population did so; and of the holidays spent within the country the greatest number were taken by the sea. In 1962, seventy-two percent of all British holiday-makers went to the coast. Swimming was and is by far the most actively pursued sport, engaged in by young and old alike. In 1965, no other single sport even approached half the number of swimming adherents.[3] But, as E. W. Gilbert has pointed out, the popularity of swimming and the beaches is a fairly recent happening: Britain's insularity has not in itself encouraged any precocious cultivation of the pleasures of the coast. It was the growing reputation of sea water and of sea bathing for health that turned the attention of health seekers from the inland spas of ancient fame to the beaches. The power of sea water owed much of its credibility to a Dr. Richard Russell of Lewes and Brighton. In 1750 he published a book on the use of sea water in treating the diseases of the glands which found favor among hypochondriacal and pleasure-seeking Europeans for the next century. The rapid growth of seaside resorts, particularly from the 1850s onward, was made possible by the spread of railroads. The one-day, weekend, and seasonal surges to the sea, a post-World

---

[3] J. Allan Patmore, *Land and Leisure in England and Wales* (Newton Abbot, Devon: David & Charles, 1970), p. 60.

War II phenomenon, reflects the increasing affluence of the lower-middle and middle classes, and the sharp rise in the use of automobiles.[4] Economic and technological factors explain the accelerating volume of the movement to the sea, but not why people should have found it attractive in the first place. The origin of the movement to the sea is rooted in a new evaluation of nature.

In the United States inland spas again preceded the seaside resorts as centers for pleasure and health.[5] Although bathing in the sea already appeared toward the end of the eighteenth century, it was much later that it became at all popular. From the first, sea bathing had to overcome prudery. Manufacturers advertised machines of a "peculiar construction" which enabled the bathers to get in and out of the water unseen. Swimming also aroused suspicion because it was a sport for mixed company. Bathers of the late nineteenth century waded into the sea in full attire. Social mores, however, do change: common sense eventually overcomes prudery. Since the early years of the twentieth century swimming has been, and remains, the greatest outdoor recreation for Americans. The east coast beaches have been seasonally packed since the 1920s. Swimming, unlike many competitive sports, minimizes the physical and social differences among human beings. The sport is suited to the entire family. It requires no expensive equipment. The infants, the old, and even the lame can enjoy the benevolent world of the seashore. The sport's popularity is good litmus for the strength of a country's democratic sentiment.

THE VALLEY

The valley or basin of modest size appeals to human beings for obvious reasons. As a highly diversified ecological niche it promises an easy livelihood: a wide variety of food is available from the river, the floodplain and the valley slopes. The human being is greatly dependent on easy access to water: he has no means of retaining it in his body for long periods. The valley holds water in its streams, pools, and springs. If the stream is large enough it also serves as the natural route way. Farmers appreciate the rich soils on the valley floor. There are, of course, disadvantages, especially to early man with simple tools. The tangled growths of the floodplain, besides sheltering dangerous animals, may be difficult to clear. The plain may be poorly drained and malarial; it is subject to floods and to temperature fluctuations greater than those experienced on higher slopes. The soils, though rich, are heavy. Some of these difficulties could be avoided or

---

[4] E. W. Gilbert, "The Holiday Industry and Seaside Towns in England and Wales," *Festschrift Leopold G. Scheidl zum 60 Geburtstag* (Vienna, 1965), pp. 235–47.

[5] Foster R. Dulles, *A History of Recreation: America Learns to Play,* 2nd ed. (New York: Appleton-Century-Crofts, 1965), pp. 152–53, 355–56.

mitigated. Large swampy plains subject to violent floods were shunned, and where possible the settlements were located on dry gravel terraces and at the foot of the valley flanks. It was in valleys and basins of moderate size that mankind took the first steps toward agriculture and to sedentary life in large village communities.

Symbolically the valley is identified with the womb and shelter. Its concavity protects and nurtures life. When the primate ancestors of man moved out of the forest to the plains they sought the physical and (one might guess) psychological security of the cave. Artificial shelters are man-made concavities in which life processes might function away from exposure to light and to the threats of the natural environment. The earliest constructed dwellings were often semisubterranean: the digging of the hollow minimized the need for a superstructure and at the same time brought the inhabitants into closer contact with the earth. The valley is chthonic and feminine, the *megara* of biologic man. Mountain tops and other eminences are ladders to the sky, the home of the gods. There man might build temples and altars but not his own dwellings except to escape from attack.

THE ISLAND

The island seems to have a tenacious hold on the human imagination. Unlike the tropical forest or the continental seashore it cannot claim ecological abundance, nor—as an environment—has it mattered greatly in man's evolutionary past. Its importance lies in the imaginative realm. Many of the world's cosmogonies, we have seen, begin with the watery chaos: land, when it appears, is necessarily an island. The primordial hillock was also an island and on it life had its start. In numerous legends the island appears as the abode of the dead or of immortals. Above all, it symbolizes a state of prelapsarian innocence and bliss, quarantined by the sea from the ills of the continent. Buddhist cosmology recognizes four islands of "excellent earth" situated in the "exterior sea." Hindu doctrine tells of an "essential island" of pulverized gems on which sweet-smelling trees grow; it houses the *magna mater*. China has the legend of the Blessed Isles or the Three Isles of the Genii which were believed to be located in the Eastern Sea, opposite the coast of Chiang-su. The Semang and Sakai of Malaya, forest dwellers, conceive paradise as an "island of fruits" from which all the ills that afflict man on earth have been eliminated; it is located in heaven and has to be entered from the West. Some Polynesian peoples envisage their Elysium in the form of an island, which is not surprising. But it is in the imagination of the Western world that the island has taken the strongest hold. Here is a brief sketch.

The legend of the Island of the Blessed first appeared in archaic Greece: it was described as a place that provided heroes with unusual harvests thrice a year. The Celtic world, remote from Greece, had a similar legend: Plutarch relates the story of a Celtic island on which no one toiled, its climate was exquisite, its air steeped in fragrance. In Christian Ireland, certain pagan romances were converted into edifying tales of saintly endeavor. Especially popular throughout medieval Europe was the legend of St. Brendan, in which the Abbot of Clonfort (d. 576) became a seafaring hero who discovered insular paradises of blissful ease and abundance. In a twelfth-century Anglo-Norman version of the tale, Brendan was made to search for an island described glowingly as a home for the pious that lay beyond the sea, "where no tempest revels, where for nourishment one inhales the perfume of flowers from paradise."

The imagination of the Middle Ages peopled the Atlantic with a large number of islands, many of which persisted well into the age of the great explorations, and indeed one, Brasil (Gaelic term for blessed), persisted in the mind of the British Admiralty until the second half of the nineteenth century.[6] By 1300 the classical Fortunate Isles came to be identified with the islands of St. Brendan. The cardinal Pierre d'Ailly, whom Columbus regarded as an authority on geography, seriously inclined to the view that the Earthly Paradise was located on or near the Fortunate Isles because of the fertility of their soil and the excellence of their climate. Ponce de Leon was reported to have searched for the Fountain of Youth in Florida, and by thinking of Florida as an island he followed the tradition of identifying enchantment with insularity. In 1493 the New World dawned on the European imagination as small delectable island-gardens. By the seventeenth century the New World had stretched to an interminable continent, and the original vision of isles of innocence and sunshine turned to incredulity as colonists stood before the immeasurable and the horrifying.[7]

The fantasy of island Edens received a new lease of life in the eighteenth century, as the somewhat ironic consequence of scientific expeditions to the South Seas. Unlike early explorers, Louis de Bougainville did not believe in any literal Eden, but his glowing account of Tahiti made the island an acceptable substitute. The voyages of Captain Cook largely confirmed the desirability of the South Sea islands. George Forster, a naturalist who accompanied Cook on his second voyage, believed that they owed much of their special appeal to contrast with the prior experience of tedium over the empty seas. In the nineteenth century, missionaries assaulted the Edenic image of tropical islands. On the other hand eminent writers who visited them—including Herman Melville, Mark Twain, Robert Louis Stevenson, and Henry Adams—upheld their reputation. The islands tri-

---

[6] Carl O. Sauer, *Northern Mists* (Berkeley and Los Angeles: University of California Press, 1968), pp. 167–68; W. H. Babcock, *Legendary Islands of the Atlantic: A Study in Medieval Geography* (New York: American Geographical Society, 1922).

[7] Howard Mumford Jones, *O Strange New World* (New York: Viking, 1964), p. 61.

umphed over adverse propaganda: tourists continued to flock to them. They acquired another meaning, that of temporary escapism. Gardens of Eden and island utopias have not always been taken seriously, least of all in the twentieth century. But they seem needed as make-believe and a place of withdrawal from high-pressured living on the continent.[8]

greek environment and topophilia

Images of topophilia are derived from the surrounding reality. People pay attention to those aspects of the environment that command awe, or promise support and fulfillment in the context of their lives' purposes. The images change as people acquire new interests and power, but they are still taken from the environment: facets of environment, previously neglected, are now seen in full clarity. Consider the role of environment in early Greek, European, and Chinese topophilia.

The sea, fertile land, and islands figured prominently in the imagination of the ancient Greeks.[9] This is hardly surprising since the Greeks depended on the sea and on the small pockets of fertile soil for their livelihood; and islands were anchors of security or oases of life in the ocean waters.

Attitude to the sea was ambivalent. The sea had beauty and use but it was also a dark, threatening force. The sea appeared frequently in the Homeric epics.[10] It was often described as a highway. When calm it showed a "wine-dark" beauty, when angry it swallowed ships and sailors. By the sixth century B.C., the Greeks had mastered navigational techniques to the extent that the much used Aegean had the familiarity of home waters. Athenians viewed it with confidence and joy. Aeschylus in his writing proudly made the Persian elders confess that it was from the Greeks that their countrymen "learnt to look upon the ocean plain, when it whitened with the tempest." In *Prometheus* he spoke of the "multitudinous laughter" of the ocean. In the works of Euripides, as in those of his predecessors, the sea, whether calm or violent, provided the most common type of simile for the conditions of human life.[11] Alexandrian poetry continued to purvey the charm of the sea. Theocritus made Daphnis sing beneath the rocks, "looking out upon Sicilian waters." On the dark side, the sea stood for nature's

8 Henri Jacquier, "Le mirage et l'exotisme Tahitien dans la littérature," *Bulletin de la Société des Oceaniennes,* 12, Nos. 146–147 (1964), 357–69.
9 H. Rushton Fairclough, *Love of Nature Among the Greeks and Romans* (New York: Longmans, Green & Co., 1930).
10 F. E. Wallace, "Color in Homer and in Ancient Art," *Smith College Classical Studies,* No. 9 (December 1927), p. 4; Paolo Vivante, "On the Representation of Nature and Reality in Homer," *Arion,* 5, No. 2 (Summer 1966), 149–90.
11 H. Rushton Fairclough, *The Attitude of the Greek Tragedians toward Nature* (Toronto: Roswell & Hutchison, 1897), pp. 18–19, 42.

cruel indifference to man; it served as the image for all that was hard and unfeeling. In the *Iliad*, Patroclus accused Achilles of being born not of human parents but of the gray sea and the sheer cliffs, so untoward was his spirit. Works of a much later date, collected in the *Greek Anthology*, are full of laments over the unknown graves of shipwrecked mariners.[12]

The gray image of the sea served to enhance the desirability of land— of "Phrygia's fruitful fields" and "Dirce's green lands of rich tilth," as Euripides put it. In Homer's *Odyssey* (Book 5), the hero was struggling wearily in the sea when a wave tossed him to its crest and he saw dry land just ahead. The bard explained:

> To Odysseus the sight of those fields and those trees was most welcome. It was like the relief that a man's children would feel in the return to life of the father who has been stretched on a sick bed, pining all too long in severe agony beneath the onslaughts of some angry power. As the children rejoice when the gods relax their father's pain, so also did Odysseus gladly swim hard forward to set his feet on dry land.

In the *Greek Anthology*, a characteristic expression of attachment to land and fear of the sea was put in the mouth of a dying husbandman:

> I charge you, dear children, that you love the mattock and the life of a farmer. Do not look with favor on the weary labor of those who sail the treacherous waves and on the heavy toil of perilous sea-faring. Even as a mother is sweeter than a stepmother, so is the land more to be desired than the gray sea.[13]

Attitude to the island, like that to the sea, was ambivalent. In the Homeric epics few islands were rich in grass, and where an island yielded abundant fruit, there lurked also the threat of the Cyclopes. On the other hand, archaic Greece gave birth to the legend of the Island of the Blessed, where heroes led easeful lives. And Ithaca, an island of no special distinction, received encomiums not only from Odysseus but also from Telemachus and Athena in the *Odyssey*. Its image was of a mountainous island rising out of the sea, a haunt for goats rather than for horses, and yet a good nursing-mother, watered by springs and blessed with good soil.

landscape and landscape painting in europe

Topophilic sentiments of the past are irretrievably lost. We can gain some understanding of them now only through the literature and through

---

12 Samuel H. Butcher, "Dawn of Romanticism in Greek Poetry," in *Some Aspects of the Greek Genius* (London and New York: Macmillan, 1916), p. 267.
13 *The Greek Anthology*, trans. W. R. Paton (New York: Putnam's, 1917), III, 15.

the art works and artifacts that have survived. In chapter 12 we shall try to evoke past environmental attitudes and values from the evidence of the physical setting—streets and houses—that people lived in. Here we attend to the evidence of visual art. At first it may seem that the early paintings which include landscape in their composition would give us clear insight into the environment and landscape tastes of former times. The evidence of painting however is not easy to interpret, for the artist acquires his skills from a school: what he depicts reveals his learning more directly than it does his own experiences in the world of man and nature. Only roughly do painted landscapes image external reality. We cannot depend on the visual arts to provide us with clues as to how particular places looked in the past; nor can we depend on them for what the artists personally delighted in, but we can take painted landscapes to be special structurings of reality that for a time enjoyed a measure of popular acclaim.

Landscape painting is an arrangement of natural and man-made features in rough perspective; it organizes natural elements so that they provide an appropriate setting for human activity. Thus defined, landscape painting appeared relatively late in the history of European art. A precocious example, dating back to the fourteenth century, is a work called "Good Government in the Country" by Ambrogio Lorenzetti. For the first time, according to Richard Turner, an Italian painter had clothed bare rock with soil and planted upon it trees and crops. Also for the first time the picture suggested great distances.[14] The purpose of the painting however was not pictorial accuracy but didactic, to show the benefits of good government. One such benefit was a prosperous countryside and if we look at the Lorenzetti picture closely we can detect in it elements of the Tuscan landscape. When did a clearly recognizable landscape first appear in a European painting? A case can be made for the year 1444, when the Swiss artist Konrad Witz painted his "Miraculous Draught of Fishes." It shows the dramatic event against a background scene that accurately portrays the lakeshore of Geneva.

Why does the artist choose to depict certain facets of reality and not others? The answer cannot be simple for among the influences that impinge on the artist are his academic training, the technical skills available to him, the nature-symbolism of his time, and the scenes that surround him. In the early stages of landscape art, the "river-in-a-valley" is a popular theme perhaps because it allows the artist to show rudimentary perspective without much difficulty. Mountains are useful in providing the vertical dimension. They are also apt symbols of threatening wilderness. From Hellenistic to late medieval times mountains are shown as bare, sheer, and grotesque; remote, forbidding, and wrapt in mystery. It is not easy, however, to dis-

[14] A. Richard Turner, *The Vision of Landscape in Renaissance Italy* (Princeton, N.J.: Princeton University Press, 1966), p. 11.

entangle the symbolic from the representational elements. Consider the landscapes of Leonardo da Vinci. Many show peaks and naked mountain walls that are almost as weird as those done by medieval artists. Without doubt mountains of a certain type captured Leonardo's imagination. But unlike medieval artists and most of his own contemporaries Leonardo was a keen observer of nature. Painting for him was a science, that is, a rigorous way of knowing reality rather than aesthetic indulgence.[15] The earliest sketch ascribable to him was a representation of the Arno Valley (1473). Later he made many sketches of the Alps, deliberately selecting for portrayal those intransigent aspects of geological reality that conformed to his inner being. Some mountains of dolomitic limestone in the Mediterranean basin in fact have the bare and sheer walls that appear in Leonardo's landscapes.

Besides mountains and river valleys, forests made an early impact on the sensibility of European artists. Forests still covered large stretches of the continent despite the extensive clearance undertaken during the medieval period. Hunting, which was popularized in the courts of France and Normandy from about 1400, opened up a new environment for the pleasure of the nobles. It was through the instinct to kill that the upper classes learnt to appreciate sylvan beauty. Pictures that showed exuberant biological nature appeared first in manuscripts on sport. The Avignon frescoes portray hunting, fishing, and falconry. The illuminated manuscript, *Très Riches Heures* (1409–1415), depicts episodes of the chase. "Primeval" forests persisted longer in northern and central Europe than in the south. While the Italian masters were engaged in great portraitures, the German artist Albrecht Altdorfer (1480–1538) painted a scene called "Landscape with St. George and the Dragon," in which St. George almost disappears in the luxuriance of the forest. It reveals the artist's awareness of the overwhelming complexity of biological nature. There is in the scene a feeling of "the fulness of the primeval forest, its solitude and stillness interrupted only by the battle between St. George and the dragon protagonist."[16] The choice of an immense forest setting for the battle reflects the influence of the Biblical conception of wilderness as the domain of danger and evil; on the other hand the artist's attention to the forest interior—his rendering of the delicate opening of the treetops to wind and sunlight—shows a sensitivity to the aesthetic qualities of the forest even when it dominates man.

In the visual arts as in literature the appreciation of wilderness came very much later than the appreciation of gardens, productive farmlands, and bucolic scenes. Before hunting became popular and took the nobles and

---

15 See André Chastel (ed.), *The Genius of Leonardo da Vinci: Leonardo da Vinci on Art and the Artist* (New York: Orion Press, 1961).

16 Benjamin Rowland, Jr., *Art in East and West* (Boston: Beacon Press, 1964), p. 74.

their ladies into the woods, the garden was the safe and desired setting. The garden however was a pure artifice: its design and image showed greater debt to religious symbolism than to the actual configurations of nature. In portraying farmlands and rural scenes, something of the reality of environment comes through. Lorenzetti's landscape of rounded hills covered by patches of trees and cropland is a recognizable Tuscan scene. More than half of the months in *Très Riches Heures* represents work of the fields in realistic detail, contrasting sharply with their background of bizarre mountains. In Giovanni Bellini's (ca. 1427–1516) *St. Francis*, we have an example of radiant topophilia. No attempt was made to transcribe an actual scene: on the contrary the artist moved St. Francis from the rugged site of the stigmatization in La Verna to a landscape more congenial to him, which is a Venetian scene of green fields and neat plane trees set against a backdrop of dolomitic foothills.[17]

Academism inhibits the perception of reality. The English Augustans saw the countryside through the eyes of Virgil and Horace. English landscape painters seldom painted what we now think of as typical English landscapes —the Chilterns, Cotswolds, Kent. They went on the Grand Tour and returned to paint formalized scenes reminiscent of Claude Lorrain (1600–1682) and Salvator Rosa (1617–1673), with classical ruins, pines, and cypresses substituting for English nature. Even Gainsborough (1727–1788), who proved that he had an observant eye for the native scene in the background of "Mr. & Mrs. Andrews," gradually gave up the natural landscape in favor of an artificiality that transformed Suffolk into Cytherea.[18] The Dutch have strongly influenced the English painters in the direction of closer observation of nature and away from the dreamy romanticism of literary landscapes. Both Crome and Constable, according to Nikolaus Pevsner, were inspired by "the Dutch landscape painters of the seventeenth century who combined probity with a feeling for atmosphere stimulated by the climate of their country." Pevsner goes on to say,

> The climate of England is similar, the closeness to the sea as noticeable in the air. So Girtin and Turner as well as Crome and Constable turned to the study of atmosphere, allowed it to animate the English everyday country scene, and developed an open and sketchy technique to interpret an ever-changing nature.[19]

Topophilia is richly informed by the reality of environment when it combines with religious love or scientific curiosity. Bellini saw nature through

17 Turner, *Vision of Landscape*, p. 60.
18 Kenneth Clark, "On the Painting of the English Landscape," *Proceedings of the British Academy*, 21 (1935), 185–200.
19 Nikolaus Pevsner, *The Englishness of English Art* (New York: Praeger, 1956), pp. 149–50.

the eyes of *caritas*. No object was slighted; every object in his landscape, from the donkey's ears to joints in the bedrock, is depicted with sharpness and accuracy. His scenes have the clarity and freshness of the countryside after cleansing showers. If they seem archaic it is because, unlike modern landscape paintings, they are often bathed in an other-worldly light that bears no relation to the moods of weather or time of day. Leonardo, on the other hand, depicted nature with scientific objectivity: his pictures of animals and mountains rested on his solid knowledge of anatomy and geology.[20]

Nature did not enjoy wide appeal among well-to-do Europeans until late in the eighteenth and early in the nineteenth century, when more and more members of the leisured class took it up. Observing nature became a fashionable pastime, the thing to do. Ladies and gentlemen, while strolling along the beach, picked up pebbles and fossils, made notes on the flora and the state of the sky. The scientific posture of detached observation was admired and imitated by artists and men of letters. Consider the influence of Luke Howard on the efflorescence of the genre of cloudscapes. In 1803 Howard devised a classification of condensed vapors. This work made an impact not only on the infant science of meteorology but also on the aesthetic sensibility of his time. In Germany Goethe was sufficiently impressed to write poems on the newly recognized family of clouds—the stratus, the cirrus, and the cumulus. Carl Gustavus Carus (1789–1869), a natural philosopher and amateur artist, urged his contemporaries to attend to the laws of weather and geology in his tract "Nine Letters on Landscape Painting" (1831), a tract that Goethe honored with an introduction. Carus's ideas influenced German artists such as Clausen Dahl (1788–1857) and Karl Ferdinand Blechen (1798–1840). Blechen, for example, turned away from an affected Romanticism—a concern with landscapes populated by monks and knights-errant—to the study of nature.[21] In England, Luke Howard's classification played a role in turning John Constable's attention to the sky and to clouds. He sketched clouds in all their moods. On one sketch he wrote: "5th of September, 1822, 10 o'clock, morning, looking southeast, brisk wind at west. Very bright and fresh grey clouds running fast over a yellow bed, about half way in the sky. Very appropriate to the coast of Osmington." In a letter (1835) Constable wrote: "After thirty years I must say that the sister arts have less hold on my mind...than the sciences, especially the study of geology."[22] Such remarks suggest a degree of detachment that is misleading, for Constable was also moved by a deep

20 Kenneth Clark, *Landscape into Art* (London: John Murray, 1949).
21 Kurt Badt, *John Constable's Clouds*, trans. Stanley Godman (London: Routledge & Kegan Paul, 1950).
22 L. C. W. Bonacina, "John Constable's Centenary: His Position as a Painter of Weather," *Quarterly Journal of the Royal Meteorological Society*, 63 (1937), 483–90.

sense of religion to know nature intimately. Nature for Constable, as for Wordsworth, revealed God's will: conceived in a humble spirit the portrayal of landscape was a means of conveying truth and moral ideas.

chinese environment and topophilia

China's physiographic mien bears little resemblance to that of Europe. In western and northern Europe farmlands generally show a rolling topography. The slight undulations correspond to the different kinds of glacial deposition, and the belts of higher relief to the bedrock scarplands. Rich farms in the broad valleys merge with grass-covered downs, and in areas of heavy soil, heavy stands of deciduous woodland remain. China, by contrast, lacks a rolling topography, and except in marginal country it has no "parkland" scenery of open grassland, dotted with wood lots. Bucolic scenes and mamillate landforms are rare. The bulk of the Chinese population lives in a land of sharp contrasts: alluvial plains, on the one hand, and steep-sided hills and mountains, on the other. Mountains look taller and more sheer than they are because of the lack of a foothill zone: alluvium creeps up to the mountain flanks. The Ssu-ch'uan basin is the only densely populated region in China that is not an alluvial plain. Its topography, with local relief of up to 1,000 feet, is more rugged than the scarplands of northwestern Europe.

As in Europe, feelings for place and nature appeared in poetry long before they did in the visual arts. Since at least the Han dynasty, poetry evoked the mood of specific places. Poems carried such titles as "From the city-tower of Liu-chou" or "A message from Lake Tung-t'ing." They were concise and focused, unlike the genre of English topographic poetry that provoked Jonathan Swift to denounce its many works as "Descriptions tedious, flat and dry/And introduc'd the Lord knows why." In China poetry showed a far greater range of nature sentiment than did landscape painting. Poets sometimes attended to evanescent scenes that painters chose to ignore: for example, the pool of moonlight on the bedroom floor that was mistaken for frost, and cliffs made scarlet just before sunset. Poets also took care to describe the countryside and recorded ordinary events on a farmstead that painters tended to neglect. In a characteristic poem, Tao Yuan-ming (A.D. 372–427) describes his return to his country home with its three pathways (almost overgrown with weeds), its pine trees, and its chrysanthemums. He wanders about in his garden and pauses to look at the clouds climbing the valleys and the birds returning to their nests. "Light thickens, but still I remain in the fields, caressing with my hand a solitary pine."[23]

---

[23] Tao Yuan-ming, "The Return;" see Robert Payne (ed.), *The White Pony: An Anthology of Chinese Poetry* (New York: Mentor, 1960), p. 144.

Tao's poem is pictorial in effect. The images it evokes—the clouds climbing the valley, the cottage, and the lone scholar caressing a solitary pine—could be the verbal rendering of a typical landscape painting. Yet such imagery did not appear in painting until some five hundred years later. Landscape was gaining importance as a pictorial theme in Tao Yuan-ming's time, but the scenes depicted were far from naturalistic. Even in the T'ang period (A.D. 618–907), clouds looked stiff and formal and mountains were emblematic spires. Palaces and human activities tended to dominate the foreground. By the beginning of the Sung dynasty (tenth century), pure landscapes began to appear. These efforts were an attempt at capturing the essence of place. The artist did not go out with easel and paint and try to copy a particular scene. Instead he entered a world, to wander there for hours or days so as to imbibe an atmosphere. He then returned to his studio to paint.[24] Nature was experienced in the penumbra of Taoist mysticism but this did not prevent the artist from observing nature with care and analytically. Kuo Hsi, who lived in the eleventh century, said that artists should not just copy nature. He noted with disapproval that painters who had been brought up in the Chê-chiang and Chiang-su provinces were prone to show the high barren landscapes of the southeast, and those who dwelt in Shen-hsi province were apt to draw the magnificent billowy tops of the Kuan Lung. On the other hand, he commended accurate observation, saying (like a geographer) :

> Some mountains are covered with earth, while others are covered with stones. If the earthy mountain has stones on top, then trees and forests will be scarce and lean, but if the stony mountain has earth on top, the vegetation will flourish. Some trees grow on mountain, some trees beside the water. On a mountain where the soil is rich, there may grow a very tall pine. Beside water where the soil is lean, there may grow a shrub only a few feet high.
>
> An inn and hut stand by a ravine and not by a delta. They are in the ravine to be near the water; they are not by the delta because of the danger of flood. Even if some do stand by the delta, they are always in a place where there is no danger of flood. Villages are situated on the plain and not on the mountain, because the plain offers land for cultivation. Though some villages are built among the mountains, these are near to arable land among the hills.[25]

The Chinese term for the art genre "landscape" is *shan shui* (mountain and water). The two major axes of landscape painting, vertical and horizontal, are abstracted from the juxtaposition of steep hills and alluvial plains that is characteristic of Chinese topography. The elements, mountain and water, are not quite equal in religious and aesthetic value: mountain

---

24 Michael Sullivan, *The Birth of Landscape Painting in China* (Berkeley and Los Angeles: University of California Press, 1962).
25 Kuo Hsi, *An Essay on Landscape Painting,* trans. Shio Sakanishi (London: John Murray, 1935), pp. 54, 55.

takes precedence despite the Taoist emphasis on the superior ways of water. Mountains have an individuality that rivers and flat lands lack. The Chinese speak of the Five Sacred Mountains but (unlike India) the great rivers have not acquired the same holy aura. The realism of Chinese landscape painting lies primarily in the faithful rendering of mountains, particularly the Hua Shan of southeastern Shen-hsi, Huang Shan of southern An-hui, Lu Shan in northern Hu-nan on the middle Yangtze, the mountains of Chê-chiang, and many places throughout South China. These mountains can be photographed so that the results look remarkably like the painting of famous landscapists.[26] Without aiming at geological or pictorial truthfulness, Chinese artists have shown their sensitivity to the facts of nature in some of their works. Joseph Needham believes that he can find a wide range of geological features among Chinese paintings, including dipping strata, anticlines, rejuvenated valleys, marine platforms, U-shaped glacial valleys (e.g., Chi-chü Shan in northern Ssu-ch'uan province), and karst topography.[27]

Landscape gardening is an art closely allied to painting and poetry. In all three art forms the influences of Shamanism, Taoism, and Buddhism can be traced. The landform elements of the garden, like those of painting, stress the verticality of the mountain against the horizontality of alluvial plain and water. To Western observers the weathered blocks of limestone used to represent mountains, and perhaps the entire composition, may seem unreal and remote from their experiences of real landscapes in Europe and North America. Yet it is ironic and of historical interest to note that the Danish geographer, Malte-Brun (1775–1826), faulted the Chinese precisely for their lack of imagination, their habit of imitating nature.

> If they have discovered a sort of beauty in the arrangement of their gardens and the distribution of their grounds, it is because they have copied with exactness nature in a strange though picturesque form. Projecting rocks, as if threatening every moment to fall, bridges hung over abyss, stunted fir scattered on the sides of steep mountains, extensive lakes, rapid torrents, foaming cascades, and pagodas raising their pyramidal forms in the midst of this confusion; such are the Chinese landscapes on a large, and their gardens on a small scale.[28]

---

26 Arthur de Carle Sowerby, *Nature in Chinese Art* (New York: John Day Company, 1940), pp. 153–68.
27 Joseph Needham, *Science and Civilization in China* (Cambridge: Cambridge University Press, 1959), III, 592–98.
28 Conrad Malte-Brun, *A System of Universal Geography*, trans. J. G. Percival (Boston: Samuel Walker, 1834), I, 413.

CHAPTER TEN

from cosmos
to
landscape

In Europe, some time between 1500 and 1700 A.D., the medieval conception of a vertical cosmos yielded slowly to a new and increasingly secular way of representing the world. The vertical dimension was being displaced by the horizontal; cosmos was giving way to a flat nonrotary segment of nature called landscape. "Vertical" here means something more than a dimension in space. It is charged with meaning. It signifies transcendence and has affinity with a particular notion of time. A world model that lays stress on its vertical axis coincides often with a cyclical conception of time; a culture with a sharply articulated calendar of festivals is likely to conceive a highly stratified cosmos. Corresponding to this geometric bias toward the vertical and temporal bias toward the cyclical (and eternal) is a special view of human nature—one which discerns a vertical dimension in the metaphorical sense. Human nature is polarized. Man plays two roles, the social-profane and the mythical-sacred, the one bound to time, the other transcending it. These roles may be enacted by members of different classes or castes in which case we have social stratification. Or they may be enacted in the same person but on different occasions.

Although the idea of the vertical cosmos began to weaken in Europe during the age of the great explorations, this secularizing trend had as yet little effect on the rest of the world and on those parts of Europe remote from the literate culture of the cities and from commercial values. The bulk of mankind, peasant farmers in particular, lived in a stratified world and experienced cyclical time, and this state continued into the first half of the twentieth century.

stratified cosmos

Primitive views concerning the cosmos have certain traits in common. Consider, first, the Bushman and his world. Here is a people of very simple material culture, living inconspicuously in the bare environment of the Kalahari desert. A typical socioeconomic unit is a band of about twenty people. Such a band might live off an area of a few hundred square miles. The horizontal space, the lived-space of the Bushman, is poor in resources and limited in size. Geographical limitations, however, are compensated by vertical spaciousness in the Bushman's world. He looks to the sky. Though forced to seek for food almost daily, and compelled to focus his eyes on the ground for signs of edible roots and the spoors of wounded animals, the heavenly bodies are yet a part of his world. The stars participate in the human drama. Their motions are sometimes interpreted with poetry. The Gikwe Bushmen say of the morning star that it is chased by the sun across the sky to melt eventually under the sun's fierce heat. The stars also have their use as time pieces. Elizabeth Thomas relates how one night in a Gikwe camp she came across a fellow roasting a plucked and trussed bird over the fire. She asked him whether it was about done. The Bushman looked at the intruder, then at the bird, then up at the sky, and shook his head. No, the bird wasn't ready because the star had not risen high enough.[1]

The vertical axis of the Bushman's world has thus a simple geometric interpretation. It can also be interpreted metaphorically to mean that which transcends the demands of social and biologic life. The Bushmen, in order to survive, have developed a net of interdependence that requires the suppression of individualism, possessiveness, and aggressive feelings. Good behavior and the cooperative spirit are essential to survival. The horizontal or biosocial plane of existence rules the pattern of the Bushman's life. But mundane activities are interrupted periodically by acts of another kind, not tied to physical necessity and out of step with the normal rhythms of human relationships. Dancing, for example: dancing, which always takes place at night and around a fire, reaches great intensity, during which the constraints and obligations of daily life are put aside. On such an occasion a mother may sit peacefully with her infant in one moment, and in the

---

[1] Elizabeth M. Thomas, *The Harmless People* (New York: Vintage Books, 1965), p. 220.

next sweep the infant to the ground and rush to join the dance like a person possessed.

Broad horizons and flat open landscapes characterize Siberia and Central Asia; yet here among the nomads one finds numerous conceptions of the stratified cosmos. The structure of Siberian and Central Asian worlds is multistoried, with the three basic levels of sky, earth, and underworld linked together along a central axis. Altaic folk-poetry speaks of the sky as made up, variously, of three, seven, nine, and even twelve hemispheres stacked one on top of the other below the polar star. The heavens are often pictured in a concrete way. To the Yakuts they are a succession of tightly stretched skins. To the Buriats the sky is shaped like an overturned cauldron, rising and falling; and in rising, an opening appears between the sky and the edge of the earth through which the winds blow. The Turko-Tartars imagine the sky as a tent or a roof, protecting the earth and life on earth. The stars are holes through which the light of heaven penetrates. Meteor light is a "crack in the sky" or "the door of heaven," and its appearance is an auspicious time for petitioning. Heaven's roof is supported by a pillar, which is also the axis of the rotating stars around Polaris. The world of the Central Asian nomad is not only vertical but vertiginous. The heavenly pillar is sometimes likened to a tethering post at which the gods fasten their rotating stars.

The shelter is a microcosm. The round tent or yurt represents the vaulting sky. The opening in the roof that lets out the smoke leads to the polar star, which on the cosmic level is variously interpreted as the stake that holds up the celestial tent, or as sky holes in the multistoried heavenly vault. To the Altaians, a central axis passes through the holes and through the three regions of sky, earth, and underworld. Along it the gods descend to earth and the dead to the subterranean regions. Along the same axis the soul of the ecstatic shaman may fly up or down. In preparation for the rites the shaman erects a special tent. A birch is put up in the center so that the crown of the tree sticks out of the air hole in the middle of the roof. Nine divisions are cut into the birch, symbolizing the nine heavens, up which the shaman is expected to climb.[2]

Cosmographic beliefs among subsistence farmers of the middle latitudes probably do not differ very much fundamentally. Their lives are ruled by the seasonal rhythms of nature. Seasons are directly related to the changing heights of the sun and to the position of the stars. Life on earth depends on events in the sky. The sun and the stars dip below the horizon, which suggests the existence of an underworld, a counter-heaven. Earlier I

[2] Uno Holmberg, *Siberian Mythology,* IV, in J. A. MacCulloch (ed.), *Mythology of All Races* (Boston: Marshall Jones Co., 1927); Schuyler Camman, *The Land of the Camel: Tents and Temples of Inner Mongolia* (New York: Ronald Press, 1951); Mircea Eliade, *Shamanism: Archaic Techniques of Ecstasy,* trans. W. R. Trask (New York: Pantheon, 1964).

have described the stratified worlds of such agricultural peoples as the Pueblo Indians, the Egyptians, and the Sumerians. It is unnecessary to multiply examples. Peasant farmers live in confined space. Few know much of the world beyond their village, their neighboring communities, and the market town, all of which may lie within an area of twenty square miles. Constraint in horizontal space is compensated by the intimacy of knowledge and by the height of the ceiling. The peasant world is surprisingly resistant to the influence of modern ideas. In China, for example, modernization introduced under the Communist government had not, in the early 1960s, shattered the vertical cosmos of the villagers, nor their cycle of festivities. The villagers' cosmos will collapse only when they are fully aware that their lives are governed not so much by the motion of the sun and moon over-head as by events (reflecting the laws of supply and demand or government policy) in other parts of the country on the same horizontal plane. Seasonal festivals will also wither to be replaced by holidays as contrived as those that city people in the Western world now celebrate.

nature, landscape, and scenery

The axial transformation in world view from cosmos to landscape may be traced in the changing meaning of the words "nature," "landscape," and "scenery." In modern usage the three words share a common core of mean-ing: scenery and landscape are often used interchangeably and both imply nature. However, the confluence is achieved at a sacrifice. Nature keeps company with scenery and landscape by ceding most of its semantic domain, and the last two words are nearly synonymous through the loss of precision in meaning.

Of the three words, the meaning of nature in popular usage suffered the greatest demotion. Insofar as it acquired the meaning of the "physis" of the pre-Socratic Greeks it designated the All or Everything. To talk of nature philosophically is still "To talk of many things; Of shoes—and—ships—and sealing wax, Of cabbages and kings—" Nature is "The heavens above, the earth beneath, and the waters under the earth." In the Middle Ages the nature of scholars and poets (adapting the Aristotelian cosmos) underwent a constriction to signify no longer the All but merely the sub-lunary regions of mutability. Though the heavens above the orbit of the moon were excluded nature remained stratified. Its major axis remained the vertical and it extended downward from the region of fire, through air and water, to earth. In the last few centuries nature has lost further ground.[3] To speak of nature today is to speak of the countryside and the wilderness; and wilderness, as we have already noted, is a word that has

[3] C. S. Lewis, "Nature," in *Studies in Words* (Cambridge University Press, 1961), pp. 24–74.

ceded almost all its power to evoke awe. Nature has lost the dimensions of height and depth; it gained the less austere qualities of charm and picturesqueness. In this diminutive sense, nature evokes images similar to those of countryside, landscape, and scenery.

The meaning of scene or scenery has suffered the least change. The scene is the stage, originally of the Greek or Roman theater. A second meaning, now the most widely accepted, is that of a landscape or view, a picturesque scene, or the pictorial representation of a landscape. A now obsolete meaning of scenery is "a moving exhibition of feeling" and this reminds us of the primitive association of the word with the stage and drama. There remains the expression "don't make a scene!" But scenery now can seldom command much emotion. The scenic spot along the highway presents us with a picture-window glimpse of nature which, sublime as it often is, rarely moves us to any response more strenuous than the taking of a snapshot.

Scenery and landscape are now nearly synonymous. The slight differences in meaning they retain reflect their dissimilar origin. Scenery has traditionally been associated with the world of illusion which is the theater. The expression "behind the scenes" reveals the unreality of scenes. We are not bidden to look "behind the landscape," although a landscaped garden can be as contrived as a stage scene, and as little enmeshed with the life of the owner as the stage paraphernalia with the life of the actor. The difference is that landscape, in its original sense, referred to the real world, not to the world of art and make-believe. In its native Dutch, "landschap" designated such commonplaces as "a collection of farms or fenced fields, sometimes a small domain or administrative unit." Only when it was transplanted to England toward the end of the sixteenth century did the word shed its earthbound roots and acquire the precious meaning of art. Landscape came to mean a prospect seen from a specific standpoint. Then it was the artistic representation of that prospect. Landscape was also the background of an official portrait; the "scene" of a "pose." As such it became fully integrated with the world of make-believe.[4]

the axial transformation
of the european world view

To the man in the Middle Ages, absolute up and down made sense. The earth occupies the lowest place in the heavenly hierarchy: movement to it is downward movement. In the modern view the stars are at a great

---

[4] J. B. Jackson, "The Meanings of 'Landscape' " *Saetryk af Kulturgeografi,* No. 88 (1964), pp. 47–50; M. W. Mikesell, "Landscape," in *International Encyclopaedia of the Social Sciences,* 8 (Macmillan and Free Press, 1968), 575–80.

distance. To look out on the night with modern eyes, as one scholar puts it, is to survey a sea that fades away into mist. To the medieval man the stars are not so much at a great distance as at a great height. To look up at the towering medieval universe is like looking at a great building. The medieval cosmos is immense but finite. Its poetry does not recognize agoraphobia. Pascal's feeling of dread before the eternal silence of infinite space is foreign to the man of the Middle Ages.[5]

EVIDENCE OF PHYSICAL SCIENCE

The axial shift in European world view is manifest in different spheres of European culture and learning. Take the hydrologic cycle. It was, and is, a widely accepted system for ordering the physical facts of the earth. We now see it primarily as the exchange of vapors and water between the sea and the land. This concept, which emphasizes geographical patterns and the horizontal component of motion, is no older than the later part of the seventeenth century. Earlier, the hydrologic cycle was conceived as having essentially only one dimension, the vertical. Aristotle's *Meteorologica* and the storied cosmos of the Middle Ages imparted the bias. "To air extenuated waters rise; To air, when it itself again refines, To elemental fire extracted shines. They in like order back again repair..." (Ovid, *Metamorphoses*). This ancient theme of the transmutation of substances along the vertical axis was a progenitor of the idea of the hydrologic cycle, which limited itself to noting the transmutations of water along a segment of the axis. The physical process served as a popular image of the transcendental relations between the human soul and God. The soul as dew drop or water seeks to be drawn up and absorbed into heaven; and God on high provides spiritual sustenance to the parched soul like rain to the parched earth. When the hydrologic cycle acquired its horizontal dimension it lost its metaphoric power. It became a purely physical process devoid of transcendental and symbolical overtones.[6]

EVIDENCE OF LITERATURE

That medieval painting was deficient in perspective is well known. In literature, too, poets showed little interest in the strict illusionism of later periods. For Chaucer nature was all foreground; he did not describe landscapes. C. S. Lewis notes that in dealing with foreground objects the medieval and even the Elizabethan imagination was vivid as to color and action, but it seldom worked according to scale. There were giants and dwarfs but their sizes lacked consistent definition. The careful maintenance of scale in

5 C. S. Lewis, *The Discarded Image* (Cambridge University Press, 1964), pp. 98–100.

6 Yi-Fu Tuan, *The Hydrologic Cycle and the Wisdom of God,* Department of Geography Research Publication No. 1, University of Toronto Press, 1968.

Gulliver was a great novelty.[7] Medieval artists were familiar with the principle that objects seemed smaller as their distance from the observer increased; they recognized but made little use of perspective. Marshall McLuhan believes that the use of three-dimensional perspective in the literary portrayal of landscape appeared late, not perhaps until Shakespeare's time. In *King Lear* we have a very early instance.[8] Edgar in the play seeks to persuade the blinded Gloucester that they stand atop the cliffs of Dover. He describes the awesome view before them thus:

> *Come on, sir; here's the place: stand still. How fearful*
> *And dizzy 'tis to cast one's eyes so low!*
>
> . . .
>
> *The fishermen that walk upon the beach*
> *Appear like mice; and yond tall anchoring bark*
> *Diminish'd to her cock; her cock, a buoy*
> *Almost too small for sight: The murmuring surge,*
> *That on the unnumber'd idle pebbles chafes*
> *Cannot be heard so high. I'll look no more,*
> *Lest my brain turn and the deficient sight*
> *Topple down headlong. (Act 4, scene 6).*

EVIDENCE OF LANDSCAPE PAINTING

It is in the history of European landscape painting that we find the most persuasive evidence of change toward the horizontal vision. A tapestry hanging on the wall decorates that wall; it does not destroy the vertical plane. A landscape painting on the wall, however, has the effect of opening a window through which a person can penetrate the vertical plane and direct his gaze outward to the horizon. The walls of Italian villas of the Renaissance period were painted with landscapes, not only so that their owners could boast of the extent and variety of their estates, but also that they might enjoy the illusion of expansive vistas.

Crude beginnings in the representation of spatial depth appeared in the paintings of England and France during the fourteenth century. These were early attempts to depict people as sentient beings standing on small horizontal spaces of their own. Later, as the human figures were modeled into three-dimensional personalities, their settings were drawn so as to give the illusion of spatial depth.[9] In the fifteenth century, true prospects and views began to acquire a measure of popularity. A new way of looking at space and light appeared which was scientific to the extent that it emphasized the geometry of perspective and the use of a consistent scale to depict

---

[7] Lewis, *The Discarded Image*, pp. 101–2.
[8] Marshall McLuhan and Harley Parker, *Through the Vanishing Point: Space in Poetry and Painting* (New York: Harper Colophon Books, 1969), p. 14.
[9] D. W. Robertson, Jr., *A Preface to Chaucer: Studies in Medieval Perspectives* (Princeton, N.J.: Princeton University Press, 1962), p. 208.

the size of objects. Dutch artists in the fifteenth century learned how to impart an air of spaciousness even to their miniature paintings. They achieved the effect partly by applying the rules of perspective and partly by the new use of light and shading. Hubert van Eyck's "Landing of Duke William" is an example of how the sense of spaciousness could be produced within a small frame. The foreground of the picture is centered on Duke William and his white horse. Recession to the distant horizon, where the sea meets the sky, is emphasized by the curvature of the beach and the diminutive size of the boats.

For maximum effect, perspective depends on convergent straight lines. Nature offers few straight lines. Two solutions were popular with European artists in their effort to exploit geometry. One was to organize the objects in the landscape along convergent orthogonals. For example, in Paolo Ucello's picture of the hunting party in the wood, the trees and the hounds were arranged along orthogonals that focused on a central vanishing point. Another technique was to use the background of a river valley for the human figures. A river valley, with its convergent flanks and the diminishing width of the river upstream, offers the closest approximation in nature to the artificial conditions of one-point perspective.

Light and color can be exploited to enhance the effect of spatial recession. Consider the position of the sun. In medieval art the sun is shown as a golden disc high up in the sky. It casts no shadow and plays no unifying role in the picture. By the fifteenth century the sun has been brought down to the horizon and made to shine on the landscape. Kenneth Clark credits Gentile da Fabriano with painting the first picture in which the sun is more than a symbol in a composition. The "Flight into Egypt" (1423) shows the sun at the horizon. In this small landscape the pattern of light and shade is unified and focused on the sun as the source of light.[10] The background is lit up and imparts a sense of depth to the scene. In the seventeenth and eighteenth centuries, the golden disc is displaced by streaks of pale blue at the horizon and from this bright background, light and color dim to the mellow browns and dark greens of the foreground. Warm colors are supposed to "stand out" while cool colors "recede."

comparison with chinese attitudes

Unlike the European tradition, Chinese landscape painting as it flourished in the eleventh and twelfth centuries put little emphasis on the horizontal, or on surface recession to a flattish horizon. To begin with, Chinese landscapes are often drawn on vertical scrolls. Just as the written

10 Kenneth Clark, *Landscape into Art* (London: John Murray, 1947), pp. 14–15.

characters—an integral part of the art work—run up and down the scroll, so the elements of the landscape are arranged in tiers. Several important differences in the organization of nature are worth noting. In a Chinese landscape painting the human figures are very small. Mountain peaks provide the vertical dimension. Mountains are a staple of nature in the Chinese view. A painted scene is not so much a *land*scape, a unit of land, as *shan shui*—an arrangement of mountains (*shan*) and water (*shui*). By contrast, in the early stages of European landscape painting, the human figure, cathedral tower, or cross dominate the vertical plane: these bear the burden of meaning. The landscape in the background provides the horizontal dimension. Another difference is that the Chinese have never developed linear perspective with the mathematical rigidity that for a time found favor in European painting. Perspective existed but from shifting standpoints. There is no single horizon. Elements in the landscape are drawn as though the eye were free to vary the horizontal direction along which it looks into the depth of a picture. Note further that it is difficult to tell the time of the day in a Chinese landscape painting. No setting or rising sun, no predawn or twilight glow appears to direct our attention to the horizon.

architecture and the landscape garden:
toward spatial extension and the visual response

THE MEDIEVAL CATHEDRAL

Architecture and landscape gardens reflect, as with painting, certain basic religio-aesthetic attitudes to the world. Medieval ideals in Europe find their most exalted architectural expression in the cathedral. The vertical cosmos of medieval man is dramatically symbolized by pointed arches, towers, and spires that soar. The Gothic cathedral baffles the modern man. A tourist with his camera may be impressed by the beauty of the nave with its aisles, transepts, radiating chapels, and the span of the vaults. Should he seek a position to set up his camera, he will find that there is no privileged position from which all these features may be seen. To see a Gothic interior properly one has to move about and turn one's head. Outside the cathedral the modern tourist may be able to get a good picture of the total structure from a distance. But in medieval times this was seldom possible. Other buildings cluttered around the edifice and blocked the distant view. Moreover, to see the cathedral from a distance would diminish its impact of bulk and verticality. The details of its facade would no longer be visible. The medieval cathedral was meant to be experienced; it was a dense text to be read with devout attention and not an architectural form to be merely seen. In fact some figures and decorations could not be seen at all. They were made for the eyes of God. By contrast, consider the Washington Cathedral in Washington, D.C. The nave axis departs from the axis of the choir by 1° 11′ 38″. The architect deliberately introduced this deviation in order to enhance the view of the visitor who enters the building by the west portal.[11]

ISOMETRIC GARDENS

Gardens mirror certain cosmic values and environmental attitudes. The Chinese garden evolved in antithesis to the city. Poised against the rectilinear geometry of the city are the natural lines and spaces of the garden. In the city of man one finds hierarchical order, in the garden the complex informality of nature. Social distinctions are discarded in the garden where man is free to contemplate and commune with nature in neglect of his fellow human beings.[12] The garden is not designed to give the visitor a certain number of privileged views; seeing is an aesthetic and intellectual activity that puts a distance between the object and the observer. The garden is designed to involve, to encompass the visitor who, as he walks along a winding trail, is exposed to constantly shifting scenes.

The history of landscape gardening in the Near East and Europe is complex. A trend that supports the thesis of axial transformation from the vertical to the horizontal lies in the progressive emphasis on privileged views, on the extension of lines of sight to the distant horizon by means of straight paths, rows of trees, and linear ponds. Ancient gardens in the Near East and in the eastern Mediterranean basin had no privileged dimension. They were roughly square in shape: the wall compound itself was squarish as well as the subdivisions for orchards, tree groves, and ponds. Nebuchadnezzar's legendary hanging gardens of Babylon (ca. 605 B.C.) were likened to a green mountain when seen from afar. This type of garden probably developed under the combined influence of terraced hillside gardening and the ziggurat. Symbolically the ziggurat linked earth to heaven.

The cloisters and gardens of monasteries were places of contemplation. The technical term for the enclosed garden or the cloister was "paradise." The fountain at its center and the streams of water rising out of the fountain symbolized the geography of Eden. Monastic gardens also provided fruits, vegetables, and herbs for the monastic community. They were not places where one sought for pleasant views nor were they designed as a setting to flatter the human ego. The characteristic shape was square. According to Petrus Crescentius, who wrote at the end of the thirteenth century, the ideal garden should be created on flat ground and should be

---

11 Richard T. Feller, "Esthetics of Asymmetry," *Science,* 167, No. 3926 (March 1970), 1669.
12 Nelson I. Wu, *Chinese and Indian Architecture: The City of Man, the Mountain of God, and the Realm of the Immortals* (New York: Braziller, 1963).

square and have sections for fragrant herbs as well as flowers. And a fountain was to be placed in the middle. In this basic pattern Crescentius did not distinguish between gardens for humble people and those for noblemen and kings. The difference was essentially one of size. A lordly garden, for example, might enclose twenty acres and contain natural springs.[13]

PERSPECTIVE GARDENS

Little is known about the gardens of the ancient Greeks and Romans. By the beginning of the fifth century B.C., the Athenians were too gregarious and too fond of public life to retreat into the shelter of private gardens. However, the use of trees in public meeting places probably transformed some of them into parks. Religious worship often took place at a sacred grove, spring, or grotto in the countryside. As to the Romans the stern philosophy of the Republic discouraged the blossoming of anything so frivolous as pleasure gardens. These made their appearance toward the end of the second century B.C., when Hellenistic influences began to penetrate Roman society. The villas of emperors and nobles in the first century A.D. were enormous estates. They included formal gardens in a pseudo-Greek style as well as little modified landscapes. Not much is known of their precise plans.

Pompeian gardens were small since they were city, not suburban, artifacts. They showed two features that the more sumptuous grounds in suburban villas probably also had: the interpenetration of house and garden and axial planning. The main living room of a Pompeian house opened characteristically to the center of the garden portico and from the house one could see down the entire length of the garden. The effect of length was sometimes augmented with a perspective scene, complete with trees and fountains, painted on the wall at the far end. Renaissance villas and gardens were patterned after their Roman prototype: both stressed views.[14] Landscapes painted on the walls of Renaissance villas played an ever larger role in producing the illusion of distance and space. The rugged Mediterranean topography, however, hindered the creation of vast man-made vistas. Gardens were arranged in tiers. The designer might orient the tiers so that they encompassed distant natural features as part of the view. A sense of spatial grandeur was achieved by adapting the garden to the lineaments of the natural setting.

It was on the flatter landscapes of northwestern Europe, and in a later period, that the urge for the horizontal extension of space and vistas found its most extravagant expression. The art of André le Nôtre made a

[13] Quoted in Julia S. Berrall, *The Garden* (New York: Viking, 1966), p. 96.
[14] Georgina Masson, *Italian Gardens* (New York: H. N. Abrams, 1961), pp. 15–16.

caricature of the belief that man could impose his aesthetic taste on nature. The garden was for show: it glorified man. From the royal bedroom at Versailles the Sun King of France could gaze down a long central vista, which was made to seem even longer by the flat sheets of water and the sentinel of trees. Such a show of human will in formal design left no sense of nature or of the divine. There was no lack of statues of gods and goddesses at Versailles but they stood meekly by, like lackeys, in stony servitude to a human conception. When ministers advised Louis XIV not to embark on a project that could deplete his treasury and that, moreover, had to overcome great obstructions in the lay of the land, the king was undeterred. "It is in overcoming difficulties," he observed complacently, "that our powers are manifest." England could also boast of grandiose landscapes of the Versailles type. One of the most ambitious in conception was the estate of the Duke of Beaufort at Badminton, which had twenty radial avenues stretching far into the country. It was reported that certain gentlemen who wished to court the duke's favor planted the trees in their estates so as to extend the duke's vistas.[15]

In the eighteenth century, so-called natural landscaping became popular in England. The natural landscape was as much a work of art and the achievement of engineers as the formal landscape. It eschewed straight lines, great avenues, and linear ponds, but the aim toward pleasing and imposing views had not changed; only the means to achieve them were more subtle. Lancelot Brown, for example, designed splendid, uninterrupted views from the house, using clumps of trees as wing screens to emphasize the receding perspective. He also considered the view in reverse and from several directions, so that the natural gardens had many more privileged points for viewing than had the formal gardens.

In this capsule survey of landscaping,[16] emphasis is put on the increasing tendency to see the garden as an environment for the house, the garden as a place of controlled aesthetic experience from a limited number of standpoints. The garden caters primarily to sight. Of human senses sight is the most discerning spatially: the habitual use of the eyes leads us to appreciate the world as a spatial entity of well-defined lines, surfaces, and solids. The other senses teach us to perceive the world as a rich unfocused ambiance. Neither the formal gardens of the seventeenth century nor the "natural" landscapes of the eighteenth century make much appeal to the senses of hearing, smell, and touch. Confined spaces are necessary to communicate the

15 Edward Malins, *English Landscaping and Literature 1660–1840* (London: Oxford University Press, 1966), p. 8.
16 Two well known books on the history of Occidental gardening and landscaping are: Richard Wright, *The Story of Gardening* (New York: Dover, 1963), and Derek Clifford, *A History of Garden Design* (London: Faber & Faber, 1966).

subtle effects of sound, fragrance, and texture: in such confined spaces the only unimpeded view is upward to the sky.

symbolism and sacredness: premodern responses

The aesthetic attitude to nature gains importance as nature sheds its numinous aura. Landscapes serve as background for commonplace human activities when they no longer harbor the spirits of the earth. The cosmos of premodern man was multistoried; nature was rich in symbols, its objects could be read at several levels and evoke emotion-laden response. We are aware of ambiguity in language. The language of ordinary discourse, and *a fortiori* of poetry, is rich in symbols and metaphors. Science, by contrast, strives to remove the possibility of multiple readings. A traditional world has the ambiguity and richness of ordinary and ritual speech. The modern world, on the other hand, aspires to be transparent and literal.

SYMBOLICAL DEPTH

Symbolical interpretation and the attribution of sacredness to places and landscapes are two closely related and characteristic ways of responding to the world in the prescientific age. As an example of symbolical interpretation, consider the medieval artists who, unlike the more literal-minded artists of later times, saw no contradiction in representing spiritual events and circumstances with the most commonplace of material objects. In the same picture human figures, costumes, and artifacts could appear as pedestrian facts and as epiphanies from a spiritual world. Almost any fresco of the Last Judgment might show a farm cart doing the service of Elijah's fiery chariot on its way to heaven.[17]

Metaphorical thinking ignores the sharply set limits of scientific classification. As scientific terms, "mountain" and "valley" are types in a topographical category. In metaphorical thought, these words carry simultaneously the value-laden meanings of "high" and "low," which in turn implicate the idea of male-female polarity and antithetical temperamental characteristics. In chapter 3, we have noted how people order their world as coordinated systems. To an outsider the elements of one system may seem unrelated to those of another. To the natives they show a natural affinity. The Chinese, the Indonesians, and the Pueblo Indians of North America have very different ways of coordinating one set of phenomena with another: they share, however, the practice of relating the world's elemental sub-

---

[17] Owen Barfield, "Medieval Environment," in *Saving the Appearances* (New York: Harcourt Brace Jovanovich), pp. 71–78.

a. Open landscapes and the vertical aspiration

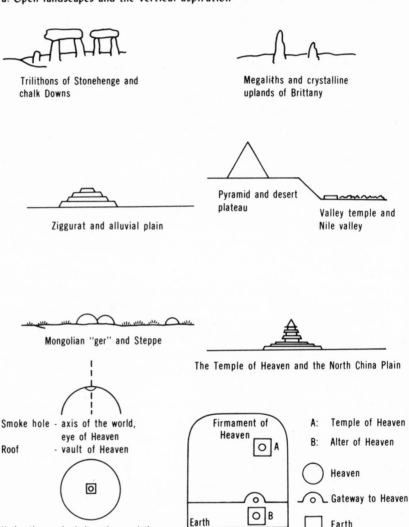

Trilithons of Stonehenge and chalk Downs

Megaliths and crystalline uplands of Brittany

Ziggurat and alluvial plain

Pyramid and desert plateau

Valley temple and Nile valley

Mongolian "ger" and Steppe

The Temple of Heaven and the North China Plain

Smoke hole - axis of the world, eye of Heaven

Roof - vault of Heaven

Under the smoke hole and around the central hearth is a square area marked off by narrow boards; it represents the earth

Firmament of Heaven

Earth

A: Temple of Heaven

B: Alter of Heaven

Heaven

Gateway to Heaven

Earth

Figure 10 Symbolic landscapes.

b. Triumph over earth forces

Parthenon. From the Pynx "Athena . . . took her stand upon the highest place and lifted her aegis like a shield over the city and a warning to its enemies, human and divine."

Saint Michel on top volcanic neck, Le Puy, France

c. Sacred landscapes

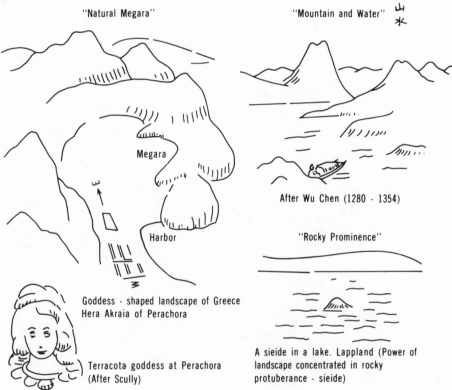

"Natural Megara"

"Mountain and Water" 山 水

Megara

Harbor

Goddess - shaped landscape of Greece
Hera Akraia of Perachora

Terracota goddess at Perachora
(After Scully)

After Wu Chen (1280 - 1354)

"Rocky Prominence"

A sieide in a lake. Lappland (Power of landscape concentrated in rocky protuberance - sieide)

Figure 10 Continued.

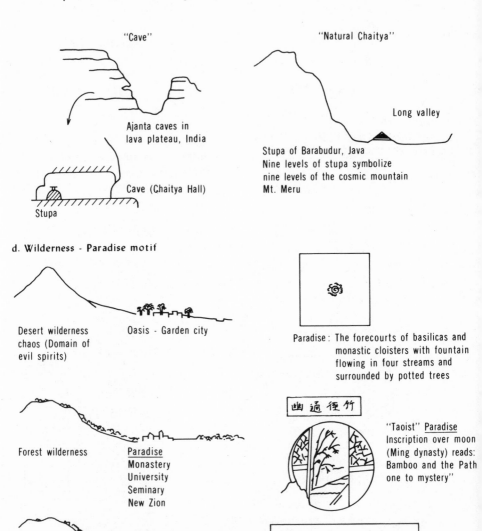

"Cave"

Ajanta caves in
lava plateau, India

Cave (Chaitya Hall)

Stupa

"Natural Chaitya"

Long valley

Stupa of Barabudur, Java
Nine levels of stupa symbolize
nine levels of the cosmic mountain
Mt. Meru

d. Wilderness - Paradise motif

Desert wilderness
chaos (Domain of
evil spirits)

Oasis - Garden city

Paradise: The forecourts of basilicas and
monastic cloisters with fountain
flowing in four streams and
surrounded by potted trees

Forest wilderness

Paradise
Monastery
University
Seminary
New Zion

"Taoist" Paradise
Inscription over moon
(Ming dynasty) reads:
Bamboo and the Path
one to mystery"

Protected wilderness
"Paradise"

Modern metropolis
"Wilderness"

Rock - and - sand garden
Zen garden of contemplation (Kyoto) ca. 1500

Figure 10 Continued.

stances such as earth, water, fire, to colors, directions, the seasons, and to some personality or cultural traits. Thus the Chinese associate metal with the autumn season, the direction west, the color white, and the mood of sorrow. In the modern world the linking of discrete phenomena by feeling remains strong. Scientists will associate autumn and the setting sun with melancholy, spring with hope, in their off guard moments.

A symbol is a repository of meanings. Meanings arise out of the more profound experiences that have accumulated through time. Profound experiences often have a sacred, other-worldly character even though they may be rooted in human biology. Insofar as symbols depend on unique events they must differ from individual to individual and from culture to culture. Insofar as they originate in experiences shared by the bulk of mankind they have a worldwide character. Natural phenomena such as sky, earth, water, rock, and vegetation are interpreted in similar ways by different peoples. Specific objects and places like pine tree, rose, spring, or grove probably have unique interpretations.

Consider the symbolic significance of the garden. At the deepest level, it may stand for the vulva of the earth, expressing humanity's yearning for ease and the assurance of fertility.[18] Specific designs and contents, however, have culturally-given meaning. For example, the monastery garden of medieval Europe is designed to be a model of paradise. Its ideal embodiment, more commonly realized in paintings than in the landscape, is packed with symbols that recall events sacred to the Christian tradition: white lilies suggest purity, red roses divine love; strawberries are the fruits of righteousness, their trefoil leaves symbolizing the trinity; and on a table in the garden are apples reminding man of his fall and his redemption by Christ.

In China, the imperial park of the Han emperors, built outside Ch'ang-an around the second century B.C., is one of the earliest landscaped enclosures of which we have a descriptive account. It was very large. Mountains, forests, and marshes lay within its circular wall, but also palaces and artificial landscapes built to reflect Taoist magical beliefs. For example, pyramidal islands were constructed in the middle of man-made lakes in imitation of the three legendary Isles of the Blest. The entire park may be seen as an idealized Taoist and shamanistic microcosm. In it the emperor enjoyed both secular and religious activities. He hunted lustily. After the slaughter, he and his entourage feasted and were entertained by dancers, clowns, and jugglers. At the end of the festivities he might climb up one of the great towers which commanded the landscape, and there commune with nature in solitude.[19]

---

[18] Paul Shepard, "The Image of the Garden," in *Man in the Landscape* (New York: Knopf, 1967), pp. 65–118.

[19] Michael Sullivan, *The Birth of Landscape Painting in China* (Berkeley and Los Angeles: University of California Press, 1962), pp. 29–30.

Gardens, together with nature poetry, found favor among the Chinese gentry from approximately the fourth century A.D. onward. Buddhism contributed to the increasing awareness of nature and to garden design, enriching its symbolic content. Unlike Occidental gardens those of China remained richly semiotic until the second half of the nineteenth century when traditional values suffered rapid decay. A garden built in the Republican period may retain many of the old symbols, though they probably say little except to the literati. In such a place the gate with the shape of the full moon invokes the idea of perfection. Animal designs of the dragon (*lung*), the bird of paradise (*feng huang*), the deer, the crane and the bat are all intended to convey meaning. Rocks and water symbolize the ancient concept of duality in nature, counterpoised in harmony. Flowers, changing with the seasons, deliver their own messages. Some are emblems of truth, purity, grace, and virtue; others speak of good fortune, longevity, and good fellowship. Willows and pines, the peach and the plum are among the popular garden trees: each is potent with meaning as, for example, the willow which represents grace and the sentiment of friendship. To walk into a Chinese garden and be aware of even a fraction of its total meaning is to enter a world that rewards the senses, the mind, and the spirit. The numerous symbols complement and enrich each other: in the idealized landscape their overall message is peace and harmony.

SACRED PLACES

The garden is a type of the sacred place. Generally speaking, sacred places are the locations of hierophany. A grove, a spring, a rock, or a mountain acquires sacred character wherever it is identified with some form of divine manifestation or with an event of overpowering significance. If Mircea Eliade is right, an early and fundamental idea in the sacredness of place is that it represents the center, the axis, or the navel of the world. Every effort to define space is an attempt to create order out of disorder: it shares some of the significance of the primordial act of creation and hence the sacred character of that act.[20] Not only the building of a sanctuary, but the building of a house and of a town traditionally called for the ritual transformation of profane space. In every instance, the spot was sanctified by some outside power, whether it be a semidivine person, a dazzling hierophany, or cosmic forces that undergird astrology and geomancy. The sign for the signal event might itself be very humble: for instance, the appearance of ants or mice could be taken as evidence of divine action. Places where charismatic leaders, endowed with divine attributes, were born or had died

20 Mircea Eliade, "Sacred Space and Making the World Sacred," in *The Sacred and the Profane* (New York: Harper Torchbook, 1961), pp. 20–65.

acquired some of their sacredness of being. Holiness was centered on the shrine or on the tomb but the sacred aura diffused over the neighboring space, and everything in it—the trees and the animals—were elevated by the association. In China it was long the custom to treat the grounds around the tombs of the sacred emperors as natural parks, in which all living things partook of the holy character of the spirit of the deceased. Such places answered the human need for religion and recreation.[21]

To the ancient Greeks the formal elements of any sanctuary were, first, the specifically sacred region in which it was set, and second, the buildings located within. "As for this place, it is clearly a holy one" (Sophocles, *Oedipus at Colonus*). The land was not a picture. To the modern eye the sites of Greek sanctuaries appear to have been selected for their pictorial qualities, but to the Greeks before the fourth century B.C. land was a force embodying the powers that ruled the world.

Vincent Scully tells us how the perception of the earth as force had undergone a gradual change between the Cretan and Mycenaean bronze age and the end of the archaic period. Cretan palaces were built so as to adapt to the forces of the earth. The ideal site included an enclosed valley in which the palace was built, a conical hill to the north or south of the palace, and a higher double-peaked mountain located some distance beyond the hill. The enclosed valley was the natural megaron, the sheltering womb. The cone symbolized the earth's motherly form; the double-peaked mountain suggested horns or breasts. The Mycenaean Greeks of the mainland shared this attitude to landscape. They too sought for the protective forms of the earth goddess. A departure was suggested by the location of Mycenae itself: this seat of pride and power lay on a hillock in the valley. The Mycenaeans were overthrown by their cousins the Dorians, who were impatient of the earth goddess. Dorians went far toward destroying the simple tie between man and land. In place of the goddess, they strove to substitute their own thunder-wielding sky god. On Crete, Dorian strongholds were built on mountains, not in the lap of valleys. Doric temples acquired a sculptural and monumental quality and appeared in all kinds of terrain, although sanctuaries dedicated to goddesses retained their traditional locations in topographical hollows. Temples dedicated to Apollo and Zeus challenged the chthonic forces. Apollo's greatest sanctuary, Delphi, lay on the lower slopes of a mountain in the heart of the Parnassus massif. Zeus was the true successor to the earth mother. His shrines occupied the tops of the highest mountains. Mount Olympus itself was his northern embodiment. Temples dedicated to Zeus were placed in the largest megara. They often

21 E. H. Schafer, "The Conservation of Nature under the T'ang dynasty," *Journal of the Economic and Social History of the Orient*, 5 (1962), 280–81.

seem to dominate, rather than adapt, to the landscapes in which they were set.[22]

In the traditions of Taoist China and pre-Dorian Greece, nature imparts virtue or power. In the Christian tradition sanctifying power is invested in man, God's vice-regent, rather than in nature. The church does not adapt to the spirit of the land: it imparts spirit to its environs. The placing of the sanctuary at the east end of the church is not an attempt to harmonize with the natural order but rather to make use of a fact (the sun rises in the east) as a symbol for the doctrine of the resurrected Christ. Christendom has its share of sacred places in grottos and near springs. Such places owe their numen not to any indwelling spirit of nature but to the miraculous appearances of martyred saints or of the Virgin Mary.[23] The monastic community in the wilderness was a model of paradise set in an unredeemed world. Wilderness was often perceived as the haunt of demons but in the neighborhood of the monastery it could acquire some of the harmony of redeemed nature and the animals in it, like their human suzerains in the monastery, lived in peace.

cyclical time and linear time

The ancients believed that movement in nature was disposed toward the circular path. The circle symbolized perfection. The moderns, following Newton's revolutionary thought, postulated the straight line as the natural path of all moving matter. Cosmos yielded to geography and landscape. The theme has many variations. It remains to add a comment on the relation of this change to the notion of time.

Time is commonly modeled on the recurrent phases of nature, those of the stars or those of the earth in rotation and revolution. Modern man recognizes these recurrent phases but for him they are little more than waves in the directional time stream. Time for him has direction, change is progressive. The eschatological viewpoint of Christianity is believed to have promoted the sense of progressive change. Yet the medieval man's sense of time, mirroring his vertical and rotary cosmos, was essentially cyclical. Not until the eighteenth century did the linear, directional concept of time become important. By then the isometric frame of space had yielded to axial lengthening and to the "open space" concept of the radial plan in architecture and landscaping. It was also the period of far ranging explora-

22 Vincent Scully, *The Earth, the Temple, and the Gods: Greek Sacred Architecture* (New Haven: Yale University Press, 1962).
23 Ernest Benz, "Die heilige Hohle in der alten Christenheit und in den ostlich-orthdoxen Kirche," *Eranos-Jahrbuch* (1953), pp. 365–432.

tions when the known geographical space of the Europeans covered nearly the whole world.

Long-distance travel and migrations may in themselves have had an effect in breaking up cyclical time and the vertical cosmos, substituting for them linear time and horizontal space. The traveler is dependent on the stars, but not so much to measure time as distance. The time differential is of importance to the navigator because it can be converted into units of distance. To various peoples of the northern hemisphere the polar star symbolized the axis of the world and of eternity. The ancient Egyptians believed it to be the final destination of the dead, since alone of the heavenly quarters the region about the polar star did not sink below the horizon. But for the explorers, traders, and emigrants moving south across the equator the polar star proves to be mortal. Sedentary peoples of the middle latitudes tend to accept the course of the seasons as an inexorable fact of nature: like the movement of the stars it is an apt image of eternity. But travelers and colonists who move along the meridians experience the flux, not only of the seasons, but of seasonal rhythms, so that at the equator the seemingly universal successions of nature disappear and beyond it, in the southern hemisphere, they are reversed.

the ideal city
and
symbols of
transcendence

The city liberates its citizens from the need for incessant toil to maintain their bodies and from the feeling of impotence before nature's vagaries. It is an achievement that we now tend to denigrate or forget. As ideal, the city seems largely lost to us while its defects as a physical environment, particularly since the Industrial Revolution, become increasingly obtrusive. In the past the city was looked up to for different reasons. Ancient settlements that arose as ritual centers promised the permanence and order of the cosmos to fragile human beings. The Greek polis provided the opportunity for free men to achieve immortality of thought and action, and so rise above their biological servitude. "City air sets a man free" is a German proverb of the Middle Ages: free men lived within the city wall, serfs outside in the country. The supremacy of the city as an ideal over rural life is woven into the meaning of words. Since the time of Aristotle, "city" to philosophers and poets stood for the perfect community. The citizen inhabited the city; serfs and villeins (villains) lived in the countryside. The city of man, where the bishop had his seat, was an image of the City of God: in the remote country or heath were the heathens; in the rural district or village (*pagus*) were the peasants or pagans.

emergence of the city ideal

In this book we are interested in the city both because it represents a human and environmental ideal (chapter 11), and because it is an environment (chapter 12). The origin of the city is a complex question that we cannot explore here. But the question may not be brushed aside altogether, for what we think is the primitive nature of the city will influence our evaluation of its importance as an ideal. If, for example, the economic interpretation is accepted without qualification, we should be at a loss to explain the city's power to command awe and allegiance. The economic interpretation sees the city as a consequence of economic surplus: the products that local villages cannot consume are exchanged at a convenient place, which eventually develops into a market town and city. Obviously cities have to be supported by their surrounding countryside. But an area may give rise to thriving agriculture and high population density without generating urbanism. On the highlands of New Guinea agriculture can support population densities of up to 500 persons per square mile, but this does not mean that urban life is about to develop. Incipient urbanism may in fact appear in areas of relatively low per acre productivity. The essential requirement is the existence of a central bureaucracy that has the power to command food and services from the people of the countryside. As Paul Wheatley put it, "the human frame [is] almost infinitely extensible and that, consequently, it [is] almost always possible to wring from even the most wretched of cultivators yet another exaction for the support of the central bureaucracy."[1] Power is seldom expressed directly as a physical force even in the animal world. In the human world it is exercised through the recognition and acceptance of the symbols of legitimacy. The priest-king is such a potent symbol. He is a semidivine being, an intermediary between heaven and earth, the co-creator of the cosmos and the guarantor of order.

When urbanism is traced back to its primary centers and into the distant past, we find not the marketplace or fortress but the idea of the supernatural creation of a world.[2] The agent is a god, a priest-king or hero; the locus of creation is the center of the world. That center is usually marked in some way. Beginning perhaps as a tribal shrine, it develops into massive and extensive ceremonial complexes that include different combinations of such architectural elements as platforms, terraces, temples, palaces, court-

---

[1] Paul Wheatley, "Proleptic Observations on the Origins of Urbanism," in *Liverpool Essays in Geography,* R. W. Steel and R. Lawton, eds. (London: Longmans, Green, 1967), p. 324

[2] Paul Wheatley, *The Pivot of the Four Quarters: A Preliminary Enquiry into the Origins and Character of the Ancient Chinese City* (Chicago: Aldine-Atherton, 1971).

yards, stairways, and pyramids. The city transcends the uncertainties of life; it reflects the precision, the order, and the predictability of the heavens. Before literacy is at all widespread, a world view is sustained by oral tradition, ritual, and (not least) the semiotic potency of architecture. Life may be more demanding in an ancient city than in a Neolithic village; but among the rites and the architectural splendor, a man in the city, however humble, has something that the villager does not have—a share in the pageantry of a far larger world.

Ceremonial centers did not always draw permanent settlers to their fringes. For example, some of the Maya shrines and those of the Dieng plateau in Java were located in places either so remote or so agriculturally unproductive that they probably never attracted large stable populations. Other than priests, caretakers, and craftsmen these ceremonial complexes were empty for most of the year. They came to life only during seasonal festivals. From the secular perspective of modern times, it surprises us to see how far peoples in the past would go toward the construction of cities of imposing edifices largely for ceremonial and symbolic reasons. Consider Persepolis, built ca. 520–460 B.C. A generally accepted view is that Persepolis was planned as the royal residence of the Achaemenid kings, the capital of an empire in which the magnificence of the palaces proclaimed royal power and pride. Yet the inscriptions and documents found among the ruins were religious rather than political or economic in nature. They declared in solemn language that the city was erected by the grace of God; that the buildings attained supreme beauty and perfection; and that under the inspiration of Ahura Mazda, the Persian kings mediated between the divine and the human worlds. Ancient peoples of the Near East were acutely conscious of the fragility of life. They sought to attain a sense of order and permanence through participation in cosmic events, in the seasonal rites performed by a mediator-ruler in a resplendent setting. Persepolis was not a political capital nor even a luxury abode of the monarch, for it was rarely occupied. It was a ritual city, a *Civitas Dei* on earth.[3]

On the Indian subcontinent, Palitana is the outstanding example of a city that was built for the gods alone. Its shrines in squares and stately enclosures—half palace, half fortress—cover the twin peaks of the sacred Shetrunja hills in Kàthiawar. One visitor describes Palitana as

> truly a city of temples, for, except a few tanks, there is nothing else within the gates, and there is a cleanliness withal, about every square and passage, porch and hall, that is itself no mean source of pleasure. The silence, too,

3 Arthur Upham Pope, "Persepolis as a Ritual City," *Archaeology* 10, No. 2 (1957), 123–30.

is striking. . . . The top of the hill consists of two ridges, each about 250 yards long, with a valley between. Each of these ridges, and the two large enclosures that fill the valley, are surrounded by massive battlemented walls fitted for defence. The buildings on both ridges, again, are divided into separate enclosures, called *tuks,* generally containing one principal temple, with varying numbers of smaller ones. Each of these enclosures is protected by strong gates and walls, and all gates are carefully closed at sundown.[4]

Palitana is a monument to the piety of the Jains from all parts of India. It is raised in marble splendor upon the lonely and majestic Shetrunja hills; like the mansions of another world it is far removed from the ordinary tread of mortals.

symbols of cosmos and urban forms

As a symbol of the cosmos, the city takes on the regular geometric shape of a circle, square, rectangle, or some other polygon. An architectural index of the vertical such as the ziggurat, the pillar, and the dome also serves to highlight the city's transcendental significance. The circle divided into four sectors by two axes symbolizes heaven. The quadripartite circular city, an Etruscan ideal, was the celestial *templum* transcribed to earth; planning within the four sectors was tied to the art of reading omens. Some scholars take the term *Roma quadrata* to mean quadripartite and that Rome at its founding was a circular city with the *mundus* (the place of departed souls) at the center. The ancient notions of center, the intersecting axes, and the four quarters of the heavenly vault were intermixed in the Christian era with images of the cross and heavenly Jerusalem. Werner Müller believes that some of these elements can be discerned in the plans of certain late Medieval and Renaissance cities.[5]

The circle is a figure with an infinite number of sides. In practice, peoples in different parts of the world have found it convenient to reduce infinity to four, to the four sides of a rectangle, the four quarters of heaven and earth, the four seasons, and the cardinal directions. Mathematically it is easier to represent the cosmos by a square than by a circle. The meanings of the circle and the square overlap but they do not coincide. In China, for example, where they appear together as an architectural complex the circle represents heaven or nature, the square the earth or the artificial world of man (Figure 11).

[4] *Imperial Gazeteer of India,* XIX (Oxford: Clarendon Press, 1908), p. 363.
[5] Werner Müller, *Die heilige Stadt: Roma Quadrata, himmlisches Jerusalem und die Mythe vom Weltnabel* (Stuttgart: Kohlhammer, 1961).

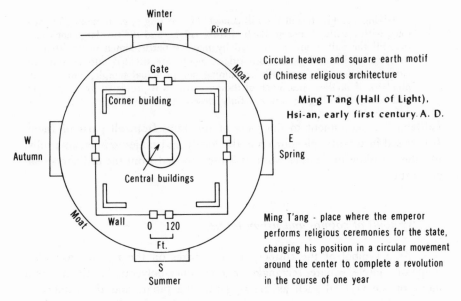

Winter

N   River

Gate

Corner building

W
Autumn

Central buildings

E
Spring

Wall   0   120

Ft.

S

Summer

Circular heaven and square earth motif
of Chinese religious architecture

Ming T'ang (Hall of Light),
Hsi-an, early first century A. D.

Ming T'ang - place where the emperor
performs religious ceremonies for the state,
changing his position in a circular movement
around the center to complete a revolution
in the course of one year

Figure 11   The symbolism of the circle and the square in architecture.

CIRCULAR AND RADIAL-CONCENTRIC IDEALS

Plans and diagrams of ideal cities often show them as circular—real ones rarely are (see Figure 12, p. 160). What can we say about circular cities of antiquity? Perhaps the earliest of which we have any evidence are the walled, circular settlements of predynastic Egypt. The hieroglyphic determinative of "town" is a circular enclosure divided into four parts by two intersecting axes. Was the Egyptian city, like the ideal Etruscan city, a model of the heavenly vault? It seems most unlikely, and we have no way of knowing. In the ancient world, Hittite towns of Anatolia seem to have been planned primarily with defense in mind. They were built at strategic locations. Their walls, oval or polygonal in shape, made skilful use of topography. Their residential quarters grew mainly uncontrolled through "natural" agglomeration. However, some Neo-Hittite settlements displayed plans of great regularity, thus inviting the conjecture that their design reflected symbolic intent. A striking example is Sam'al (Cincirli), founded near the beginning of the first millennium B.C. and incorporated into the Assyrian empire some two hundred years later. It was enclosed by two nearly perfect concentric circular walls, each provided with a hundred rectangular towers. These circular walls, unlike those of earlier Hittite cities, appear to have been built with little regard to the topography of the land. They were entered through three equally spaced double gateways, of which the strongest lay in the south. The south gate led to the citadel which stood on a mound slightly off the center of the city. A stone wall with round towers protected it. Secondary walls divided the citadel into four zones: four palaces with their dependencies and a barracks complex occupied the upper levels.[6]

Herodotus described Ecbatana, capital of the Iranian Medes, as a city of concentric circles. His story of its founding encapsulates certain steps in the transition from villages to ideal city: it is a model of the noneconomic interpretation of city origin. According to Herodotus, at the time when the Medes threw off the yoke of Assyria they lived in scattered villages without central authority. Quarrels among the villagers were common. For lack of a judicial system, a man who had distinguished himself by the fairness of his opinions was sought out to arbitrate among the different interests of the villagers. His name was Deioces. However, Deioces eventually grew weary of spending so much time regulating other people's affairs to the neglect of his own. He withdrew, with the consequence that lawlessness prevailed over the land. The villagers in their distress resolved to appoint a king and Deioces was chosen for this office. As king, Deioces required a palace and a city to be built for him. Since none of the existing settlements measured up to the dignity of kingship, the Medes built Ecbatana which became the focus of their world. The walls of the new capital, as Herodotus described it, were of great size and strength, rising in circles one within the other. They gained in height toward the center. The nature of the ground, which was a gentle hill, favored this arrangement but it was mainly achieved by art. The number of circular walls was seven, and their battlements were colored: white for the outermost encirclement, then black, scarlet, blue, orange, silver, and finally gold for the innermost wall that surrounded Deioces' palace. It is probable that the concentric zones of the cities were occupied by different castes of society. The king and his nobles lived at the center. The successively lower orders with their more numerous members occupied the successively larger and topographically lower zones until the outermost wall was reached: beyond it lived the common people. An ordered and hierarchical cosmos, symbolized by the rising tier of seven circles, displaced the earthbound world of villagers.[7]

The ideal city of Plato combined the circle with the square. The legendary island-continent of Atlantis itself was made up of concentric rings of land and water. On the secret inner mount stood the citadel, which was surrounded by a succession of round walls. The outermost wall was covered with brass, the next with tin, and the third, which encircled the citadel, flashed with the reddish glow of copper. At the center of the citadel stood the holy temple dedicated to Poseidon and Cleiton, and made inaccessible

[6] P. Lavedan, "Les Hittites et la cité circulaire," in *Histoire de l'Urbanisme,* I (Paris: Henri Laurens, 1926), pp. 56–63.
[7] Herodotus, *History,* Book I, pp. 96–99.

by its enclosure of gold. In another depiction of the ideal world, Plato noted that the city should be placed at the center of the country. First, temples were built in a spot called the Acropolis, and surrounded with a circular wall. The parcellation of the entire city and country radiated from this point. The city was divided into twelve portions, the size of which was to vary with the quality of the land.[8] What influences lay behind Plato's idealized city plans? Little is known. In the first place Plato gave only vague descriptions of the physical layout. His prototype for the citadel on Atlantis might have been influenced by pre-Hellenic fortifications in Greece or the ring of walls encircling Mantaneia built about 460 B.C. Isolated central buildings, such as the Tholos of Epidarus, were circular for religio-aesthetic reasons. And he could have known of the concentric plan of the Persian capital. But it seems more likely that Plato's system of circles, squares, colors, and numbers reflected the cosmological doctrines of the Pythagoreans rather than what he could see in the environment of his time. Cosmological diagrams can rarely be translated, without major surgery, to the untidy terrestrial world of men. Aristophanes was aware of the concept of circular and geometric cities: in the *Birds* he made fun of Plato, his disciples, and the rigid planners.

A remarkable round city of the Islamic world was Medinat-as-Salam (Old Baghdad), the capital of the Abbasid caliphs (see Figure 12). Since the circular form was not characteristic of the Islamic tradition, the design of the Abbasid capital probably showed the influence of the circular cities of the Sassanian Persians: for example, the circular plan of Ctesiphon to the southeast of Baghdad, and the concentric city of Firuzabad where the main cross roads were oriented to the compass points and the twelve sectors were named after the signs of the Zodiac. Construction on Medinat-as-Salam began in A.D. 762. One hundred thousand workers built with such speed that the caliph al-Mansur was able to move in his government the following year. Al-Mansur's city had three perfect circular walls: gates were placed at the four intercardinal points. At the center of the round city stood the great palace. Its area covered a space measuring 200 yards square, and its central structure was crowned by a great green dome the summit of which, topped with the figure of a horseman, reached a height of 120 feet above the ground and could be seen from all quarters of Baghdad. Next to the palace stood the Great Mosque. Other buildings in the Round City included various public offices such as the treasury, armory, chancery, the land tax office, the chamberlain's office, and the palaces of the younger sons of the caliph. Residential quarters lay within the walls but merchants were discouraged from establishing themselves in the perfect astronomical order. They had their own quarters along the river quay. Like all circular

[8] Plato, *Critias,* pp. 113, 116; *Laws,* Book V, p. 745.

cities Medinat-as-Salam did not survive long in its original form. Within a century of its founding sprawling suburbs grew up beyond the gates and overwhelmed the Round City, which was allowed to decay.[9]

The theocentric world view of the European Middle Ages might be expected to favor the establishment of radial-concentric towns. St. Augustine's City of God was circular. Numerous graphic depictions of Jerusalem in the medieval period showed the temple located at the center of a circular walled city. In fact the idea had little impact on urban form. The great majority of medieval towns were market settlements that had elementary privileges of self-government. Their preurban nucleus might be noneconomic: a secular or ecclesiastical stronghold around which traders and farmers congregated for protection. Unplanned growth could well have brought about a radial-concentric pattern of shops, residences, and roads, focused on the castle or abbey, and enclosed by a round wall. The central edifice of stone towered over its base skirt of lesser substance, and where the focal point was a church its liturgical orientation further imposed a certain regularity to the arrangement of houses and streets. "The circular shape of a medieval town is not unusual," says Gutkind. Bergues, Aix-la-Chapelle, Bram near Carcassonne, Malines, Middleburg, Nördlingen, and Aranda de Duero are well-known examples. The ground plan of some settlements, however, had the geometric order of the ideal city. Take the French town of Brive: its center was the abbey and its spacious square. The abbey, the town's *axis mundi,* was oriented to the east. The wall enclosing Brive was roughly circular, and pierced by seven gates. The town had concentric roads and seven main streets radiating from the ecclesiastical center. But Brive departed from the genuine ideal city in that it grew from the center outward, and not from the periphery (the defining walls) inward.[10]

Between 1150 and 1350 numerous fortified towns (*bastides*) were built, particularly in southern France, in response to the need for defense during the Albigensian wars and the long wars between the English and the French. Liberal charters as well as security attracted country people to these centers. Bastides were the planned towns of medieval Europe. Their shapes varied. Most had grid patterns, some had no regular shape, and some were radial-concentric. Members of the last type were usually grouped around a central element, be it church or open space. The new towns (*villes neuves*) lacked cosmological symbolism despite their beginnings as asylums protected by the Truce of God. There was, however, the custom of marking the town's

9 Guy Le Strange, *Baghdad during the Abbasid Caliphate from Contemporary Arabic and Persian Sources* (Oxford: Clarendon Press, 1924); Jacob Lassner, *The Topography of Baghdad in the Early Middle Ages* (Detroit: Wayne State University Press, 1970).

10 E. A. Gutkind, *Urban Development in Western Europe: France and Belgium* (New York: Free Press, 1970), p. 41.

boundary by four crosses at the four points of the compass, within which the future settlement was traced on the ground.[11]

Far more than the Middle Ages, the Renaissance and the Baroque were periods of idealistic town planning.[12] The movement began in Italy with the works of people like Alberti (1452–60), Filarete (1460–64), Cataneo (1554–67), and continued later in France and Germany. The circle and the square stood for perfection: combinations of these figures were prominent in idealized planning. For example, the basic design of Filarete's ideal town Sforzinda consisted of a circle and two squares. Within the outer circular wall lay an eight-pronged star made of two squares, one oriented to the cardinal directions and the other to the intercardinal points. Church, town hall and other public buildings stood at the center. Streets radiated outward from the central complex of buildings to the inflection points of the star. The ideal towns of Giorgio Martini (mid-15th century), Girolamo Maggi (1564), and the German architect Daniel Specklin (1589) were all eight-pointed, radial-concentric in design. Vincenzo Scamozzi's ideal town of 1615 had twelve points, and was round in general outline, but the street pattern within the fortifications followed a grid pattern.

Few circular designs of the Renaissance were actually built. An example of the translation of an ideal into reality was Palmanova, fortress city under the rule of Venice. Work on it began in 1593. The basic shape of a nine-sided polygon acquired the complex outline of a star through the addition of fortified triangular protrusions. The central market, with its prominent tower, was a hexagon. Streets were concentric and radial. The design of Palmanova owed much to Filarete's Sforzinda. Scamozzi was probably its architect. From the time of Alberti onward, Renaissance planners favored round fortifications and ideal towns of roundish outline with polygons nestling inside. This bias was reenforced by renewed interest in Vitruvius and Plato. In construction, however, the radial and circular paradigm often had to give way to the simpler design of grid-pattern streets and to cities of rectangular and irregular outline.

The bounded circle suggests completion and wholeness; the open sector of a circle suggests the possibility for infinite extension. In the seventeenth and early part of the eighteenth century, planners introduced two design elements that came to be identified with the Baroque style: radiating sectors and focal points. Both were suited to express the period's fondness for display, its ideology of uninhibited energy, and the move toward political cen-

11 Joan Evans, *Life in Medieval France* (London: Phaidon Press, 1962), p. 43.
12 Helen Rosenau, *The Ideal City: In Its Architectural Revolution* (London: Routledge & Kegan Paul, 1959), pp. 33–68; R. E. Dickinson, *The West European City* (London: Routledge & Kegan Paul, 1961), pp. 417–45.

tralization.[13] A fanlike design allowed for unlimited penetration of the countryside. It could be accommodated only outside of cluttered cities. Versailles and Karlsruhe are outstanding examples of residential and court towns that expressed the Baroque period's sense of power and grandeur. At Versailles, three straight avenues converged on the Place d'Armes before the palace. At Karlsruhe thirty-two radial axes met before the Margrave's castle. Only nine, however, functioned as streets; the remaining twenty-three fanned through the great surrounding forest. At the heart of the town was the palace. Public buildings stood around the square before the Margrave's residence. Two-storied houses of the nobility congregated in the Innere Zirkel, beyond which stretched the one-storied houses of the populace.

The medieval core of Paris was concentric in pattern and focused on the Cathedral of Notre Dame on the Isle de la Cité. When Louis XV sought to display royal prestige in the crowded quarter of the capital city he could not hope to impose on the existent medieval pattern a radial-concentric design centered on himself. What he aspired to do, as M. Patte's prize-winning plan of 1746 showed, was to impose on Paris nineteen *places royales*. These were to be circles and squares with radiating streets, and at the center of each star was to stand a statue of the Divine Monarch. But even in the plan it was clear that the rays of the stars could not extend very far: unlike the fanning avenues of residential court towns in the suburbs, those in Paris had to end abruptly on ordinary streets.[14]

The capital city is a symbol of national pride and aspiration. When an important city or capital is built, designers tend to favor the Baroque plan of circles, plazas, and radiating avenues because of its suitability for aesthetic display: Washington, D.C. and Canberra in Australia are two well-known examples. On a smaller scale and reflecting a different social ideal are the new towns of the twentieth century: these too may adopt the circular pattern. Some of them have been inspired by Ebenezer Howard's design of 1898. Howard's diagram of the garden city is radial-concentric (Figure 12). He put the circular garden and its ring of public buildings at the center, with residences and parks beyond. This modern design for communal living is remote from the pomp of the Baroque capital and even more from the magical and cosmological symbolism of the ancient Medean capital of Ecbatana. However, they all subscribe to the circular module; they aspire toward an image of a social and spatial order that is patterned ultimately on the vault of heaven.

[13] Lewis Mumford, *The City in History* (New York: Harcourt Brace Jovanovich, 1961), pp. 386–409.
[14] Pierre Lavedan, *Histoire de l'urbanisme: Renaissance et temps moderns,* II (Paris: Henri Laurens, 1941), pp. 358–63; Sibyl Moholy-Nagy, *Matrix of Man: An Illustrated History of Urban Environment* (New York: Praeger, 1968), pp. 72–73.

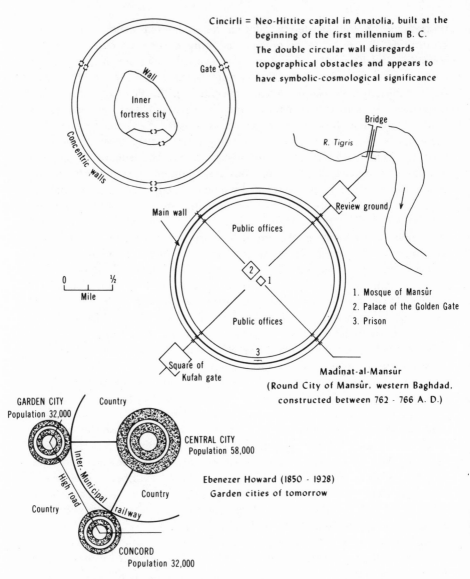

Cincirli = Neo-Hittite capital in Anatolia, built at the beginning of the first millennium B. C. The double circular wall disregards topographical obstacles and appears to have symbolic-cosmological significance

Gate

Wall

Inner fortress city

Concentric walls

Bridge

R. Tigris

Main wall

Public offices

Review ground

0 ½
Mile

2
1

1. Mosque of Mansûr
2. Palace of the Golden Gate
3. Prison

Public offices

3

Square of Kufah gate

Madînat-al-Mansûr
(Round City of Mansûr, western Baghdad, constructed between 762 - 766 A. D.)

GARDEN CITY
Population 32,000

Country

CENTRAL CITY
Population 58,000

Inter-Municipal

High road

Country

railway

Country

Ebenezer Howard (1850 - 1928)
Garden cities of tomorrow

CONCORD
Population 32,000

Figure 12   Structuring space: circular ideal cities.

RECTANGULAR IDEALS

The square in conjunction with the circle symbolizes perfection and the cosmos: alone its meaning is less clear (see Figures 13 and 14). The square, as suggested earlier, is a skeletal index of the cosmos ideally represented by the circle. When the round order of heaven is brought down to earth it assumes the shape of a rectangle with sides oriented to the cardinal directions. Yet we also know that the simplest way of dividing up the land is to survey it according to some grid system. For this reason new towns and new field plots that have been laid down by a central authority often adopt a rectangular net. Its existence does not in itself justify the interpretation that it had cosmological significance, even in the ancient world when symbolism more deeply permeated human thought patterns. The square-shaped workmen's villages and fortress towns of ancient Egypt, the rectangular plan of the Hippodamian cities of Greece, the centuriated landholdings of Rome, and the grid-patterned towns (*bastides*) of the Middle Ages appear to call for no other explanation than convenience and economy.

Yet we have evidence that, in different cultures and at different times in the past, the rectangle stood for the cosmos; it was at least accepted as the appropriate frame of the ideally organized society. In the Old Testament, for example, we find the Lord telling the prophet Ezekiel, "You shall set apart the whole reserve, twenty-five thousand cubits square, as sacred, as far as the holding of the city." The four sides of the city—northern, eastern, southern, and western—were each named after the tribes of Israel, and each side had three gates. "The perimeter of the city shall be eighteen thousand cubits; and the city's name for ever after shall be Jehavah-shammah." In *Revelations* the isometric and orthogonal character of the heavenly Jerusalem was emphasized. It "was built as a square, and was as wide as it was long. It measured by his rod twelve thousand furlongs, its length and breadth and height being equal." As in the Jerusalem foretold to Ezekiel, St. John saw that the city wall had twelve gates.

Predynastic Egypt had fortified settlements with circular walls. But unlike Sumeria, early unification of the Nile Valley under one indisputable authority left little room for the development of autonomous city-states. We have only scant evidence of the plans of ancient Egyptian towns for they were built mostly with perishable material. Stone was used in funerary monuments while dwellings, even palaces, were made with mudbrick and wood. The layout of one capital of the New Kingdom, Akhetaton, is now fairly well known. Some parts of it, rebuilt *ex novo* in 1396–1354 B.C., are rectangular. The palace in the central city is directed north-to-south parallel to the Royal way, and shows signs of planning; but otherwise Akhetaton lacks evidence of design. Important people would seem to have settled first on large plots along the main streets, followed by others of more modest means near them, while the poor built their houses in the interstices.[15]

In Egypt orthogonal planning based on cosmological principles appeared among architectural complexes designed to serve the dead rather than the living. The first great funerary assemblage of rectangular and pyramidal

[15] H. W. Fairman, "Town Planning in Pharaonic Egypt," *Town Planning Review,* 20 (1949), 33–51.

design was achieved masterfully in the temple city of the pharaoh Zoser at Sakkara, ca. 2700 B.C. During the Old and Middle Kingdoms, cities adjoining the ritual clusters of pyramids and temples were created by royal charter to house the numerous workmen and masons constructing the pyramids. After their completion the city continued to accommodate the priests performing the royal funerary services, as well as farmers and laborers who worked the land set aside to produce revenue for the maintenance of the monument and the performance of rites. Following the orthogonality and cardinal orientation of the pyramids, the layout of the adjoining city was strictly orthogonal and aligned north to south. Lahun, the largest known pyramid city to date, was built for the priests and workmen serving and working on the pyramid of Senusert II (1897–1879 B.C.). However, workmen's villages attached to cities of the living were also rectangular in form and walled as, for example, the workmen's village east of Akhetaton, built some five hundred years after Lahun. Like the streets of Lahun, those of Akhetaton village ran north-south. Again we face the problem of interpreting the rectangular design which answers both symbolic and practical needs.[16]

Assyrian city-planning in the first millennium B.C. was characteristically orthogonal (Figure 13). In this it probably showed the influence of Egypt rather than of Sumer, for the ancient cities of Sumer tended to be irregular or oval-shaped, and their internal pattern of houses and streets gave little evidence of design. Nimrud, second capital of Assyria, was built in the early part of the ninth century B.C. on a grand scale. A mud-brick wall surrounded a rectangular compound of nearly 360 hectares. A fortified inner city stood near the Tigris River: within it were palaces, temples, public buildings, and residences of the rich. The outer compound provided space for the majority of the population as well as open fields, parks, and zoological gardens. What we see here is the clear division of walled, rectangular space into an inner sacred-official precinct and an outer compound for the populace. Khorasabad, the unfinished capital of Sargon II (721–705 B.C.), was an almost perfect square, oriented so that the corners of the square pointed to the cardinal directions. Its strong wall enclosed some 300 hectares. An unexplained feature of the plan was the position of the fortified citadel with its complement of ziggurat, temples, and palace: it stood against the northwestern wall— and protruded beyond its alignment—rather than at the center.

In southern Mesopotamia, Babylon and Borsippa display the same characteristics of shape, orientation, and spatial organization as the older cities of the Assyrian north. Herodotus gives a sketch of Babylon which,

16 Alexander Badawy, *A History of Egyptian Architecture* (Berkeley and Los Angeles: University of California Press, 1968).

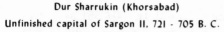

Unfinished capital of Sargon II, 721 - 705 B. C.

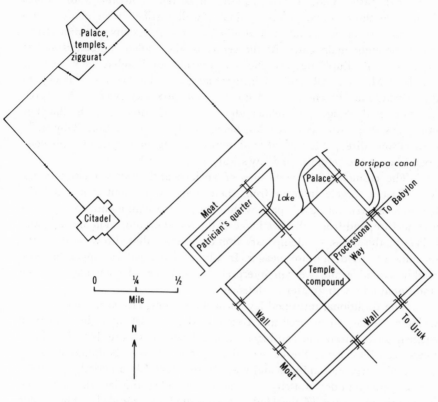

Borsippa (Birs Nimrud)
Owes final shape to Nebuchadnezzar II, 604 - 561 B. C.

Figure 13 Structuring space: rectangular ideal cities with the corners pointing toward the cardinal directions.

though inaccurate in detail, is vivid and correct in essence. He says that Babylon

> stands on a broad plain, and is an exact square. In magnificence no other city approaches it. It is surrounded, in the first place, by a broad and deep moat, full of water, behind which rises the wall. In the circuit of the wall are a hundred gates [towers?], all of brass. The city is divided into two portions by a broad and swift stream, the Euphrates. Houses are mostly three or four stories high, while streets run in straight lines.[17]

[17] Herodotus, *History*, Book I, pp. 178–80.

In fact Babylon, as the creation of Nebuchadnezzar II (604–561 B.C.), was a rectangle rather than an exact square. Its corners, however, were roughly directed to the cardinal points. A double wall fortified with many towers surrounded it, enclosing an area of 405 hectares. A system of major streets led to the eight main gates. At the center of the walled compound and to the east of the Euphrates was the holy precinct of Esaglia: in it rose the temple of Marduk, Babylon's main sanctuary, and the "Tower of Babel" or the "Foundation of Heaven and Earth." Borsippa also owed its final construction and design to Nebuchadnezzar II. Compared with Babylon, Borsippa's shape was more regular, being nearly a square. Like Babylon its corners were directed to the cardinal points; and again a square temple compound lay at the center of the city's walled enclosure.[18]

The cosmological significance of ancient and medieval cities in the Near East is largely inferred from their shape and orientation, from the hierarchical structuring of space within the walled compound, the types of architecture, and from what we know of the social organization and religious beliefs of the times. Contemporary literary sources that throw light on the meaning of city design are meager. In China, documentary support is more readily available and we can interpret the sociocosmological ideals of the traditional city with greater confidence.

The traditional form and layout of the Chinese city is an image of the Chinese cosmos, an ordered and consecrated world set apart by a massive earthen girdle from the contingent world beyond (Figure 14). In Shang times (ca. 1200 B.C.), the consecration of city site and buildings required the ritual sacrifice of animals and men. In the early Chou period (ca. 1000–500 B.C.) the founder of a city, wearing special robes and jewels, studied the geomantic properties of the land and consulted tortoise shells. The center and the circumference must be defined and consecrated. The walls, the altar of the earth, and the ancestral temple were among the first parts of the city to be built. The shape of the altar was square as the earth was square.

Until the time of major socioeconomic changes in the tenth and eleventh centuries, the design of the Chinese city retained in large measure its antique symbolism. The prolonged period of political disunion from the third to the sixth centuries, and the successive invasions of North China by non-Chinese peoples appear not to have broken down the basic rites of city building. The construction of Ch'ang-an, capital of the reunified empire of first the Sui and then the T'ang rulers, reflected the weighing of both functional and symbolic needs.

[18] Paul Lampl, *Cities and Planning in the Ancient Near East* (New York: Braziller, 1968).

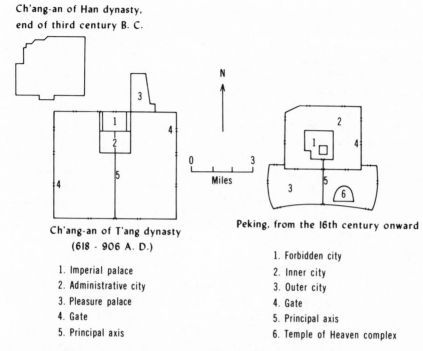

Ch'ang-an of Han dynasty,
end of third century B. C.

N

0   3
Miles

Ch'ang-an of T'ang dynasty
(618 - 906 A. D.)

1. Imperial palace
2. Administrative city
3. Pleasure palace
4. Gate
5. Principal axis

Peking, from the 16th century onward

1. Forbidden city
2. Inner city
3. Outer city
4. Gate
5. Principal axis
6. Temple of Heaven complex

Figure 14 Structuring space: rectangular ideal cities, oriented to the cardinal directions.

What were the symbolic needs?[19] As prescribed in the ritual books and absorbed into tradition, a royal city should have the following characteristics: orientation to the cardinal points; a square shape girdled by walls; twelve gates in the walls to represent the twelve months; an inner precinct to contain the royal residences and audience halls; a public market to the north of the inner enclosure; a principal street leading from the south gate of the palace enclosure to the central south gate of the city wall; two sacred places, the royal ancestral temple and the altar of the earth, on either side of the principal street. The meaning of the design is clear. The royal palace at the center dominates the city and, symbolically, the world. It separates the center of profane activity, the market, from the centers of religious observances. The ruler faces south in his audience hall, where he receives officials and conducts public business. His back is turned literally to the market. Such an ideal plan has never found complete architectural expression. Some elements are very old: for example, proper orientation. Others are relatively

[19] A. F. Wright, "Symbolism and Function: Reflections on Ch'ang-an and Other Great Cities," *Journal of Asian Studies*, 24 (1965), 667–79.

recent: for example, clearly demarcated spaces. An inner palace city that was set apart from the market and non-royal residences first came into existence, it would seem, only with the construction of Lo-yang as the capital of the Northern Wei dynasty (A.D. 495–534).[20]

The magnificent city of Ch'ang-an did not comply strictly with the ideal pattern. During the T'ang period the city was a vast rectangular enclosure, measuring six miles east-west and five miles north-south. It displayed the proper orientation, and had three gates on each of three sides of the enclosure; its altar of earth and royal ancestral temple were correctly located with respect to the central north-south axis. However, the palace quarter was backed against the north wall instead of being placed at the center; and this departure preempted the space for the official market, which in T'ang Ch'ang-an was divided into two sections and established in the eastern and western parts of the city.

Kublai Khan's capital of Cambaluc (forebear of modern Peking) was built under the supervision of an Arab architect. Yet its plan closely followed the canons of the traditional Chinese city. When Marco Polo visited Cambaluc in 1273, it appeared to him as square-shaped with the prescribed set of three gates along each side of the walls. The streets were straight and wide and laid out in squares like a chessboard. Within the outer enclosure were two walled precincts, the innermost of which housed the Khan's palace. Under the Ming emperors, the walls of Peking were shifted slightly to the south. The shift altered the shape of the wall from square to rectangle but it also brought the inner precincts closer to the center. The enclosure of suburbs which grew up outside the south wall further disturbed the simplicity of the original shape. Notwithstanding these departures, Peking remains an impressive specimen of traditional Chinese city planning.

Cosmic symbolization in the design of cities found more explicit expression in China than perhaps in any other civilization. The Chinese imperial capital was a diagram of the universe. The palace and the principal north-south axis stood for the Polar star and the celestial meridian. The Emperor in the interior of his courts surveyed the southerly world of men. In Peking's Forbidden City the Wu or Meridian Gate pierced the south wall. The Emperor was borne through the Meridian Gate into the Forbidden City while civil and military officials entered by the east and west gates. The Four Quadrants in the heavenly vault became the Four Directions or Four Seasons of the terrestrial grid. Each side of the square may be identified with the daily position of the sun or with each of the four seasons. The east side, with the blue dragon as its symbol, was the locus of the rising sun and of spring. The south side corresponded to the sun

20 Ho Ping-ti, "Lo-yang, A.D. 495–534: A Study of Physical and Socio-Economic Planning of a Metropolitan Area," *Harvard Journal of Asiatic Studies,* 26 (1966), 52–101.

at its zenith and to summer, symbolized by the red phoenix of *yang* ascendancy. At the west side the white tiger stood for autumn, twilight, weapon, and war. The cold region of the north lay behind man's back, and was symbolized by hibernating reptiles, the color black, and the *yin* element of water.[21]

Such a terrestrial model of the cosmos embraced the aristocracy and the farmers. It had meaning to an agricultural people persuaded to depend on some central authority for the regulation of calendar and of waterworks. But it had little to say to the craftsmen, whose work was not ruled by the cycles of nature, and even less to the merchants. These professions ranked low in the social hierarchy. Ideal cities patterned after some heavenly model tended to be unsympathetic to the idea of trade. They stood for stability while commerce made for growth and change. Time and again the frame of the ideal city yielded to the pressure of economic and population expansion: it assumed new shapes that reflected the laws of the market rather than those of heaven. In China the ideal pattern broke down repeatedly in the past. Yet a distinctive fact of Chinese urbanism was the persistence of the "cosmicized" city as a paradigm of design.

On the Indian subcontinent, city-building flourished on the Indus plain in prehistoric times. The architectural monuments and towns of the Harappan culture matched those of lower Mesopotamia in size and technological advance. Perhaps as a result of the excessive exploitation of the natural environment, the Indus urban tradition suffered decline and was finally disrupted by the invadnig Aryans whose material culture was less sophisticated than the civilization they displaced. The newcomers were mostly farmers and herders without any proud architectural heritage. In the Brahmanical caste system architects and builders ranked rather low on the social scale. The later Aryans, however, engaged in town planning and building, perhaps as the result of having absorbed the urban values of the people who preceded them. In the *Shilpashastras,* sacred tradition extended very high regard to the architectural profession. By the early part of the Gupta period (A.D. 320–480), and probably much earlier, the higher Hindu artificers claimed spiritual equality with the Brahmans.[22]

Indian town planning was vested with sacred and scriptural authority. "The proper place for each kind of building was strictly prescribed, as well as the measurements of the actual buildings down to the smallest mouldings.

[21] F. Ayscough, "Notes on the Symbolism of the Purple Forbidden City," *Journal of the Royal Asiatic Society,* North China Branch, 52 (1921), 51–78; R. Heidenreich, "Beobachtungen zum Stadtplan von Peking," *Nachrichten der Gesellschaft für Natur und Volkerkunde Ostasiens,* 81 (1957), 32–37; T. C. P'eng, "Chinesischer Stadtbau, unter besonderer Berücksichtigung der Stadt Peking," *Nachrichten der Gesellschaft,* No. 89/90 (1961), 42–61.

[22] Amita Ray, *Villages, Towns and Secular Buildings in Ancient India* (Calcutta: Firma Mukhopadhyay, 1964).

The whole was modeled upon the plan of a city in heaven; when the king desired to build, he called his architect, saying, 'Send to the city of the gods, and procure me a plan of their palace, and build one like it.' "[23] Idealistic town plans, which began to appear in the post-Mauryan era, called for rectangular or square-shaped cities oriented to the cardinal points. Each city had four gates, with four main roads converging on the palace at the center. According to the *Manasara,* streets were planned so as to divide the settlement into quarters suited to different caste and occupational groups. Indian town-planning ideals thus resembled those of other ancient civilizations.[24] On the other hand, insofar as one can tell from architectural remains, Indian views concerning the cosmos found explicit expression more in the design of shrines and temples than in the layout of city complexes. The idea that the human settlement represented a microcosmos certainly existed by the Mauryan period, but it took shape more often in literature than in brick and mortar.

architectural symbols of transcendence

Although the city plan was in itself a two-dimensional model of the cosmos, its link to heaven needed reenforcement in the form of architectural symbols of the vertical such as terraces, towers, pillars, ziggurats, arches, and domes. Sumerian cities displayed little of the geometric simplicities of the ideal plan. They were neither circles nor squares. Individual buildings of importance showed the concern of the architect for symmetry and balance, but they did not appear to be part of any larger composition. The cardinal points made no visible impact on design. Palaces and citadels were often located in the northwestern part of the city but this was apparently in response to the direction of pleasant winds. The cosmic symbolization of the city lay less in the plan than in the progressive elevation and isolation of its most sacred component, the temple complex. In the fourth millennium B.C., the temple complex stood open to the believers: multiple entrances led into the sanctuary. Slowly, in the protoliterate and formative periods of Sumer, the distance between the temple and the people widened. First a few steps were introduced, and then a raised platform as at Al 'Uquair and Uruk in the early part of the third millennium B.C. The culmination of this trend was the ziggurat which appeared around 2000 B.C. At Ur, the three terraces of the ziggurat reached a height of 70 feet. Temples were built on

23 A. K. Coomaraswamy, *The Arts and Crafts of India and Ceylon* (New York: Noonday Press, 1964), p. 106.
24 E. B. Havell, *The Ancient and Medieval Architecture of India: A Study of Indo-Aryan Civilization* (London: John Murray, 1915), p. 1–18.

the summits but not always: some had simply a pair of horns and served as sacrificial altars. The ziggurat had multiple symbolic meanings. It was the solid rock that emerged out of chaos; the mountain which represented the center of the universe; the earthly throne of the gods; the monumental site for the offering of sacrifices; and the ladder to heaven.[25]

The great age of the Egyptian pyramids lasted only a few centuries. Ziggurats, by contrast, continued to be a dominant architectural form in Mesopotamia until the collapse of the Neo-Babylonian empire in 538 B.C. Mesopotamian cities of the first millennium B.C. like Khorsabad (Dur-Sharrukin) and Babylon were squarish in shape with corners pointing north-south, east-west. Their internal spatial organization was also more differentiated and structured than that of the Sumerian city in the third millennium B.C. In addition, Neo-Babylonian cities had vertical architectural components that served as reminders of their transcendental nature. The famous "Tower of Babel" in Babylon was a huge ziggurat rising to a height of 200 feet, and called *E-temen-an-ki,* "the Temple Foundation of Heaven and Earth." Khorsabad had two vertical monuments, the ziggurat and the palace which stood on a fifty-foot high platform overlooking the wall.

In China the capital of the Former Han dynasty, Ch'ang-an, was not rectangular in shape. Though roughly oriented to the cardinal points, its wall, particularly at the northwestern corner, sported several bends. These have inspired the scholarly speculation that they conformed to the pattern of the northern and southern "Dippers." A more probable interpretation is that the bends adapted to the irregularities of the terrain. Within the walled compound, elevation rather than central location assured the stature of Wei-yang palace. It had been erected on the summit of a quintuple terrace of rammed earth, fifty feet above the surrounding fields.[26] The use of multiple platforms and high terraces to emphasize height and the link with heaven disappeared in later periods. Locational centrality symbolized height. In Peking the imperial palaces and halls were placed at the center of a succession of walled compounds. The emperor on his throne in the Audience Hall looked "down" to the south; conversely, the long southern avenue leading through a succession of gates to the palace signified not only direction inward by also upward.

Symbols of the vertical take different forms (see Figure 10a, p. 142). Pointed structures like the obelisk, the spire, and the dome stress one direction. The circle is a two-dimensional translation of heaven to earth. The dome is a three-dimensional symbol of heaven. It may be a nomad's tent

---

[25] S. Giedion, *The Eternal Present: The Beginnings of Architecture* (New York: Pantheon, 1964), pp. 215–41.

[26] C. W. Bishop, "An Ancient Chinese Capital: Earthworks at Old Ch'ang-an," *Annual Report, Smithsonian Institution,* 12 (1938), 68–78.

on the steppes of Central Asia, the Temple of Heaven in Peking (with its roof of blue tiles), Santa Sophia in Constantinople or St. Paul's Cathedral in London. They are all images of the heavenly vault. For technical reasons domes made of timber or stone could not exceed a certain size. In the future, transparent geodesic domes can perhaps span entire cities, but their purpose will not be to direct attention to heaven so much as to keep it out.[27]

Belief that the ancestral shelter represented the cosmic house was worldwide. Several ancient civilizations associated the heavens with the ceilings of their most revered shelters. Hence blue ceilings with stars had become traditional in Egyptian tombs and Babylonian palaces, and star-studded coffers continued to be used in Greek and Roman temples. The tent, particularly that of the shaman, was a cosmic house in the Central Asian tradition. Achaemenid kings of Persia held audiences and festivals in a cosmic tent although they lived for the most part in palaces built of wood, brick, and stone. From Persia Hellenistic kings acquired the idea of the divine tent. Pre-Islamic Arabs, and perhaps all Semites, believed in the sacredness of a domelike shelter made of leather. The dome was of great symbolical importance to Christians. During the first centuries, Syrian churchmen adopted the dome for their martyria and baptisteries partly in imitation of Hellenistic and Roman domes built over their mausolea, commemorative monuments, and thermae. By the fifth and sixth centuries the dome was used with increasing frequency in regular churches. The domical tradition in Byzantine architecture and the interpretation of the church as a replica of heaven upon earth reflected the influence of Syria, and Syria received influences from Iran, India, Palestine, and the pagan classical world. Throughout the Byzantine period, to as late as the fifteenth century, theologians viewed the church as the image of the universe: the vault was heaven and the ground the paradisial earth. Renaissance architects perpetuated the importance of the dome out of respect for Roman architecture and from an awareness of its intricate cosmic symbolism. Byzantine and Renaissance cities might deny other-worldly interpretation, but not their churches with their heaven-pointing domes.[28]

brasilia—a modern ideal city

In this sketch of the ideal city, its religious foundation and cosmic symbolism, we seem to be exploring a world of values totally alien to modern values and concerns. This is not, however, the case. Modern cities, when

---

27 E. Baldwin Smith, *The Dome: A Study in the History of Ideas* (Princeton, N.J.: Princeton University Press, 1950).
28 Karl Lehmann, "The Dome of Heaven," *The Art Bulletin* (March 1945), pp. 1–27.

they are established *ex nihilo,* retain some of the ancient conceptions regarding man's place in the cosmos. As de Meira Penna has recently pointed out, not only traditional Peking but futuristic Brasilia is laden with symbols expressive of a common and deep-seated desire to order the earth and establish a link between terrestrial space and the overarching sky.[29]

Politically, Brasilia is built in the interior to break the hold of the sea on Brazilian civilization, to give status to agriculture and the rural population, to exploit the interior's indifferent soils and possible mineral riches, and to instill in the citizenry the sense of Brazil as a continental nation of vast extent and potentiality. The capital stands for a country's collective Ego. This new awareness of the Ego is to burgeon in the thick of Brazil's green wilderness. The capital's location is already touched by myth. In the last quarter of the nineteenth century, while traveling through Brazil, Dom João Bosco was blessed with a prophetic vision. He reported seeing "a great civilization rising on a plateau on the shores of a lake between the 15th and 20th parallels." João Bosco was an Italian educator whom the Catholic church canonized. It now seems that the saint not only correctly foretold the city's general location but also its site next to a lake. No lake in fact existed there. It was created artificially to provide a pleasing setting as well as water supply for the capital. The lake was planned before the city itself.[30]

Founders of ancient cities consulted astrologers and geomancers; they gave little thought to the economics of their "cosmicizing" ventures. Following this tradition the rational accounting of financial and economic realities played no overriding role in the creation of modern Brasilia. President Kubitschek set aside costs and budgets in the pursuit of his vision. Since the president was not a god-king, his precipitate act provoked much controversy. The architect, Lucio Costa, was also criticized for rejecting the view that a new capital could be built only after a careful study of the region, and even after a slow development of communication facilities. For him the artificial capital is not an organism that slowly grows up from the ground but a fully-conceived world to be laid down on the soil. City founding, he writes, "is a deliberate act of possession, a gesture in the colonial tradition of the pioneers, of taming the wilderness."

Costa's design for Brasilia is a simple cross. It recalls, on the one hand, the tradition of the first Portuguese colonizers who raised a Cross to seal their possession of a newly discovered country: Christ the Kosmokrator overcame chaos. On the other hand, it recalls the old and sacred tradition of dividing the land by two intersecting lines pointing to the cardinal directions.

[29] J. O. de Meira Penna, *Psychology and City-Planning: Peking and Brasilia* (Zurich, 1961), pp. 20–47.
[30] Philippe Pinchemel, "Brasilia—ville symbole ou le mythe devenu réalité," *La Vie Urbaine,* 3 (1967), 201–34.

One of the axes of Brasilia is curved. The design, then, has often been compared to the shape of a bird or an airplane. The north and south wings are the residential sections and the monumental east-to-west axis is the body. Brasilia is a bird come down to earth, a new Jerusalem descending out of heaven from God. In Jungian psychology the bird is also a saving symbol, a token of spiritualization. Out of the green potentiality of Brazil's interior wilderness the spirit of man soars skyward. If this reading of the city design seems strained, we can turn to Niemeyer's cathedral—a more explicit symbol of transcendence. The cathedral is a soaring structure of sixteen paraboloid buttresses holding the transparent roof. To enter it the worshiper must first go through the bowls of the earth and pass, symbolically, through "the valley of the shadow of death." Within he is suddenly illuminated from without: his eyes are led by the surge of the buttresses to the source of light and of benediction.

physical setting and urban life styles

Most cities, perhaps all, make some public gesture toward the transcendent, displaying a monument or a fountain, a square or a boulevard that is more spacious than the requirements of mundane traffic. In the post-Renaissance period of the Western world these symbols tend to lose significance in the growing sprawl of the city. Here and there a powerful ruler may impose a geometric regularity to mirror his sense of grandeur; but it tends to be swallowed in "brickish skirts" of tangled lanes and rickety dwellings.

environments and life styles

The life style of a people is the sum of their economic, social, and ultramundane activities. These generate spatial patterns; they require architectural forms and material settings which, upon completion, in turn influence the patterning of activities. The ideal is one aspect of the total life style. We know the ideal because it is often verbalized and occasionally substantiated in works that last. Economic and social forces contribute overwhelmingly to the making of life styles, but unlike idealistic impulses they lack self-awareness. Life styles are rarely verbalized and consciously acted out. In most cases we can acquire some understanding of a people's life style, including their attitude to the world, only through the cumulative evidence of daily acts and through the character of the physical circumstances in which they occur. In attempting to describe the attitudes of non-literate peoples toward their environment, I have noted their legends and cosmographies as well as their physical settings and the activities that take place in them. The environmental values of urban peoples in the past can be known to us in no other way. We can only guess, basing our surmise on the stated ideals and on the people's daily patterns of work and play in an urban milieu. The ideals of the powerful and of integrated communities may find large-scale material expression: this is a theme of the previous chapter. Here we take note of the attitudes and life styles of ordinary citizens, whose capacity to alter the world they inhabit is limited.

A large city offers many types of physical environment. Let us focus on the street scene. The street would seem to be a fairly specific type of physical environment but in fact its character and use can vary enormously. At one extreme, it is a narrow crooked lane, unpaved or paved with cobble, packed with jostling people and carts, a place that assaults the senses with noise, odor, and color. At the other, it is a wide straight avenue, bordered by trees or blank walls, an imposing space that is almost devoid of life.

How people respond to the street scene depends on many factors. For passers-by the means of conveyance is important. Until the very recent popularization of the motor car, most people walked. True, the wealthy could always afford to travel otherwise and see urban life from the vantage point of the horseback, from the privacy of a sedan chair or wheeled carriage, but few were wealthy. In Europe, since the middle of the nineteenth century, more and more people from the middle and working classes took advantage first of the horse-drawn omnibus, then of the tram, and in the last fifty years, of the motorized bus and private car. Roughly speaking, we see the following shift in the balance between walking and other means of locomotion. In the Middle Ages pedestrians rich and poor jostled each other in the crowded lanes. Social hierarchy was rigid but it did not find orderly spatial expression in where the people lived or how they moved. From the seventeenth century onward the increasing use of carriages by the wealthy resulted in spatial as well as social separation among the people. There was less and less mingling of the social orders in the streets and marketplaces. Sidewalks, which were paths marked off by posts from the central thoroughfare, appeared in England in the eighteenth century. They were designed to protect the pedestrians against the unruly wheeled traffic. However, even at the beginning of the Victorian era pedestrians rather than carriages dominated the street scene. Clerks, tradesmen, and workers thronged the sidewalks on their way to and from work in central London. Some 100,000 people a day, for example, walked over the toll-free London Bridge across the Thames, and about 75,000 over the toll-free Blackfriars Bridge.[1] By the second half of the nineteenth century, vehicles of all kinds frequently caused congestion in London's streets, but vehicles still carried only a small portion of the total traffic of people. The contrast with a modern American boulevard is striking. In Los Angeles, streets may be jammed with cars while the sidewalks are relatively bare; and even in the middle of the twentieth century sections of Los Angeles have no sidewalks. As in a medieval lane, so on a modern boulevard people in different stations of life mix freely, but on the modern thoroughfare there is no contact, for each person (or each small group of persons) is encased in a motorized metal box.

The hours at which we make use of city streets affect our perception and evaluation of them. Much has been said about the aesthetic poverty of modern built-up areas as compared with the visual splendors of traditional cities. But how would we judge them at night? Until the introduction of street lamps powered by gas, which were not at all common before the later part of the nineteenth century, cities—however colorful under the sun—were plunged into gloom after sunset. Streets and market squares that were noisy but friendly in daytime became places of danger. In medieval times curfew after dark was not uncommon: to ensure peace, gates and doors were locked and the public places emptied of people. The rhythm of urban life was dictated by the sun. Like farmers, city people rose early and retired to the privacy of their ill-lit homes soon after dark. This was as true of Imperial Rome as of T'ang Ch'ang-an; as applicable to Renaissance Florence as to Georgian London. The spectacles that Imperial Rome provided its populace necessarily took place in daylight hours. Private feasts lasted well into the night but, as Petronius has shown, inebriated guests returning home risked losing their way in the maze of dark, unnamed streets. In striking contrast, the popular imagination now almost equates city life with night life. The social whirl in the modern city accelerates after dark. And it is after dark that even drab city streets, with their rows of nondescript "eat" places, gas stations, and second-hand car lots, take on an aggressive glow of light and color that would have surely astonished cosmopolites of the gaslight era. We may turn to individual cities for a more detailed look at the varieties of urban life style.

ch'ang-an and hang-chou

In traditional China cities were of two main types—political and commercial. Political centers arose primarily in response to the political philosophy of centralized administration, commercial centers to the requirements

[1] G. A. Sekon, *Locomotion in Victorian England* (London: Oxford University Press, 1938), p. 9.

of a market economy. Ancient views concerning man and society in the cosmos left their imprint on the political city. We have seen how its geometry and spatial hierarchy conformed to cosmological beliefs. The keynote was order. In comparison, the commercial city lacked both social and spatial order. Colorful urban life rather than architectural splendor distinguished it. Political cities were built quickly after an idealized pattern. By contrast, the physical frame of the commercial town grew slowly to accommodate the gain in population. As economic activity and population increased, the political city lost its simple rectangular geometry. Within the city walls shops spilled beyond their designated quarters; beyond the city gates new markets and suburbs sprang up to submerge the original nucleus of planned symmetry in the sprawl of new growth. A commercial town might subsequently be chosen as an administrative center or even as the imperial capital. Such a change of status, however, was seldom accompanied by any large-scale transformation of the urban frame.

During the Han period (202 B.C.–A.D. 220) the political and idealized city had the character of a succession of walled-in rectangles. Within the city enclosure the settlement was partitioned into wards, the number of which varied with the size of the town. Ch'ang-an in the Han dynasty had 160 wards, separated from each other by walls and intervening streets. Each ward opened to the street through only one door in Han times, and contained up to 100 households, each of which was again surrounded by a wall. Very narrow lanes led to the gates of the individual households. To get out of town, the inhabitants would have to pass three sets of gates: that of their house, that of their ward, and that of their town. Moreover, all the gates were guarded and closed at night. The city showed some of the characteristics of a vast prison. In the course of T'ang dynasty (A.D. 618–907) the rigid rules governing city life were somewhat relaxed. The wards were allowed four gates each instead of one, and by the second half of the eighth century the market quarters could remain open at night.[2]

The Ch'ang-an of the T'ang emperors was huge. The city wall enclosed an area of some 30 square miles, divided by a grid of broad avenues, eleven of which ran north-to-south, fourteen east-to-west. More than 100 enclosed quarters lay among the interstices of the avenues. Nearly one million people lived within the walled compound. Functionally the city was partitioned into a central and northern official precinct, two officially designated markets serving the western and eastern halves of the city, and the residential quarters which were separated from each other by walls and the great avenues. Walls, as in the Han city, were ubiquitous. Gates and doors closed at sunset and

2 Ichisada Miyazaki, "Les villes en Chine à l'époque des Hans," *Toung Pao,* 48 (1960), 378–81.

opened at sunrise. Private life of the well-to-do was private indeed. Rooms opened to interior courts and gardens. Beauty was hidden from the public eye which, from the lanes and the streets, could see only blank walls. Within the confines of the private domicile one can envisage all kinds of sensuous delight: the intimacy of human relationships, the intimacy of the private garden which opened to the world beyond only by way of the sky, and in the general silence and stillness an intensified awareness of delicate sounds and fragrances inside the house, but also from the outside drifting in through the gate and over the walls. By contrast, the markets reflected the needs and vitality of a cosmopolitan city. The western market, the more prosperous of the two, was a busy, noisy and multilingual cluster of bazaars and warehouses. People came not only to buy but to meet friends and gossip; students argued philosophy and politics. In addition, visitors and clients were entertained by prestidigitators and illusionists of every nationality as well as by storytellers, actors, and acrobats.

The market bustled with life. The great avenues, though carefully maintained, were quiet. Footpaths, drainage ditches, and fruit trees lined the principal carriageways, some of which measured more than 450 feet wide (four times the width of New York's Fifth Avenue). But there were no great emporia, nor was there much wheeled traffic despite the large total population. These avenues looked curiously unlike "streets" as we usually envisage them. They were not so much passageways that linked the people in different sections of the city as open spaces that kept the people apart. If the daytime traffic on these avenues was small, it became nonexistent after dark. With the closing of the gates life withdrew into the intimacy of the houses.[3]

The political city of Ch'ang-an reflected the ideals of an aristocratic culture. In the latter part of the T'ang dynasty this culture underwent decline as the power and ideals of the bourgeoisie rose. Rules governing the behavior of society were relaxed. The busy western market spilled beyond its confines into neighboring residential quarters. Gates remained open at night. Cafes and bars multiplied, as did the public houses of prostitution, to cater to the needs of young men who entered the ranks of the rising merchant class. The process of change toward a money economy continued and accelerated during the Sung dynasty (A.D. 960–1279). The Southern Sung capital was established in Hang-chou, a city that gained commercial importance before it acquired its exalted political status as the seat of the emperor. Ch'ang-an and Hang-chou were both great metropolitan centers of vast population but they displayed antipodean styles of urban life: the one

[3] E. H. Schafer, "The Last Years of Ch'ang-an," *Oriens Extremus*, 10 (1963), 133–79.

austere and imperial, the other raucous and flamboyant. The difference is suggested by the contrast in population density, Ch'ang-an's average of 55 persons per acre to Hang-chou's 200.

The formalism of the T'ang capital is barely visible in the densely built-up areas of the Southern Sung city. The walls of Hang-chou were irregular in shape. It had thirteen unevenly spaced gates instead of the prescribed twelve. The principal pig market rather than the residence of the emperor occupied the city's center. The palace compound was located at the southern end. By contrast with the sparsely used avenues of Ch'ang-an, those of Hang-chou teemed with pedestrians, horseriders, people in sedan chairs and in passenger carts. Besides roads the city was served by canals, with their heavy traffic of barges loaded with rice, boats weighed down with coal, bricks, tiles, and sacks of salt. More than one hundred bridges spanned the canal system within the city walls, and where these were humpbacked and joined busy arteries they caused traffic to congest into seething masses of carriages, horses, donkeys, and porters. Whereas the streets of Ch'ang-an were bordered by trees and the blank walls of the residential quarters, those of Hang-chou were lined with shops and dwellings that opened to the traffic. Off the Imperial Way, population density exceeded 325 persons per acre. The dearth of land forced the buildings to go up to three to five stories. Commercial activity permeated the city and its suburbs: almost everywhere a visitor could see shops selling noodles, fruits, thread, incense and candles, oil, soya sauce, fresh and salt fish, pork, and rice. Some tea houses on the Imperial Way were noisy houses of ill-fame in which singing girls entertained customers. The principal pig market was not far from the main artery. Several hundred beasts were butchered every day in slaughterhouses that opened soon after midnight and closed at dawn. Until the Mongol occupiers imposed curfew, city life in Sung Hang-chou continued with barely abated animation late into the night. Although public lighting probably did not exist, multicolored lanterns lit the entrances and courtyards of restaurants, taverns, and tea houses.[4]

athens and rome

Some five hundred years intervened between T'ang Ch'ang-an and Sung Hang-chou at their respective peaks of development. Both were great capital cities; otherwise the urban life styles of these two places had as little in common as their physical frames. Half a millennium separated Periclean Athens from Augustan Rome. During that time important changes in society

[4] J. Gernet, *Daily Life in China on the Eve of the Mongol Invasion 1250–1276* (London: Allen & Unwin, 1962).

and economy had occurred with obvious effects on people's perception of, and behavior in, their physical environment. For one thing, the population of Imperial Rome was probably ten times that of Hellenic Athens. Yet these epochal cities shared certain basic traits, of which the most evident was the maze of tortuous streets. In this respect Athens resembled Rome more than it did the Hellenistic towns that adopted the Hippodamian grid pattern. Another common trait was the importance of the agora or forum, the public institutions and markets where the peoples of Athens and Rome could congregate and experience an enlargement of their lives through participation in the symbols and realities of a greater world.

The Greeks gloried in public life. The private realm they tended to denigrate as something bound to the repetitive cycles of deedless organic nature. Activities pertaining to the private sphere of the household were of course recognized as essential to survival and welfare, but the Greeks nonetheless chose to relegate them to those who in their view lacked the full dignity of manhood: children, women, and slaves. This general attitude to life was reflected in the architecture of the older Greek cities in which the magnificence of the public buildings contrasted sharply with the modesty and misery of the private quarters.[5] The streets were narrow, tortuous, and mostly unpaved. Even the rectilinear passageways of the new Hippodamian towns seldom exceeded a few yards in width, and most of the streets in fifth-century Athens were narrower. Pavement was probably used in those sections of the street that had heavy traffic, and those that sloped and were subject to erosion. There were no sidewalks. One can imagine what it must have been like to walk the unpaved streets after rain. Aristophanes tells us how short-sighted old men groped their way along the narrow lanes, complaining of the mud and clay. The question of Athenian sanitation is wrapped in obscurity. Before the fourth century it was probably minimal. Slops and garbage of the worst description were cheerfully thrown into the road with no more warning to the pedestrians than the perfunctory cry, *existo*—"stand out of the way." Walking with dignity must have been difficult. Yet Athenians were told that they must not "stalk" or loiter; they must not be so lacking in dignity as to let their eyes loll about the street.

The temptation to linger could not have been great. There was little to see. Streets were often bordered by blank walls of houses that faced inward, and had only slits as windows where they boasted a second story. Some roads, however, had specialized activities which might have tempted the pedestrians to loiter. Cabinet makers in one street, potters in another, and the sculptors of Hermae in a third, clamored for their attention. It was at the marketplace that Athenians enjoyed the full flavor of

5 G. Glotz, *The Greek City and Its Institutions* (London: Routledge & Kegan Paul, 1965), p. 302.

urban life. The crowd itself lent color to the scene, for not all were dressed in white. Tunic and mantle were commonly whitish but the young sported attires in purple, red, frog-green, and black. Women alone could wear yellow. However, well-to-do womenfolk seldom appeared in the market-place, for men and slaves did the shopping and enjoyed at the same time the many attractions of the agora. Every kind of produce had its own stand, so that Athenians could arrange to meet their friends "at the fish" or "at the green cheese" or "at the figs." Buying and selling were noisy affairs. People haggled over prices. Vendors shouted their wares. Around the central mar-keting area were shops belonging to barbers, perfumers, shoemakers, sad-dlers, and wine sellers. In their neighborhood were the shaded colonnades. After shopping, a pleasant and leisurely occupation was to meet with one's friends to discuss the news of the day, politics, or abstract questions. The discussions frequently took place at the barber's, in the doctor's waiting room, or in some other shop, thus turning them into a sort of clubroom and classroom. After lunch the citizen might visit a gymnasium for exercise and further conversation. The Athenian, whether rich or poor, rose at daybreak and retired early. The night was quiet and those who wished to study or finish business stayed up late and worked by lamp light. Demosthenes pre-pared nearly all his speeches after dark.[6]

Imperial Rome combined a magnificence of public places with living conditions of the utmost squalor for the mass of its huge populace, which exceeded a million in the second century A.D.[7] Splendid monuments were set like pearls in a dense inchoate matrix of narrow, gloomy alleys and flimsy, warren-like houses. Monumental buildings, to the modern mind, imply resplendent vistas up and down broad avenues. But Rome, despite its well-earned reputation for road building, singularly lacked avenues to meet the needs of traffic and match the scale of its monuments. Among the dense net of Roman streets, only two inside the old Republican Wall were wide enough to allow two carts to pass each other and thus earn the name of *via*.

The roads that led out of Rome to Italy, such as the Via Appia and Via Latina, varied in width from 16 to little more than 20 feet. Ordinary city streets were much narrower. Many were simple passages and tracks. Their narrowness was exaggerated by the tall houses on both sides which cut off much of the sunlight and made the streets into tunnels of gloom. Adding perhaps to picturesqueness, but certainly not to convenience, these lanes constantly zigzagged, and on the Seven Hills rose and fell steeply. Footpaths or sidewalks were rare. Unlike Pompeii the streets of Imperial

---

6 T. G. Tucker, *Life in Ancient Athens* (London: Macmillan, 1906); A. H. M. Jones, *The Greek City from Alexander to Justinian* (Oxford: Clarendon Press, 1940).

7 This section on Rome is based on Jérôme Carcopino, *Daily Life in Ancient Rome*, trans. E. O. Lorimer (New Haven: Yale University Press, 1940).

Rome were not generally paved. Filth and refuse from adjoining houses defiled them daily. On moonless nights the streets were plunged into darkness and danger. People rushed home and barricaded the entrances. But unlike Athens the streets of Rome could be very noisy at night. The reason goes back to Caesar who, in order to ease the massive traffic congestions in Rome, decreed that no transport cart was allowed in the streets from sunrise until nearly dusk. This meant that as the night approached wheeled carts of every sort converged upon the city and filled it with their racket. According to Juvenal the incessant din of night traffic condemned sensitive Romans to everlasting insomnia.

Excessive crowding made the streets narrow and the houses tall. Domiciles in Rome were basically of two types: the horizontal houses of the rich which were influenced by Hellenistic architecture, and the apartment blocks (*insulae*) of the poor. The private house (*domus*) turned an unbroken wall to the street while the *insula* opened to the outside. The ratio of apartment blocks to the private house was twenty-six to one, so that the street scene was very much dominated by the tall and flimsy structures, which rose to five or six stories and frequently collapsed. The noise of buildings collapsing or being torn down to make way for others little better, punctuated the perpetual hum of the city. Fire was a constant threat and obsessed the rich and the poor alike.

The tall houses had large and numerous windows but they rendered little service. We forget how glass panes have so greatly extended our control over the world by allowing us to see it in comfort. Shutters, while keeping cold and rain, midsummer heat or winter wind at bay, also excluded every ray of light: the price of comfort was in effect the exclusion of the world. The insides of the apartment blocks were small, dark, uncomfortable and unsanitary: from the street, however, they could have looked attractive. A Roman living in the early part of the twentieth century would not only feel at home in one of the wider streets bordered by *insulae* but might even compare the façades favorably with what he could see in the poorer districts of his time. The exteriors of the *insulae* presented a fairly uniform front to the street. Their windows and doors were larger than those of the *casoni* of the modern period. Where the streets had sufficient width, the apartment façades were relieved by a variety of balconies and loggias resting on porticos, their pillars and railings hung with climbing plants. The ground floor of the better apartment houses was rented as a single unit to the moneyed tenant, and so acquired the status of *domus*. In the humble *insulae* the ground floor might be divided up into booths and shops (the *tabernae*) which opened to the street.

Despite the size of Rome, the stratification of society, and the chasm that yawned between the rich and the poor, the city lacked social and occupational zoning. There was no concept of the "proper district" in the Rome of the Caesars: patrician and plebeian rubbed shoulders everywhere. Even the crafts and industries were widely dispersed. The workers lived scattered in almost every corner of the city. Flimsy apartment houses and sumptuous mansions alternated oddly with warehouses, workmen's dwellings, and workshops. The noise of the city was augmented by the din of the workers' tools, the hustle of their toil, their shouts and swearing. The intense animation that flooded the Roman street after daybreak, as the *tabernae* opened for business, was vividly portrayed by Carcopino.

> Here barbers shaved their customers in the middle of the fairway. There the hawkers from Transtiberina passed along, bartering their packets of sulphur matches for glass trinkets. Elsewhere, the owner of a cookshop, hoarse with calling to deaf ears, displayed his sausages in their saucepan. Schoolmasters and their pupils shouted themselves hoarse in the open air. On the one side, a money-changer rang his coins...on a dirty table, on another a beater of gold dust pounded with his shining mallet on his well-worn stone. At the crossroads a circle of idlers gaped around a viper tamer; everywhere tinkers' hammers resounded and the quavering voices of beggars invoked the name of Bellona or rehearsed their adventures and misfortunes to touch the hearts of passers-by.[8]

Dusk did not necessarily bring peace for with sunset the carts began to invade the city. Where, then, could the Romans find a measure of seclusion and quiet? The rich could retire to suburban homes and gardens which, by the second century A.D., formed a sort of Green Belt around the central city. Ordinary people made do with the relatively tranquil places in the heart of Rome: for example, the foras and basilicas when once the judicial hearings were over, and the emperor's gardens that were accessible to the public. At the Campus Martius, the marble enclosures (*saepta*), the sacred halls and porticos provided a shelter from the sun, a refuge from the rain and wind, a place where even the most wretched could take his ease amidst works of art. The baths provided relaxation and various sorts of pleasure to rich and poor. By the first century A.D. their total number approached a thousand. The more opulent *thermae* boasted every type of bath as well as shops, enclosed gardens and promenades, gymnasiums and rooms for massage, even libraries and museums. The bulk of the townsmen were miserably poor: their dwellings and places of work were foul. Yet, compared with the unyielding labor and drab lives of the peasants the townsmen enjoyed variety, excitements, and leisure unique to Rome. Even the most wretched plebe in the city had access to the animation of the *palaestra*, the warmth of the baths, the gaiety of public banquets, the rich man's doles, and the magnificence of public spectacles.[9]

[8] Carcopino, *Ancient Rome,* pp. 48–49.
[9] J. P. V. D. Balsdon, *Life and Leisure in Ancient Rome* (New York: McGraw-Hill, 1969).

the medieval city

Street life in a large and important medieval town had the same kind of atmosphere as in ancient Rome; that is, the same overcrowding, hustle, noise, odor, and color generating a degree of animation and confusion that in modern times tends to be confined to the bazaars of African and Oriental cities. Fondness for public pageantry was another shared trait. Medieval towns could not, of course, match the grandiose spectacles of Imperial Rome but they made use of every occasion, sacred or secular, as excuses for celebration. Many such opportunities existed. In London, for example, the celebrations held on Lord Mayor's day were repeated at Easter, Whitsuntide, Midsummer, and on saints' days. Royal visits called for spectacles but even the conveyance of a prisoner from one prison to another was made the occasion of pomp.[10] Cathedrals were often the foci of pageants and processions. Apart from their prominence of bulk and height, cathedrals in the Middle Ages—like Greek temples in antiquity—stood out in their whiteness, a whiteness enhanced by contrast with the brightly painted decorative stonework and statuary. Ordinary buildings and houses, both in their interior and exterior furnishing, commonly displayed gaudy hues, and the same was true of the dresses for men and women. On a festive occasion the medieval street sustained an intensity of life, an assault on the senses that the modern man can barely conceive.

Compared with Ch'ang-an, Hang-chou, Rome, or Baghdad, in the eighth century, medieval towns were midgets. Medieval Germany might boast some 3,000 towns (i.e., settlements with "urban rights" bestowed by a lord), but 2,800 had less than 1,000 people. Only 15 had populations that exceeded 10,000. The largest city, Cologne, reached 30,000, and Lübeck 25,000, around the year 1400. Among English towns only London exceeded 10,000, attaining a population of more than 50,000 by the time of the Black Death. Paris was probably larger, but none of the medieval towns of Europe approached the giants of antiquity and of the Orient. What they had in common was a boisterous and colorful life style that derived from the dense clustering of people and occupations.[11]

Medieval settlements were individually distinct. They also shared certain morphological and architectural traits. Fortifications, for example, tended to dominate the medieval city's physical layout, particularly on continental Europe. As the visitor approached a city he would see a silhouette of towers and turrets in the distance; closer he would be confronted by a massive rampart, a ditch in front and widely projecting watchtowers at

10 Charles Pendrill, *London Life in the 14th Century* (London: Allen & Unwin, 1925), pp. 47–48.
11 Fritz Rörig, *The Medieval Town* (Berkeley and Los Angeles: University of California Press, 1961), p. 112.

regular intervals. Until well into the twelfth century the walls of even the larger cities had been simple. In the course of time they were made more elaborate and taller, reaching heights of 25 to 30 feet. Gates were few because they needed to be manned.[12] By the fifteenth and sixteenth centuries, walls and gates had lost much of their defensive value and had acquired, instead, value as symbols. Towns vied with one another in the artistic elaboration of their gates to impress visiting dignitaries. Within the walls, churches, the castle, and (somewhat later) the town hall dominated the cityscape. A forest of steeples pierced the sky of Chaucer's London: 99 parish churches stood inside the rampart that enclosed an area of less than a square mile.[13] The town hall gained importance as its functions expanded. Until the thirteenth century, the clothiers' house was the most important nonreligious public building. As the power of the burghers increased so did the architectural magnificence of the town halls, the trade halls and such public buildings as granaries, armories, and bridges.

In the medieval town, excessive crowding was not infrequently combined with open fields and spaces. Towns in which the walls had recently been extended might include vineyards and cherry orchards, vegetable and flower gardens near the walls. In medieval London, houses and shops packed the streets on both sides. Some buildings were only 10 or 11 feet wide and 17 feet deep. Yet a small garden was usually available at the rear of the house, or, where shops were built in rows, a common garden might serve the needs of all the tenants. The large open spaces in the center of medieval towns were distributed around the churches. There, in addition to the cemetery, land was available for holding markets. Many London parishes were two to four acres in size and must have included fairly large open areas. Throughways were narrow, not much more than lanes. Even in a large city like Paris the main streets measured only 17 to 19 feet wide; others were half that width. On the other hand, not all streets in the early Middle Ages were narrow. London's Cheapside was broad enough for tournaments to be held there until the time of Henry VIII. From the thirteenth century onward, however, roadways tended to grow narrower as more and more tradesmen encroached upon them.

Medieval streets were in general constricted, winding, and foul. Paving in London was limited to short stretches. Only in the fifteenth century did important towns like Gloucester, Exeter, Canterbury, Southampton, and Bristol begin street paving.[14] Rain turned some streets into canals of mud, and to negotiate them many people wore pattens, or wooden clogs supported on circlets of iron. There were no sidewalks. The street surface,

[12] D. C. Munro and G. C. Sellery, *Medieval Civilization: Selected Studies from European Authors* (New York: The Century Co., 1910), pp. 358–61.
[13] D. W. Robertson, Jr., *Chaucer's London* (New York: Wiley, 1968), p. 21.
[14] J. J. Bagley, *Life in Medieval England* (London: B. T. Batsford, 1960), p. 48.

where paved, was made of cobble stones. A gutter ran down the middle. In wider streets two parallel channels divided the thoroughfare into three strips. Down these gutters passed all kinds of garbage, including (in some streets) the blood and offal from the butcher shops. Butchers did much of their slaughtering in the public thoroughfare. The Shambles in London presented a perennial problem to the city. The entrails and waste of the slaughtered animals were carried away to be disposed of in the Fleet. Drippings from the carts created a swath of stink following the highway that offended the nostrils of prominent residents. Protests wrought little effect. Confusion and filth in medieval streets were aggravated by the pigs and chickens which were allowed to run loose and feed on the garbage.[15]

Gigantic advertisements of modern times are known to clutter up the street shoulders, block off views, and endanger lives by distracting the attention of drivers from the road. Even medieval London had to cope with the problems of aggressive advertising. Since shops in those days were unnumbered, many shopkeepers used signs to draw attention to their premises. The signs were hung out on poles projecting across the street. Trade rivalry encouraged them to grow to enormous size, thus further confining the width of passageways that had already been diminished by the encroachment of shops. In 1375 it was decreed that the length of the signs could not exceed seven feet.[16]

Noise permeated the streets of the medieval city from dawn to dusk. Florence woke to the peal of bells which called the people to attend early mass. In London bells rang incessantly. Street criers were everywhere and kept up their business at all hours of the day. In thirteenth-century Paris, at dawn criers "proclaimed that the baths were open and the water hot; then followed others crying fish, meat, honey, onions, cheese, old clothes, flowers, pepper, charcoal, or other wares. The begging friars and members of other orders were everywhere, seeking alms. The public criers announced death and any news."[17] The industries added their share to the total cacophony. At Jena it was reported "a certain cooper used to get up at midnight and made so much din putting hoops on his casks that the health of his neighbors was imperiled through the constant loss of sleep." Students who had to study complained, and they were sometimes successful in turning a noisy smith or weaver out of the house.[18] But noises added to the liveliness of the city. To the countrymen visiting their urban cousins the intensity of city life simultaneously repelled and attracted.

---

[15] Robertson, *Chaucer's London*, pp. 23–24.
[16] Pendrill, *London Life*, p. 11.
[17] D. C. Munro and R. J. Sontag, *The Middle Ages* (New York: The Century Co., 1928), p. 345.
[18] Marjorie Rawling, *Everyday Life in Medieval Times* (London: B. T. Batsford, 1968), pp. 68–69.

georgian and victorian street scenes

From the late Middle Ages to the end of the eighteenth century the quality of street life changed—and yet, in the riot of sensual stimuli, it remained essentially the same. Of the innovations the most important were the use of glass plates in shop windows and street lighting. Both developments appreciably extended the visual field of the townsman. Another major change was the introduction of wheeled traffic, leading to the setting up of posts to demarcate paths for pedestrians. In the Middle Ages carriages and even carts used for bringing produce into the market rarely pushed their way into the core of the city. People from different stations of life rubbed shoulders indiscriminately in the streets and squares. From the seventeenth century onward, however, there was less opportunity for mixing: the rich traveled in carriages in the middle of the road whenever they could while the mass of the citizenry walked. Walking the streets was thought to be unwholesome. As John Verney put it in 1685, "In London the roughness of the treading, the rubbing by the people, & the bustle of 'em, wearies the body & giddyes & dazeth the head."

Streets in eighteenth-century London were paved, which indicates an improvement over medieval times. Around 1800, high streets were covered with a layer of flat freestone while narrow roads retained their ancient cobbles hammered into the ground. Broader avenues had footpaths protected by posts, but less important streets had no posts and pedestrians were in constant danger of being run over by a cart. As in the Middle Ages a gutter occupied the center of the street; it was sometimes foul and stagnant, sometimes a rapid stream, the splashing of which, when a cart or carriage passed along, bespattered the dresses of gentle folk. Scavengers more or less maintained the throughways but they ignored the heaps of dust and filth that collected in every open space within and without the city of London. Pigs browsed upon these dumps, and the refuse was occasionally sold to market gardeners and others.[19]

In a busy street the pedestrians could neither rush nor leisurely stroll. He had to take care, for the doorsteps projected; the posts took up a large share of the footway; the cobbled stones of the pavement were dislodged here and there, leaving puddles of mud and filth. One risked falling into a cellar, for nearly every house had a cellar the doors of which were constantly thrown up for the reception of coals or merchandise. Then there were the penthouses built out in front of the shops, with potted flowers on top. Penthouses lent color to the streets but jutted into the footway forcing pedestrians to walk around them. Many of the shopkeepers resorted to the

---

19 Walter Besant, *London in the Eighteenth Century* (London: Adams & Charles Black, 1903).

ancient custom of having a boy outside bawling an invitation to buy. They had to compete with the itinerant hawkers.

> The apple woman or the tart woman set up their stalls where they pleased, the bandbox man with a pole slung with bandboxes over his shoulder cluttered the narrow street, the bellows-mender and the chair-mender did their repairs on the pavement. Men and women hawked taffety tarts and brickdust, doormats and watercresses, hot spiced gingerbreads, green hasteds (early pears), crying their wares as they went. The bear ward, with his unhappy performing beast, came lumbering down the street. He would often stop at a street corner and give an entertainment, blocking the roadway and terrifying the horses. The puppet-show man too would come, and set up where he would collecting a crowd to witness a puppet play and the antics of Mr. Punch.[20]

Adding to the clutter and the color of the streets were the signboards that proclaimed the names of the tenants. By the 1750s they had grown to monstrous size and were so heavy with ironwork that they dragged out the fronts of the buildings. The noise they made˙ as they swung ponderously in the wind swelled the general din.[21] Lawlessness constituted another danger and it undoubtedly heightened the drama of urban life. Dr. Johnson liked London, it would seem, despite the incivility of its streets. He always walked them with a stout cudgel. Many citizens went about armed and few prudent men ventured out alone after dark.

Street lighting improved slowly in the course of the eighteenth century. In 1716 every London householder whose house fronted a street or lane was obliged to hang out a candle long enough to burn from six to eleven o'clock in the evening. After eleven the city was plunged in darkness. Candles were lit only between Michaelmas (September 29) and Lady Day (March 25). The total time of lighting amounted to no more than 600 hours annually; the city had in fact no illumination for 247 nights of the year. In 1736 oil lamps displaced candles and the yearly hours of illumination increased from 600 to 5,000. The power of the oil lamps barely exceeded that of the candles. At every hundred feet or so a feeble glimmer pierced the darkness. Linkboys still accompanied night travelers whether they went on foot or by coach. Yet to some visitors London was impressively well-lit. William Hutton of Birmingham, describing his journey to the capital in 1780, spoke of the brilliant illumination of the streets, where not only the oil lamps appeared at regular intervals but the shop windows shone with candle light.[22] In 1775 Georg Christoph Lichtenberg described glowingly how Cheapside and Fleet Street looked after dark. Tall houses with plate glass windows lined

---

[20] Rosamond Bayne-Powell, *Eighteenth-Century London Life* (London: John Murray, 1937), p. 14.
[21] Besant, *London in the Eighteenth Century*, p. 89.
[22] Conrad Gill, *History of Birmingham*, I (London: Oxford University Press, 1952), 156.

the streets. "The lower floors consist of shops and seem to be made entirely of glass; many thousand candles light up silverware, engravings, books, clocks, glass, pewter, paintings, women's finery. . . . , gold, precious stones, steel-work, and endless coffee-rooms and lottery offices. The street looks as though it was illuminated for some festivity."[23] Doubtless these visitors over-enthused or were acquainted only with small segments of the city. Georgian London was a dark and dangerous place after sunset. Most shops had perhaps one or two candles next to the window and one or two on the counter. Taverns, with one candle per table, were poorly lit. The gloom that settled over the city in winter owed less to the cold than to the long hours of darkness. Early in the Victorian era the use of gaslight greatly improved city illumination. Gaslight was first introduced into the streets of London in 1807; by 1833 the city acquired some 39,500 gas lamps, lighting 215 miles of street.[24]

In the later part of the eighteenth century and in the Victorian era, observers of the street scene often commented on the density of wheeled traffic. Streets then were not packed with vehicles in the manner of modern streets; clerks and manual workers still lived close to the inner city and walked to their jobs. But people tended to be impressed by vehicular traffic. For one thing, wheeled carriages were still something of a novelty in the nineteenth century, especially since every decade or so a new type might appear. Traffic regulations were minimal and haphazardly enforced, so that at certain road junctions in London carriages created chaos out of proportion to their number. The noise was also overpowering—probably no less than what the modern city dweller has to bear despite the decibels contributed by motorbikes and airplanes. Stephen Coleridge writing in 1913 at the age of fifty said.

> London has changed very much since I was a boy. All the main streets were paved with stone blocks, and as there were no India rubber tyres, the noise was deafening. In the middle of Regent's Park or Hyde Park, one heard the roar of the traffic all round in a ring of tremendous sound; and in any shop in Oxford Street, if the door was opened no one could make himself heard till it was shut again.[25]

The hackney coach (taxicabs of the preautomobile era) appeared in London in the seventeenth century. It was unpopular among the tradesmen

---

23 Georg Christoph Lichtenberg, *Visits to England* (January 10, 1775); quoted in Hugh and Pauline Massingham, *The London Anthology* (London: Phoenix House, 1950), p. 445.
24 Besant, *London in the Eighteenth Century*, pp. 91–94.
25 John Betjeman, *Victorian and Edwardian London* (London: B. T. Batsford, 1969), pp. ix–xi.

for the vehicle hindered people from looking at shop windows, and enabled customers to escape the importuning of apprentices who could waylay pedestrians and push their masters' wares. It also made a great deal of din on cobbled streets. The early coaches were heavy and had perforated iron shutters for windows. Later, when the shutters were removed and glazed windows substituted, the carriage had sufficient appeal to be referred to as a glass coach. By 1771 London boasted nearly 1,000 hackney coaches, and in 1862 more than 6,000 of them had licenses to ply the streets of the metropolis. Eight hundred horse-drawn omnibuses, moving at five or six miles an hour served London's streets in 1855. By July 1857, buses operated on 96 routes. At the close of the Victorian era they brought daily into central London more than 48,000 people up to about 8:30 A.M.[26]

the automobile city: los angeles

Streets in preindustrial cities, unless they were residential or ceremonial in character, swarmed with people. From the seventeenth century onward, more and more wheeled carriages appeared. But it was only in the early decades of the twentieth century that vehicles began to displace walking as the prevalent form of locomotion, and street scenes were perceived increasingly from the interior of automobiles moving staccato-fashion through regularly paced traffic lights.

The automobile transformed the character of the city and man's relationship to his urban environment. Los Angeles is the supreme automobile metropolis. Since the second world war, many of its distinguishing physical traits were reproduced on a smaller scale by American cities of older foundation. Compared with other urban communities, residences in Los Angeles were (by 1930) far more widely dispersed, businesses were more extensively decentralized, electric railways approached bankruptcy faster, and private cars handled a greater share of urban transportation.[27]

More than any other city, Los Angeles is identified with its freeway system. In 1938 a special traffic study led to a state law that provided for the creation of nonstop drives, since known as freeways. Many of these were raised above ordinary street level, thus providing motorists with elevated views of the city seen at speeds ranging from zero at the bottlenecks to more than 60 miles an hour in the open stretches. Driving on a freeway can be disorienting. A sign, for example, may direct one to the far left lane for an

---

[26] Sekon, *Locomotion in Victorian England,* pp. 35–37.
[27] Robert M. Fogelson, *The Fragmented Metropolis: Los Angeles 1850–1930* (Cambridge, Mass.: Harvard University Press, 1967), p. 2.

objective that is clearly visible to the right of the carriageway. Yet it is the sign, rather than the evidence of direct perception, that must be obeyed.[28]

A typical outgrowth of the automobile age is the long, straight shopping street. Ventura Boulevard stretches 15 miles along the southern edge of San Fernando Valley. Wilshire Boulevard is of similar length and extends from the city center westward to the sea. In 1949 it was the principal avenue of eleven communities, and was intersected by more than 200 streets, places, drives, roads, avenues, and boulevards. With the advent of the automobile, a new conception of street length appeared: the various names that were tagged to different sections of the boulevard were given the one name, implying a uniformity of land use where none existed.[29]

The character of the commercial street changed through time. An early trait was the sparsity of business establishments relative to length. Ventura Boulevard in 1954 had some 1,420 different business houses occupying its 15 miles of street frontage.[30] In 1949 Wilshire Boulevard still had more vacant lots than improved ones. Another trait was the relative importance of parking lots, gas stations, garages, and automobile shops, as well as motels, hotels, and different kinds of eating places that catered largely to the needs of the automobile and to nonlocal customers. Offices of all kinds were prominent; not surprisingly, real estate offices outnumbered other types. In the need to attract the attention of motorists, many of whom came from out-of-town and were thus ignorant of what could be found, merchants indulged in extravagant advertising. They used not only gigantic billboards but also fanciful architecture to shout their wares: for example, "dairy-queens" were housed in huge ice-cream cones and short-order eating places were made to look like hot dogs. On Wilshire Boulevard some of the vacant lots and the ceilings of low buildings produced incomes of $30,000 to $50,000 a years as billboard sites. Many billboards stood on landscaped green lawns bordered by hedges, and were themselves imposing structures. In time, billboards gave way to business houses, some of which, however, served the same function of advertising the quality of their goods. The important thing was not to make local sales but to proclaim, by the prestige of the location on Wilshire Boulevard and by expensive decor, the status of the business.

The pedestrian is given little consideration in an automobile city like Los Angeles. Even in the 1970s some streets have no sidewalks; many others are long arteries scaled to the speed of the car; and in some sections pedestrians risk being picked up as vagrants. The streets are noisy. Eardrums of

28 Reyner Banham, *Los Angeles: The Architecture of Four Ecologies* (London: Penguin, 1971), p. 219.
29 Ralph Hancock, *Fabulous Boulevard* (New York: Funk & Wagnalls, 1949).
30 Gerard J. Foster and Howard J. Nelson, *Ventura Boulevard: A String Type Shopping Street* (Los Angeles: Bureau of Business and Economics Research, University of California, 1958).

pedestrians are buffeted by the ground bass of automobile traffic, the rumble of heavy trucks, the roar of motorbikes, and the scream of police and ambulance sirens responding to traffic accidents. Little of the noise is human. Indeed not many humans are to be seen. It is a curious experience to go up and down both sides of the most busy and prestigious shopping section of Wilshire Boulevard, the Miracle Mile, and observe that relatively few people pass in and out of the front entrances of shops while inside they are crowded. The action takes place at the back which, in terms of activity and the resources devoted to decor, is really the front. There, cars drive up in continuous streams, shoppers step out, and attendants drive the cars to the stores' parking lot.[31]

[31] Hancock, *Fabulous Boulevard*, p. 163.

american cities: symbolism, imagery, perception

In great metropolises, no man can know well more than a small fragment of the total urban scene; nor is it necessary for him to have a mental map or imagery of the entire city in order to prosper in his corner of the world. Yet the city dweller seems to have a psychological need to possess an image of the total environment in order to place his own neighborhood. Knowledge of a city varies enormously from person to person. Most people are able to designate by name the two extremes of the urban scale, the city as a whole and the street they live on. Intermediate divisions are, by contrast, vaguely conceived to the extent that few people can readily recall the name of their district or neighborhood. The two ends of the scale appear to express a common human propensity to dwell on two widely disparate levels of thought: high abstraction and specific responses. On the level of high abstraction, the immense complexity of a city may be encapsulated in the name itself such as Rome, or to a monument (Eiffel Tower), or to a silhouette such as the famous skyline of New York, or to a slogan or nickname such as The Queen City of the West. On the level of specific responses are the rich images and attitudes that a person acquires from his immediate environment in the course of day-to-day living.

In chapters 11 and 12, I have discussed first the city as an ideal and then the city as perceived in daily commerce. The ideal or symbolic aspect of a city is known to us through literary sources and from what we know of the people's religion and cosmology reflected, often, in the city's spatial organization and architecture. What people see in their urban environment, how they respond to it, cannot be known directly for cities of the past—nor, in fact, are they known for the bulk of the world's present-day metropolises— because surveys, interviews, and in-depth observations do not exist. However, something can be gleaned from the physical characteristics of that world and from the different life styles that have evolved in it. The last chapter summarizes some of the results. Now we focus on American cities, and the approach is a similar one for we shall move from American cities as idealized concepts—symbols or metaphors for what a civilization can achieve—to the people's attitudes toward particular neighborhoods acquired through habitation and habituation.

symbols and metaphors

The dominant myths of America are nonurban. They are often anti-urban: the image of paradisiac New World stands against the image of European sophistication and corruption. A later date saw the development of antinomic values within the New World itself, contrasting a virile, democratic West with an effete, autocratic, Mammon-worshipping East. The dominant spatial metaphors for American destiny, particularly in the nineteenth century, are the garden, the West, the frontier, and wilderness. The city, by contrast, stands for the world's temptations and iniquities. Beginning with Jefferson, the intellectuals, though they come largely from an urban background, have persistently enforced the agrarian myth to the detriment of the environment that nurtured their learning and elegance. The farmers themselves are understandably pleased. It has become an unthinking reflex for Americans to see the city as the farmer and the intellectual see it: Babylon- den of iniquity, atheistic and un-American, impersonal and destructive.

What has happened to the image of the city as the New Jerusalem, to the idea that the city in its monumentality and glory is a symbol for world society and cosmos? We have seen the importance of the idea of the city as a transcendental symbol in the Old World. Has none of it been transferred to the New? The idea did take root in America but its growth was, and continues to be, hampered by the pervasive agrarian myth. American towns acquired metropolitan stature and cosmopolitan traits in the nineteenth century, at a time when not only the transcendental symbolism of the city had long been buried in Europe but also the urban enthusiasms of such Enlightenment figures as Voltaire, Adam Smith, and Fichte. Romanticism, posing images of Gothic urban horror against the sunlit landscapes of the countryside, was regnant among the intellectuals. American Romantics in fact showed a greater respect for urban values than did their European counterparts.

The American urban vision borrowed from Old World sources, particularly the Bible; the works of Augustine, Dante, and Bunyan were also influential. To the Puritans the city served as metaphor for the ideal community, the New Jerusalem. As John Winthrop put it, "we must consider that we shall be as a City upon a Hill, the eyes of all people are upon us." Not only was the city to be a model community to which the eyes of the people could turn, but the Puritans intended it also as a community from which the saints could look down upon all the people; it was built not only to be an example to the world but a perspective on the world.[1] However, the Puritan's city did not aspire to cosmic symbolization. It made no effort to simulate the geometric order and mineral purity of the New Jerusalem of Revelations. Cosmic cities of antiquity shared the cosmic faith of the countryside, but in the cities the faith was made brilliantly visible in monumental architecture and through the performance of royal-sacerdotal rites. This was not the ambition of the early Puritans nor of their town-founding descendants in the nineteenth century. From the beginning, the Puritan's "City on a Hill" shared the farmer's values and accepted his cosmos; and it was far from the Puritan's mind to translate these values into urban life styles and design.

Yet it is a mistake to think that the image of the city in America has been consistently bad. In the New World no less than in the Old, the city stood for the heroic achievements of man. Not all intellectuals have denounced it. Some poets and scholars have praised its vitality and creativeness. Moreover, the American city has had its share of extravagant boosterism, particularly in the middle portion of the nineteenth century when such places as Cincinnati, St. Louis, and Chicago competed with each other for settlers and grew with extraordinary rapidity.[2]

Whatever the image, cities have in fact played a vital role in the development of the United States since the founding of the nation. Indeed,

---

1 Michael S. Cowan, *City of the West: Emerson, America, and Urban Metaphor* (New Haven: Yale University Press, 1967), pp. 73–74.
2 Frank Freidel, "Boosters, Intellectuals, and the American City," in Oscar Handlin and John Burchard (eds.), *The Historian and The City* (Cambridge: M.I.T. Press, 1966), pp. 115–20; Arthur N. Schlesinger, "The City in American History," *Mississippi Valley Historical Review*, 27 (June 1940), 43–66.

as the historian Constance Green put it, "It was apprehension lest trade rivalries of city merchants of the eastern seaboard destroy the new states that led to the drafting of the federal Constitution and the formation of the federal Union."[3] As early as the seventeenth century, urban centers where men exchanged not only goods but ideas were emerging. The Revolution itself and the rise of the Confederation of thirteen independent states were nurtured in the cities of America. The cities were then very small and formed no more than three percent of the total population. In the nineteenth century, however, nonrural settlements grew rapidly. Rural and nonrural populations increased at a comparable rate only during the decade of 1810 and 1820. By 1880–1890 the cities acquired people at four times the rate of the countryside. Urban primacy was particularly impressive in the West where the city's economic and political substance tended to overshadow the weakly-developed personality of the state. For example, by 1880 Denver became the metropolis of a region much larger than Colorado. No other sizable town offered competition within a radius of 500 miles. Its hegemony showed that the city rather than the state was the key to the development of a new country.

As the object of allegiance the state appears to have declined in significance in the post-Civil War period. Two major causes were: the War itself which greatly heightened men's consciousness of America as a nation; and the rise of urban power in the last decades of the nineteenth century. Americans who reached adulthood before the Civil War had thought of themselves first as citizens of a state—South Carolina, Massachusetts, or Ohio—and only secondly as citizens of the United States. In the 1870s and 1880s they came to identify themselves first as Americans and secondly as Bostonians, Philadelphians, or Cincinnatians. Charlestonians and Chicagoans, it is true, had from the beginning marked themselves by their city. Until the mid-nineteenth century Charleston was South Carolina in essence, and a century later state officials still occasionally had difficulty in persuading elderly Charlestonians that their automobiles needed South Carolina licenses as well as Charleston plates.[4]

Writers of the first rank have often poured scorn on the city. It is easy to pick up comments such as that made by Hawthorne: "All towns should be made capable of purification by fire, or of decay, within each half-century." Or Whitman's indictment of New York and Brooklyn as "a sort of dry and flat Sahara." In fact the attitude of poets was characteristically ambivalent. Whitman, for example, did sometimes treat cities gazetteer-fashion but his better poems transformed them into ethereal visions, "gliding

---

[3] Constance M. Green, *American Cities in the Growth of the Nation* (London: Athlone Press, 1957), p. 1.
[4] Green, *American Cities,* pp. 19, 142.

wonders." Manhattan nearly always appeared to him as strangely evanescent ("... heaven-cloud canopy my city with delicate haze ..."). His indictments were offset with tributes. In one place, New York and Brooklyn might be likened to the Sahara and yet in another the poet would chant to the "Splendor, picturesqueness, and oceanic amplitude and rush of these great cities," which gave promise of a "sane and heroic life" (*Democratic Vistas*). Unlike bucolic poets, Whitman often reached lyrical heights when he affirmed man's links to both nature and the city. New York and the myriad people in it were on the scale of oceans and tides (*Specimen Days*). Hawthorne, too, saw an analogy between the city and nature. "The wild life of the streets has perhaps as unforgettable a charm, to those who have once thoroughly imbibed in it, as the life of the forest or of the prairie." Even Thoreau noted, somewhat mysteriously, that "... Though the city is no more attractive to me than ever, yet I see less difference between a city and some dismallest swamp than formerly."[5]

The American dream is compounded of profoundly ambivalent and even contradictory elements. Nowhere is the dream's dichotomy more evident than in the desire to combine, in the nineteenth century, the antithetical images of an urban empire and an agrarian nation. Emerson's lament of 1844 epitomized a strain of deep malaise in American thought. "I wish," he wrote, "to have rural strength and religion for my children...and I wish city facility and polish. I find with chagrin that I cannot have both." Nonetheless, Emerson persistently sought to reconcile the idea of high civilization with the idea of untouched nature, empire with garden. His utopia aspired to amalgamate the best elements from diverse worlds. However, the city rather than nature assumed a central symbolic position in his larger utopia. Even in his youth Emerson recognized that the good people who lived in the woodlands of Connecticut did not esteem them; and that it was often the townsmen who were intoxicated with being in the country. Many years later he argued that the "city boy" generally possessed a "finer perception" than "the owner of the wood-lots." The impulse toward the reconciliation of the rural and urban worlds was to come from the Western Cosmopolitan rather than from the Noble Savage. The master metaphor for Emerson was the City of the West, which combined urban and Western referents. Unlike the Puritan's exclusionist City on a Hill, Emerson's city was open—a place of radical equality and divine spaciousness. "O City of God! thy gates stand always open, free to all comers..."

For the Puritans as for Emerson the term "city" stood primarily for the quality of the human community; the physical frame had only secondary importance. Emerson's vision of the physical frame was expansive in con-

[5] See David R. Weimer, *The City as Metaphor* (New York: Random House, 1966).

formity with the spaciousness of the West itself. The vast hinterland offered the city scope to expand not only its boundaries but the scale of its internal components. Lecture tours enabled Emerson to visit many of the new and rapidly growing cities of the interior. He was impressed by St. Louis' "spacious squares and ample room to grow." He also praised the "magnificent" hotels of Cincinnati and Philadelphia and observed with pleasure the noble buildings and broad vistas of Washington. Vast urban scale pleased Emerson for what it could say about America. When he complained of the "miles of endless squares," he was not protesting against the spatial scale so much as man's failure to measure up to it.[6] Whitman, too, could glory in the work of man and yet find man wanting. His experience of New York made him realize "that not Nature alone is great in her fields of freedom and the open air... but in the artificial, the work of man too is equally great." This was how he felt, yet there remained the nagging question, "Are there, indeed, *men* here worthy of the name?"

specific urban symbols

The city itself can be a monument. Persepolis, the Round City of Baghdad, Palitana, and Peking are monuments. Their physical layout, their geometry and hierarchical ordering of forms, are architectural means to express an ideal of cosmos and society. In the United States, Washington, D.C., was conceived to symbolize an ideal. Not the cosmos but an image of national greatness inspired its founding and design. Pierre l'Enfant, the planner, sought to create a city of beauty and magnificence. His plan of 1791 emphasized the monumental and the symbolic. It allowed five grand fountains and three major monuments. Of the latter, one was to be an equestrian statue of Washington at the intersection of the axes from the Capitol and the President's house; another, a Naval Itinerary Column, was to stand on an open space facing the Potomac, and the third was to be an historic Column from which all distances of places through the Continent were to be calculated.[7] Such grand motifs of design were conceived to magnify the glory of despotic kings. Historians have often commented on the irony of applying them to a nation founded on democratic principles, but the irony apparently escaped the leaders of the young nation who were intoxicated with the sense of republican grandeur. Even Jefferson did not object. His agrarian and democratic beliefs seemed not to conflict with his ambitions for the capital. The urban scale of Washington, D.C. owed much

---

[6] Cowan, *City of the West,* p. 215.
[7] John W. Reps, *Monumental Washington* (Princeton, N.J.: Princeton University Press, 1967), pp. 18–20.

to Jefferson. "It was he who appointed Benjamin Henry Latrobe, one of the greatest early architects, to be supervisor of public buildings; it was he who retained the services of Giuseppi Franzoni, an Italian sculptor, to work on the Capitol; it was he who persuaded Congress to appropriate moneys for the improvement of the city and spent a third of it in laying out Pennsylvania Avenue in the manner of a Paris boulevard."[8]

Washington is the exception. Most cities in the United States owe their morphology to the convenience of the survey grid and to the economics of growth along lines of transportation. Religious and civic aspirations take visible shape as discrete architectural elements in the urban scene. Until the last quarter of the nineteenth century church steeples were prominent, if not dominant, features of the skyline even in the largest cities. The spire of Trinity Church towered over lower Manhattan and it was only in the 1890s that skyscrapers rising at the head of Wall Street threatened the church with obscurity. Houses of God were so numerous in New York City that a whole section, Brooklyn, was known as the "Borough of Churches." In the 1830s Cincinnati had twenty-four churches, Philadelphia ninety-six and New York a hundred, in each case a house of God to every thousand people. Of churches in New York, James Fenimore Cooper wrote: "I saw more than a dozen in the process of construction, and there is scarce a street of any magnitude that does not possess one."[9] Until the 1940s, church spires dominated Charleston's skyline, and even in the second half of the twentieth century they are often the most assertive architectural element in the smaller communities throughout America.

Besides churches American cities possess another prominent architectural symbol for the country's noneconomic aspiration: this is the "temple of government." Government buildings have taken the form of public palaces, built often in the grand American-Roman style. Of course Washington, D.C. has the most magnificent public palaces but imposing specimens can be found in state capitals and even in some county seats of very modest size. As two architectural historians put it:

> It is largely through these public palaces that Americans have expressed their desire for splendor, and the visitor to our cities must go to the state houses, post offices and court houses to find the mural painting, sculpture and ornament that are missing elsewhere. If it were not for government patronage of the arts, admittedly spasmodic and casual, our communities would be much farther from satisfying the need for symbols of civic and national pride,

8 Christopher Tunnard and H. H. Reed, *American Skyline* (New York: New American Library, 1956), p. 28.
9 Quoted in Christopher Tunnard, *The City of Man* (New York: Scribner's, 1953), p. 13.

which the people of a republic demand—and ours have demanded—no less than kings and popes.[10]

An urban symbol may be a functional structure like a bridge, a non-utilitarian edifice like the St. Louis arch, or a piece of land like the Boston Common. The bridge is simultaneously a utilitarian fact and a symbol for connectness or transition from one place to the next, from one world to another. *Pons* is the common Latin root for bridge and priest. Of American bridges perhaps the best known is Brooklyn bridge. From the beginning it commanded a degree of public interest that exceeded its function as a convenience of transportation. Physical dimensions contributed to the bridge's legend. Its 1,600-foot span, held up by a gauze of graceful cables, seemed to defy the heaviness of earth. Until skyscrapers went up in Manhattan in the 1890s the bridge's Gothic towers dominated the skyline. The fact that it was heavily used from the start also helped to impose its image on the public consciousness. When the bridge was opened officially in 1883, each of the two cities it joined already had about one million people. Legends surrounded the architect John Roebling, who was a philosopher-engineer and a Hegelian. He saw in his work the embodiment of the American ideal of westward movement and the linking of East and West. It is not surprising that the Union Pacific Railroad was hailed as the last link in the course westward to India that began with Columbus's vision; but Brooklyn bridge received similar acclaim. The opening ceremony was a public drama attended by the president of the United States, and designed to symbolize the union of the people with their leaders in their joint pride of achievement. For many Americans in 1883, Brooklyn bridge also proved the nation to be healed of its wounds of civil war and again on its true course, which was the peaceful mastery of nature. Effusions over the structure did not end with the closing of the ceremonies. The translation of Brooklyn bridge from fact to symbol continued in the experiences of the people who used it or moved in its ambiance, in the response of journalists and architectural historians, and in the works of the mythmakers—painters and poets. In 1964 Brooklyn bridge was declared a National Monument.[11]

The bridge is a fact that may or may not turn into a symbol. A monument like St. Louis' arch is designed expressly as a symbol—the outward sign of an inward grace, which in this instance is the city's historic role as the gateway to the West. In 1933 plans already existed to convert the site of the original village of St. Louis into a park, commemorating the Lousiana

10 Tunnard and Reed, *American Skyline,* p. 29.
11 Alan Trachtenberg, *Brooklyn Bridge: Fact and Symbol* (New York: Oxford University Press, 1965), pp. 8–9.

Purchase which enlarged the vision of America from the boundary at the Mississippi River westward to the Pacific. President Truman dedicated the site in 1950, but it was not until 1965 that the memorial's central show-piece, the Gateway Arch, was completed. This gleaming curve of stainless steel plating soars with catenary grace to a height of 630 feet, that is, 75 feet higher than the Washington Monument, as tourist guides and local residents are proud to point out. The meaning of the arch derives from ancient tradition: like the dome it symbolizes heaven, the limbs leading the eye upward to the round curve at the apex; and in analogy to the monu-mental portal that opens into the city or palace it regally beckons the traveler to enter the promised land. Historically, travel to the new frontiers began at St. Louis. The city's commerce had its beginnings in the supply of guns, saddles, wagons, tools, building material, medicine, and food to western travelers, and in marketing the furs that the mountain men sent back. Today officials at the center gently urge the tourists to go further west along the Santa Fe and Oregon trails and experience the environment, if not the hardship, of their forebears. The memorial is administered by the National Park Service which sees fit to remind the public that "Because the Gateway Arch is a National Memorial equal in dignity and grandeur to other great memorials and is becoming a symbol of St. Louis, it should be utilized in advertizing, displays, cartoons, etc., with restraint." In making use of the arch, one should ask, "Is the proposed use frivolous or ostentatious?...Is the Gateway Arch displayed in its proportionate scale to other structures? It should not be displayed in a subordinate role to other structures since not only is it the dominant physical feature of the Memorial but also it is the dominant physical feature within the City of St. Louis."[12] It seems clear that, if not to the local citizenry then to the country at large, the outstanding symbol for St. Louis will not be such old landmarks as Eads Bridge or the Old Courthouse but the soaring arch built to serve no utilitarian ends.

The Gateway Arch is designed specifically to capture a widely-shared historical sentiment. Its success depends not only on the aptness of the sym-bol but also, to a large degree, on its ability to capture the public's imagina-tion through novelty and sheer size. The green areas of Washington, D.C. contain some of the nation's greatest monuments: they are deliberately created sacred places. In contrast to these self-conscious symbols which must depend to some extent on bravura for success, Boston Common owes its status not to any intrinsic physical attribute but to its effectiveness in articu-lating and symbolizing the genuine historical sentiments of a significant portion of the community. Walter Firey has clearly shown how the spatial

---

[12] From a mimeographed sheet of the United States Department of the Interior, National Park Service, Jefferson National Expansion Memorial, May 25, 1970.

symbolism of Boston Common has exerted a marked influence on the ecological organization of the rest of the city. The Common is a 48-acre tract of land wedged directly into the heart of the business district, cramping it severely.

> Unlike the spacious department stores of most cities, those in Boston are frequently compressed within narrow confines and have had to extend in devious patterns through rear and adjoining buildings. Traffic in downtown Boston has literally reached the saturation point.... The American Road Builders' Association has estimated that there is a loss of $81,000 per day in Boston as a result of traffic delay.[13]

Many proposals have been made to relieve the congestion by extending a through arterial across the Common; however, economic rationale could not contend with the sentimental values that influential Bostonians and people throughout the State have vested in that tract of land. The Common has become a "sacred" object. Its integrity has a number of legal guarantees. The city charter forbids Boston in perpetuity to dispose of the Common or any portion of it. State legislation further prohibits the city from building upon the Common, except within narrow limits.

booster imagery—city nicknames

Civic pride and economic competitiveness have often combined to give cities labels (nicknames or epithets) that claim to capture their unique distinction. The nickname may complement the visual symbol: thus Florence is the Duomo or the Piazza della Signoria but it is also *la Fiorente.* New York is its famous skyline but also the Empire City and several dozen other competing epithets.

Cities in the United States are exceptionally rich in nicknames. The luxuriance is the result of competition among relatively young settlements which sense the need to advertize their individuality and unique virtues against the claims of rivals. Chambers of Commerce, civic leaders and businessmen, journalists and artists have all sought to bolster the reputation of their hometown with some striking image. Laudations are occasionally combined with the critical voices of disillusioned artists and visitors from rival towns. The result is a rich mix of incompatible images. Even where they all originate from some favorable source unforeseen contradictions and ironies may occur. Fort Worth, for example, is the Cow Town, the Panther

---

[13] Walter Firey, *Land Use in Central Boston* (Cambridge, Mass.: Harvard University Press, 1947), p. 151.

City, as well as the Arsenal of Democracy. New York is a gallimaufry of conflicting labels: it is the Big Apple, the Front Office of American Business, the Vacation City, the Babylonian Bedlam, the Capital of the World, and many others. Nicknames also change as the character of the city changes: thus Chicago was once the Garden City, generating an image of sylvan elegance that was not far from the truth before the great fire. Subsequent growth and prosperity transformed Chicago into the City of Big Shoulders and the Crime Capital.

The pell-mell of nicknames that accrues to a city in the course of time is a forceful reminder of metropolitan complexity. In any large urban center, multifarious interests exist and each will push for a label that suits its purpose. Crude epithets bear little resemblance to the poet's distilled metaphors, but they may be truer to the rhetoric of the man in the street. Joseph Kane and Gerard Alexander have compiled a list of American cities and their nicknames. Although the list cannot claim to be systematic or exhaustive, it provides sufficient information to show a geography of urban labels used in boosterism.[14]

Despite the fact that all large cities have many nicknames and that similar ones appear with monotonous regularity, regional differences are clearly discernible. To illustrate, of the four cities with the largest number of nicknames New York boasts its world status, Washington, D.C. its political supremacy; Chicago projects virility and San Francisco elegance. The images of Chicago and San Francisco reveal noteworthy similarities and differences. Both lay claim to the geographical location "West." Chicago is the Metropolis of the West, San Francisco the Queen City of the West. Both recognize the distinctiveness of their metropolitan setting. Chicago is the City by the Lake, the Gem of the Prairies; San Francisco is the Bay City, the City of a Hundred Hills. San Francisco asserts its cosmopolitanism and elegance: it is the Queen City, the Paris of America, the City Cosmopolitan. Chicago emphasizes by contrast its ties with the wealth of the region and its centrality within the nation: it is the Hogopolis, the Cornopolis, the Hub of American Merchandising and the Country's Greatest Rail Center. Although Chicago was known as the Garden City and the Gem of the Prairies, reflecting the earlier claim to gentility, the image of Chicago as an aggressive place where the men work hard and things get done has come to be far more prominent. Chicago makes no special pretension to elegance; indeed the City of Big Shoulders cannot also aspire to being the Queen City.

Geographical settings are recognized in the urban label if they are especially distinctive and attractive. For a small place like Carlsbad in New

14 This section on city nicknames is based on the data in J. N. Kane and G. L. Alexander, *Nicknames of Cities and States of the United States* (New York: Scarecrow Press, 1965).

Mexico the limestone caves are its only title to fame: it is *the* Cavern City. For the big places the topographic attribute is of minor importance. Some cities acknowledge the presence of "hill," "lake," "bluff," or "mountain." San Francisco is of course the Bay City and Houston the Bayou City. If, however, the geographical setting seems undesirable it is ignored. In Kane and Alexander's list of nicknames of American cities, the word "desert" appears only six times. Palm Springs and Indio in California are exceptional in that they actually exploit their desert setting. Indio calls itself the Desert Wonderland or Southern California's Desert Playground. Palm Springs claims to be America's Foremost Desert Resort or the Oasis in the Desert. Nevada and Arizona do not have any water problem to speak of, if we give credence to the self-bestowed images of their cities. Each state (in the Kane-Alexander listing) has only one city where the word "desert" appears—surrounded and all but lost in the welter of effusive epithets. Las Vegas is the Broadway of the Desert. But scarcity of any kind is not implied, for Las Vegas is also the City That Has Everything for Everyone—Anytime, and the Town Blessed By An Ideal Year-Round Climate.

City nicknames reflect and exaggerate the basic values and myths of America. In a nation that takes pride in its industrial prowess, it is not surprising that numerous places seek identification with their industries and products. We find Auto City, Beer City, Cash Register City, Pretzel City, Insurance City, and Shoe City among others. On the other hand there exist (although in far smaller number than the first group) botanical and pastoral epithets like camellia, lawn, oak, bower, palm, and sycamore. The great epic of American history is the westward migration. In Kane and Alexander's lists, no less than 183 cities boast the title "Gate" or "Gateway." A few do not use the specific word "gate" but they nonetheless emphasize their character as passageways or routes. Modesto in California, for example, is advertized as the "City that is only two hours to the Sierras or the sea." Some of the smaller towns use the word "gate" merely to draw attention to a local tourist attraction or a scenic area; thus Grand Portage, Minnesota, is the Gateway to Isle Royal National Park. There are nine "Gateways to the West," four "Gateways to the South," but none to the north or east. Naturally, if one goes westward far enough one reaches the East. Hence San Francisco is the Gateway to the Far East. Beyond the Golden Gate lies Paradise, as Hawaii calls itself. But the course of empire no longer points westward. A place like Titusville (Florida) hopes to cash in on the future by claiming to be the Gateway to the Galaxies.

We normally think of cities as centers of convergence. To motorists moving across the continent, however, cities are not necessarily destinations; they may merely be places to refuel, eat, or obtain a night's rest. Even local residents proudly declare their hometown to be a "gateway," as though it were just a place to pass through. But this apparent show of modesty is countered by the citizens' desire to advertize their town as, in some sense, the world's center. So, if there are 183 "gateways," there are at least 240 variants of nicknames in which the word "capital" appears; and the number rises several fold if we include also the "Hub," the "Home," the "Center," the "Heart," the "Cradle," the "Crossroads," and the "Birthplace." Many cities stress both their centrality—a standing that is supposedly derived from their achievement and geographical advantages—and their position as gateway, which promises the future. St. Louis is the Hub of American Inland Navigation as well as the Gateway to the West.

imageability

Boosterism aims to create a favorable image and has little respect for complex truth. But to be effective the image must have some grounding in fact. A strong trait is made to stand for the whole personality. What this is, we have seen, varies not only with the real differences among and within the cities, but with the specialized concerns of the groups that wish to draw the public's attention to a particular attribute. An epithet or a catch phrase provides the image. It cannot, however, project a clear visual image even when it tries to be descriptive as in the designations the Garden City, the City of Bridges, the Windy City, the Broadway of the Desert, and so on. Often the designations are more abstract as, for example, the Queen City of the West. Differing in approach, though not in aim, are the attempts to capture the character of a place by a specific scene or picture. Again we can point to the effectiveness of Manhattan's skyline as the emblem of New York. Anselm Strauss points out that for a film to establish its locale in New York the famous skyscraper profile needs to be flashed on the screen for only a second.[15] Many European cities have visual emblems of comparable power. London is easily recognized from a scene of Picadilly Circus or a view of the Houses of Parliament by the Thames River, Paris from the bookstalls along the Seine, Moscow from the Red Square in winter. American cities lack visual identity. Egregious exceptions like New York, San Francisco, or New Orleans remind us all the more of the visual greyness of most other metropolises. Yet even small cities sell postcards, revealing a faith in the worthiness of their main street, parks, and monuments. Postcards depict aspects of the town that are believed to do it credit. Occasionally a typical street scene is shown, but more often postcards stress the highlights—the parts that capture the attention, that have high imageability.

[15] Anselm L. Strauss, *Images of the American City* (New York: Free Press, 1961), p. 9.

Postcards tell us something about imageability. They probably reflect the values of the local businessmen. Until Kevin Lynch's book *The Image of the City* appeared in 1960, little was known about the mental maps of city dwellers. Lynch presents us with the public image of the central districts of three cities, Boston, Jersey City, and Los Angeles.[16] Members of the professional and managerial class, for the purpose of the study, constitute the public. In Boston and Jersey City the sample tested and interviewed reside in the central district; in Los Angeles so few members of the middle class live in the central district that the sample has to be made up of people who work downtown but have their homes elsewhere. Anyone who has a passing acquaintance of these cities will probably say of Boston that it has a fairly strong visual personality; of downtown Los Angeles that it shows less character, and of Jersey City that it is nondescript. Such impressions are confirmed by the local residents. Their perceptions are naturally more specific: even Jersey City has more shape and pattern than a casual visitor might think, as indeed it must to be liveable.

To most of the people that Lynch interviewed, Boston is a historical and rather dirty city of distinctive locales, red-brick buildings and crooked, confusing paths. The favorite views are usually the distant panoramas that give a sense of water and space. Residents have a good grasp of the broad spatial structure of Boston, aided by the clear edge of the Charles River and the parallel streets of the adjoining Back Bay area that lead eastward into the Common and the shopping district. Away from the edge of the river the city seems to lose precision. The regular grid of Back Bay, a common enough pattern of American cities, takes on extra visibility in Boston by contrast with the irregular grid in other parts of the city. Places that strike most people as particularly vivid are the Common, Beacon Hill, the Charles River, and Commonwealth Avenue. For many they form the core of their image of central Boston.

Jersey City lies between Newark and New York City and is crisscrossed by railroads and elevated highways. Competition has etiolated its central functions. It looks more like a place to pass through than to live in. "To the usual formlessness of space and heterogeneity of structure that mark the blighted area of àny American city is added the complete confusion of an uncoordinated street system."[17] Residents can think of few landmarks; their mental map of Jersey City is fragmented and has large blank areas. To the question of effective symbols the most common response is to point to the New York skyline across the river rather than to anything within the city. A characteristic judgment is that Jersey City is merely a place on the fringe of something else. One resident claims that his two symbols are the

---

16 Kevin Lynch, *The Image of the City* (Cambridge: M.I.T. Press, 1964).
17 Lynch, *Image of the City*, p. 25.

skyline of New York, on the one side, and the Pulaski Skyway, standing for Newark, on the other. Jersey Citians appear indifferent to their physical setting. Streets look so much alike that the choice as to which one to use is reduced to arbitrariness when saving time is not important.

As the core of a metropolis, central Los Angeles is charged with meaning and activity. It has large imposing buildings and a fairly regular pattern of streets. Regional orientation in the metropolis seems not too difficult, being aided by mountains and hills on the one side and ocean on the other, by well-known regions such as the San Fernando Valley and Beverly Hills, by the major freeways and boulevards, and, finally, by recognizable differences in the architectural style and in the condition of the structures that mark the successive rings of growth. The distinctive vegetation, too, gives central Los Angeles character. Yet its image is less sharp than that of Boston. One reason is that the title "downtown" is used of central Los Angeles largely as a matter of habit and courtesy, for several other cores compete with it in the intensity of shopping and in the volume of business. Another reason is that the central activities are spatially extended and shifting, thus diluting their impact. But central Los Angeles is far from being another Jersey City. Mental maps formed of Los Angeles are more precise and detailed. Their composite image reveals a structure centered on Pershing Square nestling in the crook of the L formed by two shopping avenues, Broadway and 7th Street. Other prominent features are the Civic Center at the end of Broadway and the historical node of the Plaza-Olvera Street. Several architectural landmarks are recognized but only two in any detail: the black and gold Richfield Building and the pyramidal top of the City Hall. The degree of attachment to the old parts of Los Angeles, particularly to the tiny Plaza-Olvera Street node, is unexpectedly strong. To judge from the few interviews, it is even stronger than the attachment of conservative Bostonians toward what is old in their city. The middle-class people in Los Angeles that Lynch interviewed are commuters. They have a vivid impression of their own residential districts, and they continue to be aware of streets, the finer houses, and flower gardens as they drive away from their home areas; but sensitivity to the urban setting declines as they approach downtown so that on the mental maps of these commuters central Los Angeles is a sort of visual island surrounded by grey spaces. An instructive conclusion of this type of study is that experience does not necessarily increase the store of urban images of motorists.[18] The regular commuter and the occasional passenger respond to roughly the same set of visual cues.

18 Stephen Carr and Dale Schissler, "The City as a Trip," *Environment and Behavior*, 1, No. 1 (1969), 24.

image, experience, and class

Charles River, so important a visual element for well-to-do Bostonians, is rarely mentioned by low-income residents of the West End district although they make greater use of its bank. It is therefore worth restating that the city images given in Lynch's work are those of a social class; and that they are sampled from the active adult age group. Members of this class are likely to exert influence on urban life far in excess of their relative numerical strength. It also seems probable that they experience a greater range of settings in their city than the very poor, the very rich, and people of moderate income but limited education. And as active adults their world is naturally far more spacious than that of either young children or fragile oldsters. To appreciate the range of urban imagery and attitudes in a large city, we need to consult works that do not operate within the tidy canons of social science. Studs Terkel's *Division Street: America* is such a work.[19] He interviewed informally people from many walks of life in different parts of Chicago: they included cab driver, policeman, barmaid, teacher, landlady, nun, domestic, window washer, corporation vice president, and lady of means—mostly people who are not in the habit of expressing their opinions in writing. College professors and other members of the pen-wielding class have not been approached since their views are relatively abundant and accessible. The people interviewed by Terkel seemed willing to unburden themselves freely before him and his tape recorder. The result is an immensely rich record of human perceptions, attitudes, and aspirations in one Midwestern metropolis. Out of this record we can extract a wealth of urban images that, in their fragmentariness, defies facile classification.

In any large metropolis people of different income and social status live in separate parts of the city. The rich very rarely seé the poorer quarters except perhaps on slumming tours inside air-conditioned limousines. They may have a clear mental map of the city but it is largely abstract knowledge. Their own residential areas they know intimately: the rich are as isolated by their wealth in their exclusive compounds as the poor in their slums and ethnic ghettos. The poor know little of the metropolis outside their own districts. They are the urban villagers, suffering many of the city's ills but enjoying few of its compensating amenities. The poor, however, do have a "backstairs" experience of the outside world. When ill they may be taken to a distant hospital for free or low-cost service, and when they run afoul of the law they spend time in a distant reformatory or jail. The poor thus

[19] Studs Terkel, *Division Street: America* (New York: Avon Books–Random House, 1968).

become aware of alien places that seem threatening even when the purpose of the institution, as with the hospital, is benign. One result of these alarming, involuntary trips to the outside world may be to increase their awareness of the identity of their own neighborhood. On a day-to-day basis, the female poor know well-to-do residential areas as maids, gaining a perspective on the world of wealth very unlike that of their employers. In contrast to lower-class housing, the front and back regions of middle-class residences are sharply differentiated. The front tends to be tidy and formal, the rear unprepossessing. Social adults enter the house through the front, while the socially marginal—the domestics, delivery men, and children—enter through the rear. In the middle- and upper-class business world, janitors and scrubwomen perceive and work in environments that differ appreciably from those of executives and their retinue of well-pressed assistants. The uniformed workers perceive the small doors that lead to the back regions of business buildings; they see and smell the "guts" of the building exposed in the basement store and heating rooms; they are well aware of the profane transportation system that moves the dirty cleaning equipment, the large stage props, and themselves.[20]

The upper-middle- and upper-class white American male lives in sylvan suburbia and works in a steel-and-glass tower downtown. The route he traverses daily is the freeway or road that passes through the better residential and business districts. The social character of the parts of the city—nodes and connecting routes—that he experiences in person is essentially homogeneous. Business trips take him to other towns but the places he visits are of the same general physical and social character. Vacations to Europe lead him to urban milieus that are different only superficially if he continues to circulate at the same socioeconomic level. True novelty is jarring, even painful; the pleasant vacation combines the security of the familiar with mere tokens of adventure. What is true of the well-to-do probably holds also for the less affluent middle- and lower-middle classes: their experiences of the city are tied to places that, however physically distinctive, tend to have similar social standing. Descent to quarters of a lower level occur as infrequent visits—to shop for specialty foods and to eat in ethnic restaurants. The emphasis here is on the very narrow range of urban experience for most city dwellers. When a family moves into a new town there is usually a brief period of exploration to become oriented to the larger setting, to locate the shopping areas, and decide on the shortest and most pleasant paths between home and places of work. But soon a routine is established that deviates very little from one work week to the next.

20 Erving Goffman, *The Presentation of Self in Everyday Life* (Garden City, N.Y.: Doubleday, 1959), pp. 123–24.

Perhaps a member of the professional middle class—a doctor, lawyer, or journalist—has greater opportunity to experience a broad range of environments and cultures than either the very rich or poor. William Stringfellow noted with surprise this unexpected bonus of freedom when, as a young graduate of Harvard Law School, he went to Harlem to live, to work as a lawyer, to take part in neighborhood politics, and to be a layman in the local church. He lived in the slum but as a well-educated white man he was not bound to the environment. In suburbia he might have submitted to its mores but in Harlem he was free and able to transcend barriers that otherwise separated people. In the course of a day, Stringfellow might spend the morning in court with an addict, then have lunch with a law professor at Columbia, "interview clients back at 100th Street during the afternoon, have a drink with some of Harlem's community leaders at Frank's Chop House on 125th Street, have dinner with clergy friends or with fellow parishioners at a midtown restaurant, stop for a bull session with some law students or seminarians, or spend the evening talking with friends from the Harlem neighborhood." Or he might "return to the tenement to read or write; or, more often than not, do a little more work in rehabilitating the place, go out late to get the *Times,* and visit with people on the street."[21]

St. Clair Drake and Horace Cayton's study of Chicago's black ghetto suggests that the "upper shadies" also experience an exceptionally broad spectrum of life styles. Upper shadies are wealthy blacks who acquired their wealth and the social status in their community that goes with it through illegal means, for example, by operating syndicates that control lottery and gambling. They also establish legal businesses in the ghetto, partly to serve as fronts and partly to earn the approval of respectable citizens. Being black and hence ostracized by the white community, the upper shadies can identify emotionally with the ghetto poor; they are recognized by the poor as Race Men, that is, supporters of black causes. Being shady they are familiar with the underground world. Being wealthy they lead lives characteristic of wealth and engage in such social rituals as formal dinners, attending the races, and horseback riding. Upper shadies like to travel, and are continually shuttling between Chicago and New York. They visit friends on the West Coast; they have summer homes in the lake regions of Michigan and northern Illinois, and they vacation in Europe. They thus live and work in a wide range of environments and can transcend many social barriers. Only racial barriers, in the period before the second world war, confined their mobility.[22]

---

21 William Stringfellow, *My People is the Enemy* (Garden City,N.Y.: Doubleday, 1966).
22 St. Clair Drake and Horace R. Cayton, *Black Metropolis,* II (New York: Harper & Row, 1962), 547.

the urban neighborhood

RECOGNITION

"Neighborhood" and "community" denote concepts popular with planners and social workers. They provide a framework for organizing the complex human ecology of a city into manageable subareas; they are also social ideals feeding on the belief that the health of society depends on the frequency of neighborly acts and the sense of communal membership. However, Suzanne Keller has shown that the concept of neighborhood is not at all simple.[23] The planner's idea of neighborhood rarely coincides with that of the resident. A district well defined by its physical characteristics and given a prominent name on the city plan may have no reality for the local people. The words "neighborhood" and "district" tend to evoke in the outsider's mind images of simple geometrical shape, when in fact the channels of neighborly act that define neighborhood may be extremely intricate and vary from small group to small group living in close proximity. Moreover, the perceived extent of neighborhood does not necessarily correspond with the web of intense neighborly contacts. "Neighborhood" would seem to be a construct of the mind that is not essential to neighborly life; its recognition and acceptance depend on knowledge of the outside world. The paradox can be put another way: residents of a real neighborhood do not recognize the extent and uniqueness of their area unless they have experience of contiguous areas; but the more they know and experience the outside world the less involved they will be with the life of their own world, their neighborhood, and hence the less it will in fact be a neighborhood.

Distinctive neighborhoods have well-defined boundaries that tend to separate them from the mainstream of urban life. They are isolated for economic, social, and cultural reasons. The districts of the extremely wealthy and the extremely poor, the exclusive suburbs and the slums, the racial and immigrant ghettos stand out sharply in the urban mosaic. However, the residents of these locales do not recognize their own uniqueness to the same degree. The very rich are well aware of the bounds of their world: "We keep ourselves to ourselves." Middle-class suburbanites can be even more sensitive of their territorial integrity, for their world, in comparison with that of the established rich, is more vulnerable to invasion by "uppity" outsiders. Colored residents of ghettos are compelled to develop an awareness of their home ground for they encounter unmistakable hostility beyond it. On the other hand, slum dwellers and residents of white ghettos (the quarters of recent European immigrants, for example) may show little appreciation

23 Suzanne Keller, *The Urban Neighborhood* (New York: Random House, 1968).

of the fact that they occupy districts of any special character with definable boundaries. Let us look at these generalizations more closely.

Beacon Hill, Boston, is a famous upper-class neighborhood. For a long time it has been a world to itself, marked off from its contiguous areas by tradition, culture, social standing, and economic power. It is keenly aware of its own distinction, a claim that is widely accepted by outsiders. In self-awareness, in the sense of community based on culture and tradition, Beacon Hill is perhaps matched by certain ethnic quarters; but the psychological differences are very great, since the one seeks isolation through its presumption of superiority whereas the other takes isolation to be the best means to cope with threat. New middle-class suburban communities try to achieve something of Beacon Hill's exclusiveness; but without the sanction of history and tradition they must depend on economic fences or walls of racial prejudice to keep out the undesirable elements. Yet Beacon Hill began as suburbia. After the Revolution upper-class families turned to the then rural and out-of-the-way Beacon Hill district. Moreover, Beacon Hill did not simply grow: it was planned to be a fashionable quarter for people of position and means. For a century and a half it was able to maintain its high status, although next to it a working class quarter (the West End) sprang up to accommodate the successive waves of poor immigrants. The fence that Beacon Hill raised about itself was not simply economic: poor relations and indigent students of the right background could live in it, but high-paying business establishments and exclusive apartment-hotels were not welcome. In the course of time Beacon Hill has become far more than a piece of real estate; it is a symbol for a mellow world that whispers rather forbiddingly of old family lineages, distinguished residents, old family houses, local antiquities, and venerable neighborhood traditions. It is as effective symbol that Beacon Hill, in the mid-twentieth century, can continue to attract and retain certain upper-class families that would not otherwise live there. Many houses on Beacon Hill belonged to famous people and carry their names. Such domiciles are permeated by the ghostly presence of an illustrious past and can bestow instant standing to people who currently live in them.

Residents of Beacon Hill are keenly aware of their neighborhood identity. The place has a rich literary heritage, and some of the energy for composition seems to have gone into pamphleteering. Articles and pamphlets in profusion have been written by residents of the Hill, extolling its charm and sacredness. Newer communities may wish to advertize themselves likewise, but since they lack the historical reality that begets self-confidence their voices tend to be somewhat shrill. The historical theme in Beacon Hill is not only an objective fact that any scholar can uncover: it lives in the minds of the residents. Two types of organization, formal and informal, contribute to neighborhood solidarity. Formally, the Beacon Hill Association exists to represent the specialized interests of the residents as a whole. Its declared objective is "to keep undesirable business and living conditions from affecting the hill district." Formed on December 5, 1922, the existence of the Association suggests that the informal means for maintaining the Hill's character have not been adequate. It is, however, the informal organizations that give vitality to the neighborhood. In Beacon Hill they center mainly around kinship ties and visiting relationships. Of a less routine and intimate nature are certain annual ceremonies on the Hill. The principal ceremony takes place on Christmas Eve and involves caroling and candle lighting. An old custom, it had lapsed during the Civil War and was revived in the present century. Eventually the ceremony attracted city-wide attention and thousands of outsiders would flock to Beacon Hill on a Christmas Eve to observe and participate. In 1939 an estimated 75,000 persons took part in the carol singing, and nearly all the dwellings on the Hill displayed lighted candles. Such events accentuated local self-awareness and enriched the public image of the neighborhood.[24]

Beacon Hill is an example of a place where the local resident and the outsider tend to agree on its essential character and limits. The resident himself easily acts the role of the passing observer who views the district from a knowledge of the world beyond. Behind the image is the reality of the neighborhood in its historical continuity and cultural distinctiveness, in its formal and informal organization. Few urban districts are communities in all the senses that Beacon Hill is a community. The internal and external images do not normally coincide: the area perceived as neighborhood by the resident is often only a fraction of that perceived by the outsider as homogeneous social space. In a study of West Philadelphia, researchers have found that the area name familiar to social workers and informants was not widely known among the inhabitants, the majority of whom (seven-tenths) considered the area simply as part of West Philadelphia in general. The lack of prestige of the name was possibly a factor in its denial, for in a racially mixed area in the same city the inhabitants of one district might adopt the name of an adjoining district if it had greater prestige.[25] Neighborhood concept seems also a vague spatial idea to the residents of a southern town. Fewer than one out of ten respondents thought of "this part of town" as "having any particular boundaries or limits." However, 29 percent of the sample could supply some kind of a neighborhood name in response

24 Firey, *Land Use in Central Boston,* pp. 45–48, 87–88, 96.
25 Mary W. Herman, *Comparative Studies of Identification Areas in Philadelphia* (City of Philadelphia Community Renewal Program, Technical Report No. 9, April 1964, mimeographed) ; quoted in Keller, *Urban Neighborhood,* p. 98.

to the question: "If someone you meet elsewhere in Greensboro asks you where you live, what do you tell him?" An equal proportion supplied a street name, but when pressed for a neighborhood designation they were able to provide it.[26]

Boston's West End illustrates the multifaceted and often ambiguous nature of the neighborhood concept. The West End was a working-class district of Italian Americans of the first and second generation, mixed with Irish and Jewish elements that at one time dominated the area. Before its destruction under a Federal renewal program, West End, in both physical characteristics and in the life style of the people, provided a colorful contrast to its neighbor, the high-class Beacon Hill. From the economic, sociological, and cultural points of view both West End and Beacon Hill are clearly defined neighborhoods. But whereas Beacon Hill dwellers are highly conscious of their own culture and geography, this seems less true of West Enders. Trained observers of the West End scene reach conclusions that appear, at first glance, to be contradictory. Fried and Gleicher say that "the sense of the West End as a *local region,* as an area with a spatial identity going beyond (although it may include) the social relationships involved, is a common perception." To the question, "Do you think of your home in the West End as part of a local neighborhood?" eighty-one percent of those interviewed replied in the affirmative.[27] By contrast, Herbert J. Gans notes that "the concept of the West End as a neighborhood was foreign to the West Enders themselves. Although the area had long been known as the West End, the residents themselves divided it up into many *subareas,* depending in part on the extent to which the tenants in one set of streets had reason or opportunity to use another."[28] Residents of this working-class district never used the term "neighborhood." Until they were threatened with eviction so that the district could be redeveloped, the West End as a neighborhood was not important to them. They lacked interest in it as a physical or social unit. Comments about it were rarely colored by emotion. The imminence of redevelopment made many of them aware of the existence of the West End as a spatial and cultural entity, but few protested its destruction. Some felt sure until the end that while the West End as a whole was coming down, their street would not be taken.[29]

26 Robert L. Wilson, "Liveability of the City: Attitudes and Urban Development," in F. Stuart Chapin, Jr. and Shirley F. Weiss (eds.), *Urban Growth Dynamics in a Regional Cluster of Cities* (New York: Wiley, 1962), p. 380.
27 Marc Fried and Peggy Gleicher, "Some Sources of Residential Satisfaction in an Urban Slum," *Journal of the American Institute of Planners,* 27, No. 4 (1961), 308.
28 Herbert J. Gans, *The Urban Villagers* (New York: Free Press, 1962), p. 11.
29 Ibid., p. 104.

DEGREE OF SPATIAL EXPERIENCE AND CONCERN

These apparently conflicting views concerning the West Ender's awareness of neighborhood can be reconciled if we recognize the degrees of spatial experience and concern. The middle-class homeowner has an intimate experience of his house. At the same time he has an abstract but intense interest in his neighborhood as a piece of real estate the quality of which directly affects the market value of his house. Beyond economic considerations the homeowner values the neighborhood and will defend its integrity because it represents a desired way of life. The artist or intellectual, like the middle-class homeowner, is keenly aware of the special quality of his district and will defend it against encroachment. However, he is not likely to possess much property and is more apt to attach value to his neighborhood for aesthetic and sentimental reasons. Herbert Gans observed that in the campaign to save the West End the Italian Americans who participated were limited to a handful of artists and intellectuals.[30] Although the artists and writers shared many of the activities of their age and kin groups in the West End, their talents and careers set them psychologically apart. Through knowing something of the greater world they could see the West End as a whole and value its distinctive traits.

The great majority of West Enders are people of the working class. Their awareness of neighborhood seems to be made up of concentric zones, highlighted in varying degrees by the type and intensity of experience they have of them. The core of awareness centers on the home and the street or a segment of the street. Within this small locale the working class of West End socialize informally with great frequency, generating in time a warmth of feeling for place rarely attained in middle-class communities. Besides the home base working-class people may identify strongly with a few other spots, usually within walking distance of home. These are the favorite recreation areas, the local bars, and perhaps the settlement houses. Sentiment is unromantic and unverbalized but real and pervasive over these fuzzily bounded areas and the web of short linking routes. By contrast, people of the urban middle class are highly selective in the use of space, and the areas familiar to them are far flung. Another difference is that their sense of home has sharp limits. To a middle-class person home may extend to a lawn or garden for which he pays taxes, but beyond it the space is impersonal. As soon as he steps on the street he is in a public arena in which he feels little sense of belonging. To a working-class man the boundary between his dwelling and its immediate environs is permeable. All channels between dwelling and environment, such as open windows, closed windows, hallways, even walls and floors, serve as a bridge between inside and outside. One observer notes:

[30] Ibid., p. 107.

Social life has an almost uninterrupted flow between apartment and street: children are sent into the street to play, women lean out the windows to watch and take part in street activity, women go "out on the street" to talk with friends, men and boys meet on the corners at night, and families sit on the steps and talk with their neighbors at night when the weather is warm.[31]

In Boston's West End, territory is differently bounded for different people. To most residents it is quite small. The boundary between the dwelling unit and the street may be highly permeable but few people venture to include much of the public realm as their private space. The street is a common unit of neighborhood sentiment. Politicians recognize this fact, for when they campaign they not infrequently trim their talks to appeal to the passions of each street. It is instructive to note that the perceived size of the neighborhood bears little relation to the extensiveness of the West End kin- and friendship net. The conclusion would seem to be that although sentiment for place is strongly influenced by the availability and satisfactoriness of interpersonal ties, it does not depend entirely on the social network.

Neighborhood is the district in which one *feels* at home. Another more abstract sense of neighborhood is that it is the district one knows fairly well both through direct experience and through hearsay. Most West Enders claim familiarity with a large part or most of West End; and many have knowledge of contiguous areas. A quarter of the people interviewed report familiarity with some distant sector of the Boston region. In other words, many residents are aware of an inner world of the West End, surrounded by a somewhat hostile outer world. We should not expect the West Enders to be able to delimit the boundaries on maps, nor that their inner worlds be much alike. They have experienced certain differences between their world and what lies beyond, and their consciousness of these differences is intensified by their perception of the outside world as not only rich and powerful, cold and lonely, but threatening. In the mid-fifties the vague sense of threat turned into reality when plans for redevelopment were announced. For a time West Enders became fully conscious of the unique character of their district, but (as we have noted earlier) with the exception of a few intellectuals and artists, their concern for the survival of West End sufficed to generate only an occasional flurry of uncoordinated protests.

NEIGHBORHOOD SATISFACTION

By and large people are satisfied with their residential area. For those who have lived at a place for many years, familiarity breeds acceptance and

[31] Fried and Gleicher, "Residential Satisfaction," p. 312.

even attachment. Newcomers are more prone to voice discontent; on the other hand, people may express contentment with their new neighborhood despite their real feelings, because it is difficult for them to admit that by moving for economic gain they have in fact made fools of themselves. People of high income most often express satisfaction, which is hardly surprising since they are where they are by choice, and they have the means to improve the quality of their neighborhood. Less affluent people are less enthusiastic: the reasons given for why they like their area tend to be general and abstract, whereas those given for disliking it are more specific and concrete. Satisfaction seems a rather weak word: it may mean little more than the absence of persistent irritations.

It is often difficult to know how to interpret "liking" or "attachment" when it is verbally given. Liking a district does not necessarily commit a person to stay in it or even to patronize predominantly its facilities and services. Keller writes:

> In one racially mixed area of Philadelphia both white and Negro residents appreciated the area for its cleanliness, quietness, convenient location, well-maintained property, and even pleasant people. However, the white residents went outside the area for shopping and recreation and refused to participate in the single community organization, thus staying in the area physically but not in spirit.[32]

Satisfaction does not mean strong attachment. In the study of residential areas in West Philadelphia, most of those interviewed considered their area as a "fairly good" place in which to live, but fully three quarters could imagine living elsewhere. Seventy-five percent of the residents of Boston's West End, before its redevelopment, said that they liked the district or liked it very much, and fully 71 percent named the West End as their real home. Yet for a large group the West End as home seems to have meant little more than a satisfying base for moving out into the world and back. Indeed many showed greater appreciation of the home base's accessibility to other places than with the home base itself.[33] Despite the claim to liking the neighborhood, including its densely built tenements and the visual and aural closeness of people, many West Enders indicated that they would gladly move to a new house in the suburb under two conditions: that the suburb be one of the older kind scattered around Boston city, and that they could move together, maintain the old social ties and the old social climate.

City dwellers put a higher value on the quality of their neighborhood than on either the conveniences of the city or on the quality of their home. In a study of two southern cities (Durham and Greensboro, N.C.), the

---

[32] Keller, *Urban Neighborhood*, p. 110.
[33] Fried and Gleicher, "Residential Satisfaction," p. 307.

researchers found that by far the greater portion of the residents, from both the central districts and the fringes and from both high- and low-income groups, expressed satisfaction with their city as a place to live in; and that their attitudes toward the city tended to parallel their attitudes toward the neighborhood. But people also showed a greater readiness to give an opinion of their neighborhood and were far more critical of it than they were of the general environment of the city. When discussion centered on the city the residents displayed much interest in roads and streets and in mobility. However, when they had to choose between "a very good but inconveniently located neighborhood" and "a less desirable but conveniently located neighborhood," the residents were three to one in favor of the good neighborhood: accessibility to other parts of the town mattered less. In both Greensboro and Durham, higher value was placed on neighborhood than on house. When the choice was between "a very good house in a less desirable neighborhood" and "a less desirable house in a good neighborhood," six to one of the people interviewed were in favor of the neighborhood over the house.[34] Middle-class residents want a good house but most would settle for a lesser one if they could have the real advantage as well as the prestige of the good neighborhood. Working-class people also attached greater importance to the neighborhood than to the dwelling but for somewhat different reasons. In the first place, low-income working people rarely enjoyed the option of selecting between "a very good house" and "a less desirable one." They also showed less concern with the symbolic status of suburbia than did members of the lower-middle class who strove consciously to better themselves. The measure of working-class preferences requires a negative scale expressing relative states of dissatisfaction. For the working class, dissatisfaction with dwelling does not necessarily mean dissatisfaction with neighborhood. For example, although half of the Puerto Rican immigrants in New York City were dissatisfied with their living quarters, only 26 percent were dissatisfied with their neighborhoods.[35] This attitude is compatible with an oft-observed tendency among working-class people: that they do not restrict their social lives to their immediate dwellings as middle-class people tend to do, nor to differentiate private from public space quite so sharply.

Satisfaction with neighborhood depends more on satisfaction with neighbors—their friendliness and respectability—than on the physical characteristics of the residential area. Complaints about inadequate housing or unsafe streets often turn out to be complaints about the habits and standards of neighbors. Social relations seem to determine how a people will respond to the adequacy of their dwellings and facilities, whether they will stay or

34 Wilson, "Liveability of the City," pp. 380–81.
35 N. Glazer and D. McIntire, *Studies in Housing and Minority Groups* (Berkeley and Los Angeles, University of California Press, 1960), p. 163.

move, and how they cope with overcrowding and other inconveniences. West Enders of Boston, as we have noted earlier, were quite willing to move if they could do it together and maintain the old social ambiance. They were content with their district because they liked the close group experience. They did not see their area as a slum and resented the city's labelling it as such. In Greensboro, North Carolina, contentment with urban living was related to the amount of participation in church activities. The proportion of highly satisfied men who were affiliated with the church was 12 percent greater than the proportion of highly satisfied men who were not affiliated, and for women the difference was 20 percent. Similar results were obtained in Durham. The dissatisfied, who made up only a tenth of the total sample, complained about the poor shopping and transportation facilities, but it was not primarily economics that distinguished the dissatisfied from the satisfied. It was rather social relationships. The dissatisfied griped about the lack of contact with friends, with the church, and about the kind of people they had to associate with, at least twice as often as among the satisfied. Women, expectedly, put greater value on friendly and suitable neighbors than did the men. They were more attached to the neighborhood and showed greater reluctance to leave it. For both men and women general satisfaction correlated with whether expectation was frustrated or fulfilled. Thus, people with less than a high school education had few aspirations and consequently few dissatisfactions. The college educated had high aspirations but these they could fulfill in large measure; they too tended to be satisfied with their neighborhood. Discontentment reached highest proportion with people possessing a high school diploma; they had had their sights raised but they lacked the means to achieve them in adequate measure.[36]

the view from below

The view from below is of a narrow, bleak, and threatening world. People with any energy, generally the young, try to compensate for it through escape into fantasy or by acts of violence. The life styles of the poor vary as much as, if not more than, those of the rich despite the fact that the poor labor under severe economic constraints. The affluent tend to submerge local differences under the glitter of an international style. The poor, on the other hand, are strongly influenced by particularistic or ethnic traditions and by the diverse socioeconomic conditions under which they are compelled to live. Chinatown, black ghetto, and Skid Row are disparate urban worlds, sharing only poverty and low social status. In this section I shall sketch some char-

---

[36] J. Gulick et al., "Newcomer Acculturation in the City: Attitudes and Participation," in Chapin and Weiss, *Urban Growth Dynamics*, pp. 324–27.

acteristic perceptions of the poor in Harlem and in Skid Row. With Harlem the views given are chiefly those of the young. The existence of the family, however disrupted, is the fundamental social fact that distinguishes Harlem from Skid Row. Their life styles have little in common, although both ghetto blacks and Skid Rowers carry the burden of poverty and live in decaying environments. Outside prisons and concentration camps the lives of the lonely men of Skid Row are perhaps the ultimate in degradation, for unlike the ghetto poor, Skid Rowers can find no relief in the animal spirits of the young, in female altruism toward her brood, or even much in fantasy and violence.

To the outsider the most striking fact about the ghetto, such as Harlem in the 1950s, is its ugliness—the filth and the neglect. "In many stores walls are unpainted, windows are unwashed, service is poor, supplies are meager. The parks are seedy with lack of care. The streets are crowded with people and refuse."[37] Some curious incongruities appear: Harlem is filthy and yet many businesses cater to beautification and tidying up. A visitor walking the streets of central Harlem is likely to be impressed by the succession of barber shops, beauty shops, and cleaning establishments. People are ill fed and yet businesses involved with eating and drinking (bakeries, caterers, grocery stores, liquor stores, luncheonettes, restaurants, bars, and taverns) abound, and dominate parts of the street scene. On a Sunday morning, Harlem residents are dressed up to go to church and the event would make a sedate picture except that the streets are stained with vomit and blood, tokens of Saturday night's rage and frustration. Public edifices housing a museum, an art gallery, or art school are nonexistent, despite the stereotype image of the Negro as artist. Five libraries contribute minimally to the enrichment of the mind, but hundreds of bars, hundreds of storefront churches, and scores of fortune-tellers cater to fantasy. Funeral homes, of which Harlem had 93 in the 'fifties, proclaim the reality of shoddy, unproductive lives too soon ended; yet their proliferation is at the same time a symptom of the people's need to dream in the teeth of death.

The street is ugly and dangerous but in summer it has a far greater appeal to Harlem residents than their cramped and airless rooms. A man, 35 years old, puts it this way:

> ...the officer said, "All right, everybody get off the street or inside!" Now, it's very hot. We don't have air-conditioned apartments in most of these houses up here, so where are we going if we get off the streets? We can't go back in the house because we almost suffocate. So we sit down on the curb, or stand on the sidewalk, or on the steps, things like that, till the wee hours of the morning.[38]

[37] Kenneth B. Clark, *Dark Ghetto* (New York: Harper & Row, 1967), p. 27.
[38] Ibid., p. 5.

What is a home? The middle-class image is typically composed of a house surrounded by lawn and separated from the public world of streets. Claude Brown, in his autobiographical novel, writes: "I always thought of Harlem as home, but I never thought of Harlem as being in the house. To me, home was the streets. I suppose there were many people who felt that." Children, in particular, find excitement in the street that makes the home seem dull and dismal. "When I was very young...I could always be sitting out on the stoop. I remember Mama telling me and Carole to sit on the stoop and not to move away from the front of the door. Even when it was time to go up and Carole would be pulling on me to come upstairs and eat, I never wanted to go, because there was so much out there in the street."[39]

Children are well aware of the sordidness of their environment. And even more than the physical decay they sense the threat of bums and drug addicts. The streets may provide excitement but a thin line separates excitement from fear. "I had been afraid in Harlem all my life," Brown recalls. "Even though I did things that people said were crazy—people who thought that I must not be afraid of anything—I was afraid of almost everything."[40] Children in a Harlem school for sixth graders were asked to express their impressions of their block. Typical responses were: "My block is a dirty crumby block." "My block is dirty and it smells terrible...it have doopedics and garbage pan is spill on the side walk and food is on the ground." "Around my block theirs no *trees* on the side walks like the Park on the outside...." When asked how they would improve their blocks, these eleven- and twelve-year olds recommended the removal of junkies and bums, building new houses with hot water "every day," planting trees, and making the streets into play streets by removing the bums and the parked cars.[41] Privacy is believed to be a characteristic value of the middle class. Working-class people are more tolerant of crowding; many even appreciate informal mixing in undifferentiated space among relatives and close friends. But a measure of privacy is a fundamental human need, and that measure is often transgressed in the crowded rooms of Harlem. Even children are keenly sensitive to the lack of privacy in their homes. For example, Herbert Kohl took six Harlem children to visit Harvard; they stayed at Brattle Inn. It soon transpired that the youngsters had little interest in Harvard; they wanted to stay in their rooms to enjoy the luxury of privacy, quiet, and their own beds.[42]

---

[39] Claude Brown, *Manchild in the Promised Land* (New York: New American Library), p. 428.
[40] Ibid., p. 201.
[41] Herbert Kohl, *36 Children* (New York: New American Library, 1968), pp. 47–49.
[42] Ibid., p. 60.

Teen-agers and children living in Harlem know very little of the outside world. Fantasy takes the place of reality. Teen-agers pretend to knowledge that they do not really have, some modelling themselves after petty criminals, others after college students. Undirected activity and violence alternate with lethargy and despair. A common mood of teen-agers in the 'sixties is revealed in the following chat between a social worker and a youth of nineteen.

How do you feel about the conditions here?
I don't know.
What do you mean, you don't know? You're out here every day.
As long as I can survive, I don't care about nobody else, man.
Is it rough out here in the streets, trying to survive?
Yes, if you don't put your mind to it, you know, to do something to survive by, it's rough.[43]

Knowledge of New York City beyond Harlem is very limited. Children in Herbert Kohl's class had no idea that Columbia University existed, even though they could see it from their classroom window. Trips downtown beyond Harlem were bewildering experiences. When the youngsters emerged from the subway they had difficulty in connecting the spectacular Park Avenue of opulent apartment buildings, doormen, and clean sidewalks with the Park Avenue they knew: "Where are the tracks? Where are the ash cans?" Claude Brown, in his autobiographical novel, described his first encounter with Flatbush. (His job as a delivery boy took him to that alien part of New York). "I'd never been to Flatbush in my life before. I'd never known there was such a pretty section in New York City. I needed to go over there when it was spring and everything was in bloom. I liked being in a place where everything was so clean. It used to make me feel like me."[44]

The Skid Rower occupies the lowest position in the status order of Western society. Few human beings are more exposed to the flagrant contempt of respectable people than the "Bowery Bum." Since no one is born to the Skid Row way of life, every denizen must have lost status when he moved there. It is the nadir of downward mobility. As an ecological setting for homeless men, Skid Row began to appear in large American cities about the early 1870s; it grew rapidly at the turn of the century and reached a peak some thirty years later during the Depression when more than one and a half million people, as a minimal estimate, were homeless. Since the beginning of the second world war, Skid Row population has rapidly declined.

[43] Clark, *Dark Ghetto*, pp. 89–90.
[44] Brown, *Manchild in the Promised Land*, p. 229.

An estimate in 1950 put the number of Skid Rowers in American cities at 100,000.

In physical appearance Skid Row is unmistakable. Near the central business district or heavy transportation facilities of almost every large city spreads a drab mosaic of substandard hotels and rooming houses; taverns, cheap restaurants, second-hand stores and pawnshops; employment agencies offering unskilled jobs and missions offering salvation and a free meal. Listless men, standing in groups or loitering around penny arcades or garbage cans, are a common sight. Their life style is so bizarre to the average citizen that the larger Skid Rows are a tourist attraction. Some see it romantically as a carefree life; most see it as the ultimate in degradation. The journalist who is after human interest stories can count on meeting Skid Rowers with Ph.Ds; the sociologist hypothesizing environmental causes invariably meet alcoholics from broken homes.[45] Marginal people do not verbalize their self-perceptions. They appear content to confirm whatever prejudices outsiders may have of them. Research tends to destroy the more romantic images. Bogue believes that Skid Row life can best be symbolized by two pictures:

> The first is that of the middle-aged or elderly man sitting in the lobby of a cubicle hotel looking vacantly into space as if waiting for someone who never comes. And the second is that of the gandy dancer or spot-job laborer bowed drunkenly over the bar, his earnings spent, trying to collect himself enough to get back to the cubicle without being picked up by the police.[46]

Street life is abundant but gray. Early in the morning, while most of the city is still asleep, the sidewalks begin to fill with men. Shuffling movements up and down the street continue until nine or ten at night; thereafter they gradually taper off. On Saturdays and Sundays sidewalks are packed with pedestrians and loiterers. The purpose is to window shop and socialize. Gazing into windows may take hours; reading the menu and choosing a place to eat is often a major decision for the day. Small knots of people collect at hotel entrances, on street corners, and near favorite taverns to meet acquaintances. Such encounters often lead into the tavern. Many lean against the walls to watch the social scene. The Skid Rower's one great wealth is time, and like all great wealth, it is a burden. After dark the most popular activity is watching television. Drinking in taverns is second in frequency. Winter in a northern city is an added challenge to survival; it also further isolates the men. The wind-swept and icy streets discourage the sort of activity that in warm weather consumes mercifully so large a portion

---

[45] Samuel E. Wallace, *Skid Row As a Way of Life* (New York: Harper & Row, 1968).

[46] Donald J. Bogue, *Skid Row in American Cities* (Chicago: University of Chicago Press, 1963), p. 117.

of the Skid Rower's time. In cold weather television is more than ever the channel for physical and psychological withdrawal. Skid Rowers also seek out the warmth of library reading rooms and in despair they will even have their souls saved at the missions for a few hours of warmth and a free meal. Next to food, a place to sleep (flop) is the vagrant's most insistent problem. To the respectable citizen, sleep could suggest only a bedroom or, under unusual circumstances, a couch or sleeping bag. But to the urban nomad of Skid Row it could mean one of a hundred possible flops—furnace room, cotton wagon, stairwell, trash box, scale house, hotel toilet, penny arcade, church, loading dock, and so on.[47]

Can we speak of topophilia? In Chicago's Skid Row a majority of the residents dislike their environment, but a large minority—perhaps a quarter —claim to like it. Most of the "likes," however, are merely adaptations to the need for survival: Skid Row offers the advantages of anonymity, cheap living, and proximity to welfare agencies and missions. Some inhabitants respond more positively to the district: they give it approval because they "feel at home," "find life here interesting or exciting," or they can be themselves and "do as they please." As to what Skid Rowers dislike, it is significant that they object to the people, to their drunkenness and low status, far more than to their decrepit physical setting.[48]

recapitulations

In this chapter we see how the valuation of the city can differ. On the abstract level the city may be identified with a boastful simple epithet calling attention to a single trait—bratwurst or sunshine; it is an emblem of human greed and degeneracy but also a metaphor for man's highest achievements. At the level of lived experience, the environmental attitudes of old aristocratic communities and those of the upward-mobile young from the lower-middle and middle classes barely overlap. Urban imagery is one thing for the commuter executive and quite another for the slum child on the stoop or the vagrant with time, but little else, on his hands. What generalizations can we draw? Four are worth noting: (1) Neighborhood is a very elusive idea. Intimate space is always restricted, though perhaps broader for working-class people than for the well-to-do occupants of suburbia. To the former, intimate space is a segment of the street, a street corner or courtyard: this is the felt neighborhood. To the middle-class suburbanite, intimate space may not extend beyond his house and lawn. As concept, however, neighbor-

47 James P. Spradley, *You Owe Yourself a Drunk: An Ethnography of Urban Nomads* (Boston: Little, Brown, 1970), pp. 99–109.
48 Bogue, *Skid Row*, pp. 134–38.

hood covers a much wider area in the mind of the white-collar executive than in the mind of the working-class poor. (2) People, irrespective of economic class and culture, tend to judge the quality of their environment more by what they perceive to be the desirability of their neighbors than by the physical condition of the neighborhood. (3) The imageability of a city, in the sense of how sharp and how many images are perceived and retained in the mind, does not necessarily improve much with experience. (4) A large city is often known at two levels: one of high abstraction and another of specific experience. At one extreme the city is a symbol or an image (captured in a postcard or a slogan) to which one can orient oneself; at the other it is the intimately experienced neighborhood.

CHAPTER FOURTEEN

suburbs
and
new towns:
the search
for environment

Suburb is an ideal. To middle-income people in the developed Western countries the word suggests a whole way of life in which the best of rural and urban living are combined without their defects. On the other hand, "suburbia," a word of much more recent coinage, appears to mock this ideal. Among well-educated and sophisticated people, attitudes to suburban living are ambivalent: a professor of literature will admit to an address in the Greenacres with the same sheepishness that he admits to owning a color TV.

Books and articles have been written on the "myth and reality" of the suburb. An environment in which more than a third of Americans live seems at times curiously elusive. This is not true of the city. Whatever we may think of the city it is real. Inverse romanticism explains in part this attitude; it persuades us to identify reality with whatever is hard and intransigent, commercial and crass, traits that we associate with urban centers. Another reason is the priority of the city experience. Images of the suburb arise in response to images of the city. When cities are viewed as cosmic paradigms or centers of civility and freedom, to live beyond them—in the suburbs—is to be beyond the pale, to be in a twilight zone where men cannot rise to their full humanity. On the other hand, when cities are described as abominations, "dins of iniquity," suburbs acquire a romantic if not holy glow. In neither case is the suburb, in relation to the city, quite real. The suburb also seems utopian (in the ambivalent sense of "desired place" and "no place") because writers tend to depict the move out of the city as a free undertaking. Sociologists take the rural-urban migration of the nineteenth century to be the result of economic compulsion, but the twentieth-century exodus into the suburbs tends to be explained by the notion of "a search for environment." In this chapter I shall attempt to describe some common responses to the suburb in dialectical relationship to the image and reality of the city.

suburb—"beyond the wall"

The traditional city, we have seen, has cosmic overtones. It is a symbol of the center; it is sacred and ordered space walled off from the profane world. When citizens of the medieval town boasted, "City air makes us free," they recognized the fact that beyond the city wall freedom was curtailed: the humbler traders huddled outside the gates, and in the countryside peasants and serfs toiled under the watch of their overlords. The medieval scholar Alanus ab Insulis compared the universe to a city. In the central castle, in the Empyrean, the Emperor sat enthroned. The angelic knighthood lived in the lower heavens, while human beings were creatures of the margin and dwelt outside the city wall. C. S. Lewis comments on the exquisite touch with which Alanus denied our species even the tragic dignity of being outcasts by making us merely suburban.[1] In the modern world the "core" character of cities is suggested in many French towns by the road signs at the city limits—*Centre-ville et toutes directions*.

City denotes civility. The word "civilization," first coined in the middle of the eighteenth century, meant at first simply the civility and urbanity that one could expect to find in the company of town dwellers. To be *sub-urban* was not quite to be the uncouth countryman but it did mean, literally, to be less than urban, less urbane, not quite civil, not fully civilized. This view had a basis in fact: the less desirable occupations, the less prestigious elements of society and the outcasts established themselves outside the bounds of the traditional city. In a dialogue from *The Canterbury Tales* (1386), Chaucer revealed something of his contemporaries's attitude toward the suburb.

> *"Where dwelle ye? if it to teele be."*
> *"In the suburbes of a toun," quod he,*

[1] C. S. Lewis, *The Discarded Image* (Cambridge: Cambridge University Press, 1964), p. 58.

"Lurkyne in hernes and lanes blynde,
Where-as thise robbours and thise theves, by kynde,
Holden hir pryvee, fereful residence."[2]

Suburbs began in England, as they did on the Continent, with the extramural settlement of persons who stood in every sense on the fringes of urban society. By the sixteenth century, France had its distinctive *faubourg* ("fore"-burg) just as England had its *"fore*-streets." They shared certain features. For instance, inns, places of amusement, minor industries, and obnoxious trades like soap making and leather tanning were established outside the city limits.[3] The poor in England flocked to the suburbs, and likewise foreign immigrants who set up industries that competed with those of the city guilds. Law and order were difficult to enforce in the London suburbs of Tudor times. In France the "fore" element of *faubourg* acquired the folk etymological interpretation of *faux*, that is, "imitation" or "sham." Although the word *faubourg* has lost its early association with the poor quarters, the word *faubourien* (suburban dweller) still retains it.

The concept of a hierarchical gradient sloping from the exalted center to the lowly margins was idealized in the Medean capital of Ecbatana. Even in the twentieth century something of a value gradient is retained in the successive zones of a great metropolis. Richard Sennett says: "Cities were arranged in rings of socioeconomic wealth, with the factories at the outskirts of town, workers' suburbs or quarters next to them, and then increasingly more affluent belts of housing as one moved closer to the center of the city."[4] At the center, monumental buildings devoted to administration, commerce, and the arts congregated. Up to the time of the second world war European cities such as Turin, Vienna, and Paris retained this pattern. In Paris one of the best residential districts lies between the Place de l'Etoile and the Bois de Boulogne. The rich could afford to remain in the metropolitan core, while rising land values since the 1870s forced the poor to move out to the suburbs. Sophisticated Europeans preferred to live close to the cultural amenities of the central city. A survey of Vienna in the 1950s showed that 82 percent of the people sampled wanted to stay in the town center. Even in the United States, great metropolitan centers like New York, Boston, and Chicago managed to retain roughly the traditional urban pattern at the opening of the present century.

So long as the central city kept its wealthier citizens and cultural status, the suburb remained metaphorically outside the wall. However, the fudging and reversal of the socioeconomic gradient became increasingly common

---

2 Quoted in H. J. Dyos, *Victorian Suburb: A Study of the Growth of Camberwell* (Leicester: Leicester University Press, 1961), p. 20.

3 Ibid., p. 34.

4 Richard Sennett, *The Uses of Disorder: Personal Identity and City Life* (New York: Knopf, 1970), p. 68.

from the time of the Industrial Revolution. In Europe, commercial and workshop cities that lacked strong cultural institutions showed congested and polluted cores where the poor lived close to their places of work; beyond them stretched suburban belts of rising affluence. In the United States, particularly among the older medium-sized cities, the downtown areas visibly decay while the suburbs and outlying shopping centers acquire wealth and glamor. It is in downtown, next to the old railway station, that one normally finds the cheap hotels, eat places, and their forlorn clients. Fancy restaurants and shiny new motels stand at the outer edges of the city boundary. The suburban man sits enthroned in his split-level home while the central city, including the town hall and its governmental agencies, sink in poverty.

suburb—reaction to the city

Athens in the fifth century B.C. was a crowded unsanitary town of narrow, tortuous streets and small, dark, poorly aired homes. The Athenian valued his public persona and the public places in the city which allowed him to perform meaningful acts. The home, family life, and the comforts of the body were held to be of less account. This, however, was only one side of the picture, for many citizens had farms in the country and lived at least a part of the year away from the crampedness, the din, and the challenges of city life. The virtues of the countryside were tacitly recognized by establishing the gymnasium and the academy beyond the city walls. Imperial Rome combined open and grand public places with a dense warren of ramshackle houses and narrow filthy streets. The homes of the aristocrats mingled with the tenements of the plebs, and to escape from the fetid city air wealthy Romans built villas in the suburbs. Roman aristocrats loved luxurious mansions that had dining rooms raised far out above the sea, and many swimming pools. "Rome of the early empire looked rather like certain parts of California."[5]

The city center was the arena of public affairs. Despite the stress and strain, city living offered rewards to ambitious men. The wealthy, moreover, could always escape seasonally. If there existed a time when the foulness of the environment quite overpowered the lingering appeal of urban amenities, it was during the early decades of the Industrial Revolution. The escape into the suburbs, which improved transportation and rising incomes in the second half of the nineteenth century made possible, needs to be seen against the degraded character of the urban cores—degraded by uncontrolled industrial effluvia, and by the extraordinary packing of workers, casual laborers, and their families into miserable, foul dwellings. Dickens had made the image

---

[5] Gilbert Highet, *Poets in a Landscape* (New York: Knopf, 1957), p. 135.

of Coketown memorable. Official reports can be equally eloquent, portraying hell through the simple device of giving the facts. A superintendent of police described the low quarters of Glasgow in these words:

> The houses in which (the poor) live are unfit even for sties, and every apartment is filled with a promiscuous crowd of men, women and children, all in the most revolting state of filth and squalor. In many houses there is scarcely any ventilation; dunghills lie in the vicinity of the dwellings; and from the extremely defective sewerage, filth of every kind constantly accumulates. In these horrid dens the most abandoned characters of the city are collected, and from thence they nightly issue to disseminate disease, and to pour upon the town every species of crime and abomination.[6]

Such was the state of urban wreckage, said Lewis Mumford, that the old cry "Women and children first" made sense. "Life was actually in danger in this new urban milieu of industrialism and commercialism, and the merest counsel of prudence was to flee—flee with all one's goods, as Lot and his household had fled from the sultry hell of Sodom and Gomorrah."[7] Unfortunately, only the moneyed and professional middle class people could make the exodus. They were escaping from the city's foulness, the threat of disease, and from the poor themselves for "dread of their unwholesomeness and dirt," as one writer put it in 1850.

What other aspects of the city seemed repellent? Cramped and airless quarters even for the aristocracy and the upper middle class. For example, the house at 28 East Twentieth Street, New York, in which Theodore Roosevelt was born, stood tight between two other houses. He described the middle room on the first floor, a library, as "without windows and consequently available only at night." City dwellers also sought to escape from the stifling conventions and compulsions of urban society. In the suburbs they could be themselves, dress informally and do what they liked in their own little worlds. This ideal has a familiar and modern ring, although Leone Battista Alberti had already said it in the fifteenth century. Another reason for moving was to escape from the new immigrants. In the United States the heavy influx of Irish, East European, and Italian settlers was beginning to dilute the Anglo-American flavor of city residences in the later part of the nineteenth century. From the viewpoint of the old residents the new immigrants suffered from the twin defects of poverty and strange, therefore unacceptable, habits. More recently, Puerto Ricans and blacks have invaded the metropolises of the northeastern seaboard. Again middle-class whites responded by taking flight when they could. This motive—now generally

---

6 Quoted in William Ashworth, *The Genesis of Modern British Town Planning* (London: Routledge & Kegan Paul, 1954), p. 49.
7 Lewis Mumford, *The City in History* (New York: Harcourt Brace Jovanovich, 1961), p. 492.

regarded as unworthy—is seldom voiced. The new suburbanites prefer to stress the positive, respectable reasons: they moved because "the suburb is good for bringing up children" and, tellingly, because they preferred to live "among their own sort of people."

A general cause of flight from the city was, and is, a nebulous fear of being overwhelmed, the fear of the confusion and richness of urban life. David Riesman describes how in one of the Chicago suburbs he had found a number of extremely capable men, active in their businesses or law firms downtown, who seem to enjoy the simplicities and apparent trivia of suburban living. They appear devoted to the small scale, and "will spend time on whether dogs should be on leash or not, on whether parking meters should be installed on the main shopping street, and on minuscule questions of zoning. These men have retreated from the great problems of the metropolis, and perhaps of the nation, to the more readily manageable ones of the periphery."[8]

the growth of suburbs

The suburban image is dominated by the comfortable residential setting of the upper middle and middle classes. Suburbs, however, come in a variety of types which reflect the socioeconomic status of the residents, the presence or absence of industry, and their age—since the suburb is commonly a step in the transformation from rural to urban life styles. To understand suburban values and attitudes, a brief excursus into the growth of suburbs is necessary. The historical perspective helps us to appreciate the range of meaning possible in the term "suburb."

Archaeological evidence suggests that by the second millennium B.C., population had already spilled beyond the walls of Ur. This is one of the earliest known examples of extramural development. If we think of the suburb as simply the growing edge of a city, then it is a phenomenon that has happened repeatedly: whenever, in fact, cities were rapidly expanding into the countryside. But, for lack of documentary evidence we can rarely say whether the distinction between "city" and "suburb" was applicable to urban areas that had long since returned to dust. Walls, what remain of them, are a means for drawing the distinction: the wall was the clearest expression of what the city builders took to be the limits of their domain. In ancient China most cities had walls. The concentric ramparts defined the successive stages of incorporation of suburban communities into the

---

[8] David Riesman, "The Suburban Sadness," in William M. Dobriner (ed.), *The Suburban Community* (New York: Putnam's, 1958), p. 383.

urban sphere. Tradesmen and artisans crowded outside the city gates, and in time their numbers reached a size that justified the protection of a wall. Suburban growth could be rapid. For example, within decades of the completion of Peking's rampart, in the 1420s, a large suburb of more than one hundred thousand families sprang up beyond the southern wall. Traders from all parts of the empire and from foreign countries established shops and homes there. By the middle of the sixteenth century (ca. A.D. 1552), a new wall fenced in the suburban sprawl to form the Outer or Southern City. Concentric enclosures were also built around old European cities like Paris which, since the late Medieval period, consistently outgrew the limits imposed by its successive walls.

Suburbs housed the poorer elements of the population including traders, craftsmen, innkeepers, and foreigners, but wealthy people found quarters there too. Some Italian cities, for example, had acquired extra-mural outskirts of cottages and villas, with ample gardens, as early as the thirteenth century. Land for a belt of three miles around Florence was occupied by rich estates with costly mansions; Venetian families had their villas on the Brenta. The suburb, Mumford observes, "might almost be described as the collective urban form of the country house—the house in the park." The suburban way of life is "a derivative of the relaxed, playful, goods-consuming aristocratic life that developed out of the rough, bellicose, strenuous existence of the feudal stronghold."[9]

At the beginning of the eighteenth century, the regular commuter appeared on the English scene. A place like Epsom was not only a rural market town and spa but a suburb of London some fifteen miles away. Businessmen set up their families in Epsom; they themselves commuted to the city daily. This adds a new meaning to the suburb. Whereas in the past the aristocrats maintained suburban villas which they occupied for extended seasons, by the eighteenth century middle-class merchants could live permanently in the suburb and do their business in town. Improvements in transportation had made commuting possible. Before 1700 the suburb embraced two extreme life styles: that of the poor who lived and worked there and that of the leisured rich who repaired to their country estates in summer. Time given over to traveling was minimal. As roads and carriers improved, villas and summer homes could be established at scenic spots with little regard to distance from the city, while suburbs, housing daily commuters, sprang up at the urban fringe within reach to the central places of business. Residential suburbs soon acquired not only respectability but a reputation for self-importance and a penchant for rural fantasies that William Cowper, in 1782, could already mock in verse.

9 Mumford, *City in History,* p. 484.

Suburban villas, highway-side retreats,
That dread the encroachment of our growing streets,
Tight boxes, neatly sash'd, and in a blaze
With all a July sun's collected rays,
Delight the citizen, who, gasping there,
Breathes clouds of dust, and calls it country air.[10]

By the middle of the eighteenth century, London was growing so fast that one of Tobias Smollett's characters was made to say (in 1771), "London is gone out of town." Prosperous suburbs also sprang up to serve England's wealthier commercial and manufacturing cities. Birkenhead, for example, came into existence after the Napoleonic Wars as a place of residence for the rich merchants of Liverpool; families were lured there "by pleasant country scenery, fine river views and the wonderful ease with which they were able to pass from the bustle of the town to the quiet of the country."[11] Southport became another residential satellite of Liverpool, and bloomed especially after the opening of the railway in 1848. Although urban growth was rapid in the eighteenth and in the early part of the nineteenth century, it could not match the "explosive" expansion of the great metropolises into the countryside in the late Victorian era and since. Two major innovations in transport made this expansion possible: first the railroad, then the motor car.

Railroad and the development of mass transit broadened the economic base of people who could afford the move to the country. The middle classes followed their social betters in the exodus. Railroads radiating from the city influenced the direction of suburban growth. New housing at first clustered neatly around the train stations that were placed some three to five miles apart. This early type of suburb was small in size, seldom housing as many as 10,000 people because, other than the wealthy who could retain horse and carriage, accessibility meant being within easy walking distance to the train station. Upper-middle and middle-class residential suburbs were strung out like beads on the railway line. Each was surrounded by country greenery. The houses themselves were spacious, set in their own grounds and, from 1850 onward, both the houses and the street plans showed an increasing tendency to abandon rectilinear urban forms in favor of romantic eccentric styles for the residences, and curved naturalistic lines for the streets. Although these affluent suburbs have been criticized as havens of social irresponsibility, environmentally they had great appeal. The railroad and the tramway also enabled the working men and their families to move out of the central cities. Unfortunately the houses built for them at the urban

---

[10] Quoted in Dyos, *Victorian Suburb*, p. 23.
[11] Ashworth, *British Town Planning*, p. 40.

fringe showed little more imagination than the crowded accommodations they had abandoned. The air over the suburb was cleaner but otherwise the working class lived in mass-produced, dreary housing estates, often large enough to make nature seem as remote as when the workers were packed deep in the urban core. Even sanitation was not much better. The idea behind suburban living was its healthier environment: in reality the advantages of country air were offset by faulty building, bad drainage, and inadequate water supply beyond the town boundaries.

The trend in metropolitan expansion initiated in the railroad era continued and accelerated with the mass production of the automobile. The motorized car, at first a toy of the rich, within three decades became a major means of transportation available to the people. This was primarily an American success story. The number of automobiles in the United States increased from 9 million in 1920 to 26.5 million in 1930 and to about 40 million in 1950. The figures imply a vast gain in people's mobility as well as an overall rise in economic welfare despite major setbacks such as the depression in the 'thirties. In late Victorian England, working-class people were able to make the suburban move not only because of the railways but, as important, because they had steady jobs, shorter hours, and better wages— in other words, the economic means. Similarly in twentieth-century America the explosive suburban growth, particularly in the 'twenties and in the post-World War II period, occurred during the phases of economic boom.

The most singular feature in modern metropolitan expansion is its speed and scale. Suburbs appeared "overnight." They have the character of a "rush." Consider Toronto.[12] In 1941 the combined population of the three outlying townships of Etobicoke, Scarborough, and North York was 66,244. In 1956 it was 413,475. Five years later it had become 643,280. Areas which had only three or four rural families might be covered, a year later, by as many as 500 to 1,000 suburban homes. In 1961 greater Toronto had about two million people, more than one-half of which lived beyond the city borders. For every person domiciled in an old built-up area in 1961, one other was living in a residential area not more than fifteen years old. Statistics of dramatic suburban growth are commonplace, and indeed there is no need to appeal to figures for a phenomenon so aggressively visible as the ubiquitous suburban sprawl. The word "sprawl" is descriptive. In contrast to the neatly planned communities of the upper-middle class, the suburbs of the lower-middle and the newly-affluent working classes are a sea of undifferentiated dwellings, street blocks, and subdivisions, beginning and ending nowhere that could be seen clearly. The suburban estates of the rich

[12] S. D. Clark, *The Suburban Society* (Toronto: University of Toronto Press, 1965), pp. 9–11.

and of the high-income professional people are utopian enclaves in the vast brickish skirt that surrounds the central city.

appearance and changes in appearance

To most people in North America, the word "suburb" is likely to evoke an image of split-level homes in a setting of winding roads, tricycle-littered sidewalks, neat lawns, and straggly trees. In reality, suburbs differ much in the circumstances of their creation, in price, size, durability, institutional complexity, and in the income, educational level, and life style of their residents. How suburbs look reflect these differences. Facts of geography also count, for example, distance from downtown and the nature of the site, whether it is wooded ridge or flat farm country. A suburb may have been, originally, a village that the city people have invaded and taken over; or it may be something wholly new, created out of the cornfields by a big business builder using modern technology. It can be an older residential area, close to downtown, and made up of spacious dwellings on relatively small plots, with venerable trees and a few quaint specialized stores; or it can be a new upper-middle class community developed on the urban fringe, with large ranch-style houses, broad uncluttered front lawns, wide sidewalks and the services of a mammoth shopping complex. A suburb may be established on a wooded ridge and consist of houses of a single basic design that depend on the intricacies of site for variety; or the developers may build it on flat open land, in which case variety must depend on artificial landscaping and the construction of houses in different sizes and styles. The suburb may be row housing of nearly identical units or high-toned residences standing on their one-acre lots.

In general, suburbs are a stage in the process of urbanization. They acquire in time not only the amenities but also the less desirable traits of the city. Rich suburbanites are aware of this process. They do their best to protect their communities (their little utopias) from the forces of change, and by virtue of organization and wealth they have been fairly successful. For most suburban dwellers changes are inevitable. In many cases they are desired and deliberately made because, unlike high-income people who could move into new estates that have complete facilities, the middle classes must often occupy raw "developments," where the numerous disadvantages of an unfinished environment offset the merits of newness and cleanness. Important changes in the appearance of a suburb, for better or worse, may occur in a mere decade. Here I shall quote two passages from William Dobriner's vivid portrayal of Levittown on Long Island: one depicts the estate in 1950 when it was brand new, and another twelve years later.

To walk down a Levittown street in the spring of 1950 was to be struck by the newness of it all: freshly painted houses with western pine exteriors; the ruts that guided the '47 Chevys and Fords up to the carports; grass, growing braver each week; skinny saplings, three to a house, standing like embarrassed sentinels along the curving sidewalks. Noise, bikes and wagons and baby carriages. Knots of housewives sitting on lawns, next to busy playpens. Gangs of three- and four-year olds shriek and giggle in and out of the houses. A milk truck purposefully hammers down the road. The women, now in silence, intently study the course of a salesman as he parks his car and tries to figure out which is number 107. Above all there is the uncluttered bowl of the sky—a great, clean, blue presence coming down all over Levittown. On a clear, bright day Levittown is brilliantly etched in blue and green and is close to the sky. Only the houses reach toward it. Everything else is young, growing, and close to the ground.[13]

A dozen years later, much of the newness has worn off. Many saplings died. Some streets have become almost treeless while others are verdantly suburban. As an outside observer, Dobriner seemed unimpressed by the amateurish efforts at improvement. We may, however, read between the lines of his description and surmise that to the residents themselves the changes were not tacky; rather they expressed that freedom to innovate which was denied them in the city. Dobriner writes:

As a group, the Cape Cods seem tired. New, they were quaint and had charm. Levitt's artist specialists carefully calculated balanced color schemes for an entire neighborhood. Now, individualism, indifference, neglect, and taste good and bad have changed the balances. Do-it-yourself paint jobs; vivid red, aqua, chartreuse, cerulean, and pink trims. Jerry-built dormers stagger out of roofs. The expansion attics are all fully expanded. You see a half-finished carport, patched concrete, broken asbestos shingles, grime and children's fingerprints ground into a peeling light-blue door, a broken picket fence, a dead shrub, a muddy trampled lawn. . ."[14]

Residential suburbs are economically and culturally parasitic on the city. Some communities have sought to diversify land use and establish cultural institutions, and so achieve a measure of independence. They welcome clean industries for the jobs they create and for relieving the burden of school taxes. Two suburbs of Minneapolis, Hopkins and Golden Valley, boast industries in their midst that supply more jobs than the local population can fill.[15] Culture on any scale, however, is difficult to maintain in even rich communities unless they pool their resources. In the New York region, Westchester County has been able to support three symphony orchestras by

13 William M. Dobriner, *Class in Suburbia* (Englewood Cliffs, N.J.: Prentice-Hall, 1963), pp. 100–101.
14 Ibid., p. 105.
15 Scott Donaldson, *The Suburban Myth* (New York: Columbia University Press), p. 84.

drawing their membership and audiences from towns throughout the lower half of the county. On Long Island, too, some suburban communities are developing closer contacts with one another to pool cultural information, organizational techniques, and even audiences.[16]

Suburbs change their character for different reasons: one may have been invaded by commerce or industry, another deliberately seeks them; one suffers incursion by minority groups, another welcomes them; and a suburb may work hard to improve its public library and other hallmarks of culture. All are steps toward a more urban way of life; they are capitulations, unwilling or intentional, to urban forces and values.

suburban values and ideals

Of the many and varied motives for moving to the suburb, the search for a healthy environment and an informal life style are among the oldest. We have noted repeatedly how the sentiment for nature and rural ways is fostered by the pressures of urban life. The city environment is simultaneously seductive and nerve-jangling, beautiful and foul. People of wealth and means have always been able to seek relief from it by escaping to their country estate. In the Western world the sentiment for nature culminated in the romantic movement of the eighteenth and nineteenth centuries. Health and physical well-being figured prominently in the romantic adulation of country life but more central to the movement was the idea of virtue. A physical setting and a means of livelihood (the farmer's) had taken on moralistic overtones. The city symbolized corruption and ultimate sterility. It was the place where men struggled for power and vainglory and yet succumbed to petty social conventions. The country stood for life: life as seen in the fruits of the soil, in green growing things, in pure water and clean air, in the healthy human family, and in freedom from arbitrary political and social constraints.

The suburb has acquired some of the values of the country. The ideal image of suburban living focuses now on nature and health, now on the family, now on the freedom to organize one's own life. Europe and America share the romantic tradition and their suburban values have much in common; but there are notable differences. In England the aristocracy inspired a certain snobbery of taste among the more ambitious members of the middle class. To have a domicile, simulating the upper-class country house, in the right location mattered more to the English bourgeoisie than to their American counterpart. Some London suburban addresses of the early Vic-

16 Philip H. Ennis, "Leisure in the Suburbs: Research Prolegomenon," in Dobriner (ed.), *The Suburban Community*, p. 265.

torian period sounded, as Dyos put it, like the "monotonous but purposeful recital of Debrett—Burlington, Montague, Addington, Melbourne, Devonshire, Bedford, and so on." Middle-class suburbanites also attempted an architectural imitation, at least in the ornamental details.[17] By contrast, the older upper-class suburbs in the United States carried unpretentious geographical names such as Westport, Shaker Heights, Grosse Pointe, Whitefish Bay, and Edina. New middle-class estates tend to evoke the rural ideal and nostalgia. Communities are called Pinewood, Golden Valley, Country Village, Codbury Knolls, Sweet Hollow, Fairlawn, Green Mansion, Victorian Woods.

The suburban image in the United States is enriched by tradition and values that are distinctive to this country: for example, agrarian ideals that trace back to the Jeffersonian icon of the independent family farm; the concept of small town democracy, and frontier lores compounded of such diverse elements as individualism, man-versus-nature, and helpfulness to one's neighbor when the need arises. Consider each in turn as it is manifest in the modern suburb.

Popular names for suburbs characteristically recall some aspect of nature or country: this may be taken as one more evidence of America's nostalgia for rural ways. The front lawn and the back garden take the place of the farm, and pets the place of livestock. As tokens of another life style, lawn and pets can be more of a burden than joy to the city man without any experience of country living. Lawn and garden, in particular, are the visible signs of a nebulous faith rooted in experiences that the city man may never have had: they are maintained at much cost in time and effort so that the suburban family can signal to its neighbors that it supports the common faith. As the American farmstead is ideally a family enterprise, so the family lies at the hub of suburban living. Amenities typical of suburbia are established to meet the needs and functions of the family. The school, the church, and the shopping-recreational center are prominent icons in the landscape. By far the most common reason given for the move to the suburb is to raise children. Not only is the city apartment lacking in space for a growing family but the city itself is seen as full of danger. Parents feel anxious when their children are in the streets or out of sight. The suburban home, by contrast, is a haven for youngsters: in the bosom of the family and in a wholesome environment they cannot fail to grow into healthy and respectable citizens.

The suburb projects the image of small town democracy. Government in the big city is perceived to be hopelessly complex and corrupt. This view became a part of America's folklore in the last decades of the nineteenth century, when influx from the countryside and foreign immigration com-

17 Dyos, *Victorian Suburb*, p. 171.

bined to flood the large urban centers. In the turmoil of human numbers, conflicting human passions and needs, the divergence between principle and practice in city government so yawned as to make mockery of the historic rationale. Since the political health of the small town is also in decline for lack of a young and vigilant citizenry, only in the small semiautonomous suburb could something of the ideal of participatory democracy be maintained. In the suburb, as David Riesman noted, the successful city lawyer or business man might happily devote his talents to the minutiae of local government. The city's attempts to annex the suburbs and include them as part of metropolitan culture and government have met with strong resistance. Upper-middle and upper-class suburbs valued their legal autonomy and cozy politics. Suburban self-rule continued to expand. By 1954 the New York region boasted 1,071 separate jurisdictions; Chicago, 960; Philadelphia, 702; St. Louis, 420; until, all in all, fourteen percent of all local governments in the United States were in the metropolitan areas.[18]

The suburb is at the frontier of metropolitan expansion. It is a society coming into being, a society undergoing change, at the end of which is urban culture. Pioneering characteristics of the new suburb are revealed in its lack of form, lack of socially differentiated structure, and in the general rawness of its living conditions: muddy streets, undependable water, primitive sewerage and garbage disposal, poor or nonexistent schools, poor transportaiton and the sense of isolation.[19] A pioneering spirit of doing things oneself is necessary when a family moves into a low-income subdivision, created— almost overnight—in the countryside; also required is the spirit of cooperation with one's neighbors in similar straits. In the poorer suburbs residents often build their own homes with their own tools. They have to learn the skills of the pioneer jack-of-all-trades. The middle-class suburbanite might move into a "finished" house, but much work remains to be done which forces him into the role of a handyman. Such a role may be entered willingly: it gives added status to the father, strengthening his image as provider to the family. It is, in any case, not a role he can adopt in the crowded city apartment where every structural change requires the approval of the landlord. In the suburban home a man may actually do little to modify his surroundings but the possibility, symbolized by the well-equipped workshop, is there. Cooperation is another frontier and suburban trait. Common needs engender mutual help. The car pool and cooperative baby-sitting are adaptive responses to the scarcity of resources. The communal construction of a swimming pool in the new suburb recapitulates the experience of barn raising of an earlier period; suburbanites now exchange lawn mowers rather than

18 Robert C. Wood, *Suburb: Its People and Their Politics* (Boston: Houghton Mifflin, 1958), p. 83.
19 Clark, *Suburban Society*, p. 14.

reapers.[20] In some packaged communities for high-income people and in the older suburbs, the frontier life is more an idea than reality—an idea symbolized by a certain casualness of dress and manner, and by the charcoal broiler in the backyard over which the head of the house engages in the manly art of sizzling steaks.

Suburbs differ greatly as physical settings; likewise the environmental values and attitudes of the people who elect to live in them. People move into the suburb for diverse reasons, some of which may have little to do with the quality of the suburban environment as such. S. D. Clark notes that young people of limited means seek for a house rather than a communal setting. The first consideration for them is a house they can afford. The physical character of the suburb matters little, for it is likely to be a vast sprawl of dwelling units without any apparent boundary or center and without any sense of community. For young people in their early married life, to leave the city entails many sacrifices but the city is felt to deny them one vital necessity—a house in which to raise a family. The older professional and upper-middle-class people, by contrast, may already live in a suburb; when they move, it is to one of higher status that is more exclusive and has more amenities. The emphasis, then, is less on the individual house than on the area and "way of life." Thorncrest Village in Toronto, for example, is a package community for people in the higher income groups. When a resident in the Village is asked for the features that attracted him to it, the answer is likely to ignore the quality of the house and to emphasize the quality of the estate such as its exclusiveness, its organized community life, restricted membership, and quiet country living in a protected area.[21]

When people seek a "way of life" in a community, their image of it may be so strong as to be quite out of step with the actual way men behave. Richard Sennett illustrates the power of projection over experience in the example of the prosperous black family who tried to move into a wealthy suburb outside a midwestern city. This suburb had a divorce rate about four times that of the national average, a rate of juvenile crime approaching the worst section of the neighboring city, and a high incidence of emotional disturbance severe enough to warrant hospitalization. Yet the people of the suburb united to deny residence to the black family, claiming that they were a community of solid families, that theirs was a happy, relaxed place kept together by strong communal ties.[22]

Man's capacity for self-delusion is great. Verbal expressions of attitudes are seldom very revealing in themselves. A family floundering in debt, suffering loneliness and the numerous inconveniences of a raw, hastily put-up

20 Wood, *Suburb,* p. 131.
21 Clark, *Suburban Society,* p. 74.
22 Sennett, *Uses of Disorder,* p. 34.

environment will nonetheless declare their satisfaction with the suburban move if there is something in their new setting that has an edge on the old, which is usually the spaciousness of the house itself. A self-conscious community, striving after some collective image, will readily deny the actualities of experience. Intellectuals who write about city and suburban life styles are not exempt from delusion and bias. At one time they denounced the big city for its impersonality and corruption, and lauded the small town and rural life for their sense of community and the ability to govern themselves. Yet when people seek to realize some of the small-town and rural values in the suburb, the intellectuals (with notable exceptions such as Herbert Gans) are not happy with the result. Many have shown their disapproval by calling suburban living "escapism," "nostalgic impotence," and, at best, a kind of "sadness," or "unpleasure." Like all human creations suburbia is flawed and criticisms are often justified. But it did and does represent an ideal, one which only developers and housing agents can now praise effusively. In 1925, however, it was still unexceptional for a scholar to express warm hope for the suburbs while recognizing their limitations. H. P. Douglass wrote:

> Because they constitute an unscrambling of an overcomplex situation, because they are largely composed of like-minded people to whom cooperation should not be difficult, and because of the environmental advantages of roominess, the suburbs, in spite of their limitations, are the most promising aspect of urban civilization.... Formed out of the dust of cities, they wait to have breathed into them the breath of community sentiment, of neighborly fraternity and peace. They reflect the unspoiled and youthful aspect of urban civilization, the adolescent and not yet disillusioned part of the city, where, if at all, happiness and worthy living may be achieved, as well as material well-being.[23]

model villages and new towns

The suburb represents one ideal in the search for environment. Model villages and new towns represent another. How do the two ideals differ? Critics who denigrate the suburb can also speak harshly of new towns and garden cities, lumping them together as romantic retreats for people who cannot face the challenges and problems—the richness—of urban society. Critics sympathetic to planned suburbs may see in their aspirations toward autonomy and a relaxed life style as similar to those of the new town but achieved without the strenuous political and educational efforts that Patrick Geddes and Ebenezer Howard thought necessary. Suburbs are not made from the same mold; neither are new towns. It is not surprising that a

[23] H. P. Douglass, *The Suburban Trend* (New York: The Century Co., 1925), pp. 36–37.

diffusely organized new town on the edge of a metropolis, with only token public institutions and places of work, should look and function rather like a residential suburb; whereas an autonomous suburban community that supports local culture and invites industrial plants to move in has embraced some of the basic values of the new town program. The differences, however, are real and derive from the social as well as environmental idealism that energizes the model village and garden city movements. Suburban growth is essentially unplanned, being a stage in metropolitan expansion. People escape to the urban fringe for places to live. Other types of land use may or may not follow. By contrast, planning lies at the heart of the new town enterprise, and its scope reaches beyond residences to a total, integrated environment in which people can live, work, and play.

A precursor of the garden city (as the new town is often called) was the mid-nineteenth-century model village of northern England. Built in the countryside beyond the polluted textile towns, the model village attested to the idealism of newly-rich industrialists whose consciences were stricken by the deplorable living conditions of their factory workers. It may challenge credibility that idealism could reside in a person of new wealth. Yet such was the case: in establishing a model village the industrialist had to make certain sacrifices in his business enterprise. A strong sense of duty incumbent on the squire, a social conscience fueled by nonconformist religion, a romantic belief in nature and in community modeled after the medieval village combined to drive the Yorkshire industrialists, Titus Salt, Edward Ackroyd, and the Crossleys to spend time, energy, and resource in the founding of their model settlements. These settlements had the following features in common: they were built "from above," that is, by leaders for people under their charge; they were built in the country; they were intended to be self-contained communities in the sense that the people both lived and worked there, and planners provided for churches, cultural institutions, infirmaries, and hospital; they reflected the faith of the planners in the benevolent influence of environment on health and morals; they were small in population.[24]

The garden city movement in England began at the end of the nineteenth century under the inspiration of Ebenezer Howard. What is a garden city? Howard said in 1919 that it is "a Town designed for healthy living and industry; of a size that makes possible a full measure of social life, but not larger, surrounded by a rural belt; the whole of the land being in public ownership or held in trust for the community."[25] In this definition we see how the new town or garden city differs conceptually from the model village

---

24 Walter L. Creese, *The Search for Environment: The Garden City Before and After* (New Haven: Yale University Press, 1966), pp. 13–60.
25 Ebenezer Howard, *Garden Cities of Tomorrow* [first published under this title in 1902], edited with a preface by F. J. Osborn, and an introduction by Lewis Mumford (London: Faber & Faber, 1965), p. 26.

on the one hand and from the suburb on the other. What they have in common is that they all stem from the belief in healthy living away from the larger metropolis. A garden city, unlike the model village, is a cooperative enterprise, and not the realized dream of one all-powerful philanthropist. The social ideals behind the garden city are a step further removed from the inspiration of religion and romantic medievalism. The garden city is much larger, its population is more heterogeneous, and its industries are far more varied; it is designed for middle class people and affluent workers. Unlike the older model villages, new towns have more greenery and roomier individual lots, reflecting the naturalistic style of landscaping that acquired wide popularity by the end of the nineteenth century. Unlike the suburb the garden city is designed to be a city. Planners strive for the idea of multiple land use and a diversified population. The new town is to become a community, not because the people in it have the same socioeconomic background but because people from different walks of life need each other's services. It has a center, the focus of public functions. And it is separated from other towns by a green belt, that is, unlike most suburbs it has a clearly visible edge.

Since the establishment of the first garden city, Letchworth (1903–1905), the new town movement has had its detractors. The garden city was confused with the packaged suburb despite its explicit urban aspirations, including the fairly high residential density that Ebenezer Howard put at 70 to 100 persons per acre. Letchworth itself gave cause to some of the criticisms for its planners showed greater concern for landscaping, for spacious residential lots and the quality of individual housing than for excellence in public architecture and the coherence of the overall plan. Emphasis on the "garden" aspect of the garden city has resulted in the excessive planting of trees. By the time the trees are fully grown their dense foliage in summer blocks out sunlight and view and can be oppressive to the residents: it is only a modest improvement to move from the asphalt jungle to the greenhouse. Lewis Mumford, for long a champion of the British new town movement, admits that Letchworth is not a great success in design and that it now looks like "a cross between a modernized country town and a spread-out contemporary suburb."[26] Welwyn Garden, built some fifteen years later, has greater coherence than Letchworth, but there too the emphasis is on ample greenery and private living than on public functions, focal meeting places, and the urbanity of close-textured design. In contrast to these pioneering ventures, new towns built in the post-second world war period show less infatuation with greenery and greater concern for achieving architec-

[26] Lewis Mumford, *The Urban Prospect* (New York: Harcourt Brace Jovanovich, 1968), p. 150.

tural form, for displaying an urban texture while avoiding high-rise buildings. Cumbernauld near Glasgow exemplifies this new trend.

The new town inspired by Howard, F. J. Osborn says, is "as much a city *in* a garden—that is surrounded by beautiful country—as a city *of* gardens."[27] In recent decades design philosophy tends to shift its focus from "garden" to "city," moving the new town away from its suburban image to approximate an urban ideal. Environmental concepts underpin much of physical planning. Two ideas in particular have guided the siting and design of model villages and new towns: one is that nature has a beneficent influence on health and morals, the other is that the architectural setting has an impact on social behavior. In England, late model villages such as Bournville and Port Sunlight and the early new towns tend to stress greenery: the planners show their trust in nature's power to temper social ills. Recently-built new towns do not neglect nature, least of all the concept of the greenbelt, but their design reflects more the confidence that planners have in architectural influence. New towns are built for various purposes, one of which is to encourage social integration. In this respect the result has not been entirely successful: people of the same class tend to segregate themselves into neighborhoods. Even more upsetting from the planner's viewpoint is the way that some middle-class people will work in one town and live in another, thus undermining the concept of the new town as a self-contained community in which people of different socioeconomic background work, play, and raise their families.

The modern search for environment in suburbs and new towns began a century ago. It was driven by urban decay and the yearning for wholesome life. The self-contained new town, surrounded by a greenbelt, rather than the suburb beckons as the more promising of the solutions to urban growth. England has pioneered this effort.[28] Other countries have followed with varying degrees of success. As more settlements are built and more countries adopt the garden city scheme, some of the original ideals and purposes of the new town tend to lose focus. Conspicuous in this respect is the changing concept of proper size. "Aristotle's conception, that there was a right size for the city, big enough to encompass all its functions, but not too big to interfere with them, was re-stated in modern terms by Howard. He empirically fixed the right number as 30,000."[29] Such early garden cities as Letchworth and Welwyn Garden City had fewer than 45,000 people in 1970. Some of the more successful ventures are quite small: Tapiola near Helsinki has only 16,000 residents on one square mile of land. But there

27 Osborn, in his preface to *Garden Cities of Tomorrow*, p. 26.
28 Frank Schaffer, *The New Town Story* (London: MacGibbon & Kee, 1970).
29 Frederic J. Osborn and Arnold Whittick, *The New Towns: The Answer to Megalopolis* (London: Leonard Hall, 1969), p. 26.

seems to be a recent move toward gigantism. In France, for example, the new town of Evry (18 miles southeast of Paris) is planned to acquire 300,000 people by 1975, and 450,000 ultimately. In the United States the National Committee on Urban Growth Policy has recommended the creation of 100 near communities averaging 100,000 persons each and 10 new communities of at least 1,000,000.[30]

Paradigmatic environmental ideals are few in number. Do they reappear in somewhat different dress during different periods of history? As ideal, the cozy neolithic village ceded to the pristine cosmic city; the growth of cities into metropolitan sprawls led to the yearning for the model village close to nature and to the new town of modest size; new towns, when they are planned to contain 500,000 to 1,000,000 people each, would seem to revert to the ideal of the cosmos-building priest-kings of antiquity.

[30] Chester E. Smolski, "European New Towns," *Focus,* 22, No. 6 (1972).

summary

and

conclusions

The study of environmental perception, attitudes, and values is enormously complex. Although I have touched on a wide range of topics, almost any reader will find that I have skimped on, or overlooked entirely, themes of central concern to him. The broad framework provided here, however, may help the individual reader to place his own interests and note how they are related to other topophilic themes. Within the compass of this survey I consider the main points to be the following:

1. A person is a biological organism, a social being, and a unique individual; perception, attitude, and value reflect all three levels of being. Humans are well-equipped biologically to register a vast array of environmental stimuli. Most people go through their lives making only very limited demands on their perceptual powers. Culture and environment largely determine which of the senses are favored. In the modern world vision tends to be emphasized at the expense of the other senses, smell and touch in particular for they require proximity and slow pace to function, and they stir the emotions. Human beings respond to the environment in numerous ways but a few are based on biology and transcend particular cultures. For example, the range in size of the objects that people are able to perceive and relate emotionally is limited; human beings attempt to segment the con-

tinua of space and time; their taxonomies of biological nature show a basic similarity; the human mind is disposed to organize entities into antinomic pairs and to seek their mediation; ethnocentrism and the concentric arrangement of emotive space are common human traits; certain colors, particularly red, black, and white, acquire symbolic meanings that overstep cultural boundaries. The individual transcends the pervasive influence of culture. All humans share common perspectives and attitudes, and yet each person's world view is unique and that not in any trivial sense.

2. The group, expressing and enforcing the cultural standards of society, affects strongly the perception, attitude, and environmental value of its members. Culture can influence perception to the degree that people will see things that do not exist: it can cause group hallucination. Where sex roles are distinct, men and women adopt different values and perceive different aspects of the environment. The perception and environmental judgments of natives and visitors show little overlap because their experience and purpose have little in common. In the same type of natural setting (the semiarid plateaus and mesas of northwestern New Mexico), five groups of people live close to each other but have maintained their distinctive world views. Reality is not exhaustively known by any number of human perspectives, although that aspect of reality called resource is subject to depletion if enough people perceive it as resource and exploit it. Attitude to environment changes as mastery over nature increases and the concept of beauty alters. In the course of time Europeans have viewed mountains as the dwelling place of the gods, ugly excrescences on the smooth body of the earth, sublime nature, scenery, health and tourist resorts.

The physical environment itself has an effect on perception. People who live in a "carpentered" world are susceptible to different kinds of illusion from those who live in an environment lacking in orthogonality. It is seldom possible to relate environmental characteristics to perceptual biases as cause to effect: culture mediates. However, we can make less precise, indirect statements of relationship. We can say that the development of visual acuity is related to the ecological quality of the environment. Thus the Gikwe Bushmen learn to identify individual plants in the dry season whereas the Kung Bushmen, living in a better endowed setting, need only learn the location of plant aggregates. Environment necessarily provides the major building blocks of autochthonous cosmologies and world views: the contrasts between Egyptian and Sumerian world views in the frame of their individual environments are revealing.

3. Despite the many surveys on people's preferences for town, suburb, or farm as places to live, and on where they go for vacation, we remain largely ignorant of the quality and range of experience in different types of physical setting under different conditions. We need a William James to study *The Varieties of Environmental Experience*. Statistics giving us the

number of people who visit the National Parks or buy summer homes are better measures of fashion and the state of the economy than of people's real sentiments concerning nature. Such data reveal little of how people make use of their opportunities in a natural environment and how they can be expected to benefit from exposure to it. Topophilia takes many forms and varies greatly in emotional range and intensity. It is a start to describe what they are: fleeting visual pleasure; the sensual delight of physical contact; the fondness for place because it is familiar, because it is home and incarnates the past, because it evokes pride of ownership or of creation; joy in things because of animal health and vitality.

Certain natural environments have figured prominently in humanity's dreams of the ideal world: they are the forest, the seashore, the valley, and the island. The furnishing of an ideal world is a matter of removing the defects of the real one. Geography necessarily provides the content of topophilic sentiment. Paradises have a certain family likeness because the excesses of geography (too hot or too cold, too wet or too dry) are removed. In all of them, plants and animals useful and friendly to man abound. Paradises also differ in their respective excellences: some are rich pastures, others are magical forests, perfumed islands, or mountain valleys.

4. The world views of nonliterate and traditional societies differ significantly from those of modern men who have come under the influence, however indirectly, of science and technology. The point has often been made that in a prescientific age people adapted to nature whereas now they dominate it. A truer distinction is to recognize that primitive and traditional peoples lived in a vertical, rotary, and richly symbolical world, whereas modern man's world tends to be broad of surface, low of ceiling, nonrotary, aesthetic, and profane. In Europe the change took place gradually from 1500 onward, and it affected not only science but art, literature, architecture, and landscaping.

5. The ancient city was a symbol of the cosmos. Within its walls man experienced the order of heaven freed of biological necessities and the vagaries of nature that made country life insecure. All cities contain public symbols of some kind that concentrate and enforce (through high visibility) the ideals of power and glory. In a modern metropolis the symbol may be a grand avenue or square, an imposing city hall or a monument that captures the city's history and identity. Cities are enormously complex but some are clearly tagged by a single image: New York's skyline and San Francisco's streetcar are among the few examples from the United States. A single piece of dramatic architecture can give identity to a metropolis, putting the older historical emblems in the shade. One thinks of the Eiffel Tower in Paris (an upstart in a city rich in monuments), Toronto's City Hall, and St. Louis's Gateway Arch.

As artifact the city reflects human purpose. To most people living in a large metropolis, however, it is an environment that is as much a given fact irreducible to particular human needs as the facts of nature. Only over a small part of the city do people feel they have control. Their own homes may express their personalities, the places where they work if these are small and privately-owned, and perhaps the neighborhood street if it is the scene of informal socializing. To appreciate how people respond to their urban settings we need to know the kinds of activity that take place in the home, in the places of work and play, and in the streets. Life styles are highly varied in any large metropolis. People live in the same city, even in the same part of the city, and yet perceive different worlds. Common to all city dwellers is the remoteness between their type of employment and the obtaining of food that sustains life.

6. Attitudes toward wilderness and the countryside, insofar as they are verbalized and known, are sophisticated responses to environment that have their origins in the city. They presuppose the existence and recognition of environmental types and a degree of freedom to choose among them. Attitudes toward all three types of environment have been ambivalent from the beginning. Wilderness signified chaos, the haunt of demons—and purity. The garden and farm represented the idyllic life, but even Eden had its snake; country estates induced melancholy; and the farm was for peasants. The city symbolized order, freedom, and glory, but also worldliness, the corruption of natural virtues, and oppression. In the West, nature-Romanticism in the eighteenth century was soon followed by the horrors of the Industrial Revolution; together they led public opinion to stress the merits of the countryside and of nature at the expense of the city. Images are reversed so that the wilderness stands for order (ecological order) and freedom whereas the central city is chaotic, a jungle ruled by social outcasts. Suburb, once perceived as the place for paupers and obnoxious trades, has now greater prestige than the decaying city core. The time-honored meanings of "core" and "periphery," "center" and "margin," are reversed. The new town movement is an attempt to combine the virtues of suburban living with the idea of the center.

Human beings have persistently searched for the ideal environment. How it looks varies from one culture to another but in essence it seems to draw on two antipodal images: the garden of innocence and the cosmos. The fruits of the earth provide security as also does the harmony of the stars which offers, in addition, grandeur. So we move from one to the other: from the shade under the baobab to the magic circle under heaven; from home to public square, from suburb to city; from a seaside holiday to the enjoyment of the sophisticated arts, seeking for a point of equilibrium that is not of this world.

index